ECONOMIC ISSUES, PROBLEMS AND PERSPECTIVES

THE STOCK MARKET: CRISIS, RECOVERY AND EMERGING ECONOMIES

ECONOMIC ISSUES, PROBLEMS AND PERSPECTIVES

THE STOCK MARKET: CRISIS, RECOVERY AND EMERGING ECONOMIES

ALLISON S. WETHERBY

EDITOR

Nova Science Publishers, Inc.

New York

For permission to use material from this book please contact us:
Telephone 631-231-7269; Fax 631-231-8175
Web Site: http://www.novapublishers.com

NOTICE TO THE READER

The Publisher has taken reasonable care in the preparation of this book, but makes no expressed or implied warranty of any kind and assumes no responsibility for any errors or omissions. No liability is assumed for incidental or consequential damages in connection with or arising out of information contained in this book. The Publisher shall not be liable for any special, consequential, or exemplary damages resulting, in whole or in part, from the readers' use of, or reliance upon, this material. Any parts of this book based on government reports are so indicated and copyright is claimed for those parts to the extent applicable to compilations of such works.

Independent verification should be sought for any data, advice or recommendations contained in this book. In addition, no responsibility is assumed by the publisher for any injury and/or damage to persons or property arising from any methods, products, instructions, ideas or otherwise contained in this publication.

This publication is designed to provide accurate and authoritative information with regard to the subject matter covered herein. It is sold with the clear understanding that the Publisher is not engaged in rendering legal or any other professional services. If legal or any other expert assistance is required, the services of a competent person should be sought. FROM A DECLARATION OF PARTICIPANTS JOINTLY ADOPTED BY A COMMITTEE OF THE AMERICAN BAR ASSOCIATION AND A COMMITTEE OF PUBLISHERS.

Additional color graphics may be available in the e-book version of this book.

LIBRARY OF CONGRESS CATALOGING-IN-PUBLICATION DATA

The stock market : crisis, recovery and emerging economies / editor, Allison S. Wetherby.
p. cm.
 Includes index.
 ISBN 978-1-61122-545-7 (hardcover)
 1. Stock exchanges--United States. 2. Stock exchanges. 3. Financial crises--United States. 4. Financial crises. I. Wetherby, Allison S.
 HG4910.S688 2010
 332.64'273--dc22
2010042637

Published by Nova Science Publishers, Inc. † New York

CONTENTS

PREFACE

This book examines the dynamic linkages among the federal budget deficit, interest rates and the stock market for the United States from 1960 to 2006. Topics discussed herein include the strategic risk assessment techniques that can be applied to investment and trading portfolios in emerging financial markets, such as in the context of the Gulf Cooperation Council (GCC) stock markets, as well as Africa's emerging capital markets and the financial crisis and whether the theory of periodically collapsing speculative bubbles can explain the dynamics of East Asian emerging stock market returns.

Chapter 1- This chapter examines the dynamic linkages among the federal budget deficit, interest rates and the stock market for the United States from 1960 to 2006 period. The empirical strategy is a structural VAR analysis. The results suggest that budget deficits negatively impact upon stock returns, which implies a violation of the Ricardian Equivalence Proposition. Further analysis shows a higher sensitivity of stock returns to corporate taxes relative to public spending. Finally, it is shown that although taxes are relevant for corporate profits in the short run, budget deficits are important for the stock market in the long run.

Chapter 2- The aim of this chapter is to fill a gap in modern risk management literature and especially from the perspective of stock markets in emerging economies. This chapter provides pioneering strategic risk assessment techniques that can be applied to investment and trading portfolios in emerging financial markets, such as in the context of the Gulf Cooperation Council (GCC) stock markets. In this chapter, key equity price risk assessment methods and modeling techniques that financial entities, regulators and policymakers should consider in developing their daily price risk management objectives are examined and tailored to the particular needs of emerging markets. This is with the intent of setting-up the basis of a modeling technique for the measurement of strategic equity price exposures in the day-to-day financial trading operations. While extensive literatures have reviewed the statistical and economic proposition of Value at Risk (VaR) models, this paper provides real-world modeling techniques that can be applied to financial trading portfolios under the notion of illiquid and adverse financial market circumstances. In this paper, the authors demonstrate a practical modeling approach for the measurement of stock markets risk exposure for financial trading portfolios that contain several illiquid equity asset positions. This approach is based on the renowned concept of liquidity-adjusted VaR (LVaR) along with the innovation of a simulation tool utilizing matrix-algebra technique. To this end, a matrix-algebra modeling technique is used to create the necessary quantitative infrastructures and trading risk simulations. This tactic is a useful form to avoid mathematical complexity, as more and more securities are added to the portfolio of assets. In addition, it can simplify the financial modeling and programming process and can allow as well a clear-cut incorporation of short (sell) and long (buy) positions in the daily risk management process. As such, the broad risk model can simultaneously handle LVaR appraisal under normal and severe market conditions besides it takes into account the effects of liquidity of the traded equity securities. In order to illustrate the proper use of LVaR and stress-testing methods, real-world paradigms of trading risk assessment are presented for the GCC stock markets. To this end, simulation case studies are attained with the aspiration of bringing about a reasonable framework for the measurement of equity trading risk exposures. The modeling techniques discussed in this paper will aid financial markets' participants, regulators and policymakers in the instigation of meticulous and up to date simulation algorithms to handle equity price risk exposure. The suggested analytical methods and procedures can be put into practice in virtually all emerging economies, if they are bespoke to correspond to every market's preliminary level of intricacy.

Chapter 3- The past two decades alone has witnessed four major shocks to the global financial system: the collapse of the European exchange rate mechanism in 1992-1993, the peso crisis in 1994-1995 and the Asian turmoil in 1997-1998. The most recent, the subprime crisis, started in the summer of 2007 in the United States and intensified in 2008 and 2009 and has since changed the face of global finance and economics. As developed economies emerge from the recession, the contagion has spilled over from Wall Street to Main Street, engulfing hitherto resilient emerging market economies. For African countries, two notions of the financial crisis have become prominent: (a) the transmission mechanism between the financial systems in Africa and the rest of the world are weak and this has moderated, if not averted a catastrophic consequence of the spillover and (b) the main effect of the financial crisis is that of a second round effect.

So far the argument has been on the real sector effects of the crisis, and the analysis, more anecdotal than empirical. However, under alternative channels of transmission, both second and first round effects are significant. The authors show with extensive analysis of recent data from various indicators of stock market, bank and real economy variables that Africa's emerging and frontier markets have suffered as much as other markets from the spill over of the 2007 slow down: plummeting equity prices, deteriorating bank balance sheets, capital flow reversals, and reduction in remittances. The authors offer important policy conundrums, including but not limited to financial market reform, improving efficiency of Africa's emerging equity markets and regional integration to exploit the benefits of scale economics.

Chapter 4- The authors investigate whether the theory of periodically collapsing speculative bubbles can explain the dynamics of East Asian emerging stock market returns. By employing three alternative measures for the deviations of actual prices from fundamental values, they estimate various two-state regime-switching models for the dynamics of excess returns of the equity markets under scrutiny. Their results indicate the existence of (usually negative) bubbles in the East Asian stock markets. While their regime-switching models seem to be able to capture the behavior of the stock markets, considerable heterogeneity among countries is evident with respect to the effect of the bubble on equity returns. Finally, their models appear to have predictive ability over the timing of a change in the state (i.e. regime) of the equity markets.

Chapter 5- This chapter investigates how the stock market reacts to the disclosure of internal control deficiencies under the Japanese Sarbanes-Oxley Act of 2006. Given that the

Japanese official agencies attempted to minimize the negative shock caused by the disclosure, the authors find no stock market reactions on the whole to the disclosure of internal control weaknesses. They also show that negative market reactions are intensified if firms have changed auditors in recent years, have uncertainties over their ability to continue as a going concern, have larger assets or fixed debts, or are listed on the emerging stock exchanges. In contrast, negative stock reactions are mitigated when firms have high ratios of foreign shareholders or current liabilities. Another interesting finding is that whether a firm engages a Big 4 audit firm does not seem to matter to investors evaluating firms with internal control weaknesses.

Chapter 6- Adaptive wave model for financial option pricing is proposed, as a high-complexity alternative to the standard Black–Scholes model. The new option-pricing model, representing a controlled Brownian motion, includes two wave-type approaches: nonlinear and quantum, both based on (adaptive form of) the Schrödinger equation. The nonlinear approach comes in two flavors: (i) for the case of constant volatility, it is defined by a single adaptive nonlinear Schrödinger (NLS) equation, while for the case of stochastic volatility, it is defined by an adaptive Manakov system of two coupled NLS equations. The linear quantum approach is defined in terms of deBroglie's plane waves and free particle Schrödinger equation. In this approach, financial variable shave quantum-mechanical interpretation and satisfy the Heisenberg-type uncertainty relations. Both models are capable of successful fitting of the Black–Scholes data, as well as defining Greeks. Based on the two models, as well as the rogue solutions of the NLS equation, the author proposes a new financial research program.

Chapter 7- The authors study dynamic and causal relations between stock returns and aggregate equity mutual fund flows in the U.S. stock market. More specifically, Granger (1969) and Sims (1972) causality tests and an ECM indicate that there is unidirectional causality from stock returns to mutual fund flows. Furthermore, if there is a deviation from long-run equilibrium, the stock returns force the deviation to go toward the long-run equilibrium. Thus, it is likely that stock returns lead mutual fund flows and appear to be the most important element explaining fund flows in the U.S. financial market.

Chapter 8- This investigation is one of the first to adopt quantile regression to examine covariance risk dynamics in international stock markets. Feasibility of the proposed model is demonstrated in G7 stock markets. Additionally, two conventional random-coefficient frameworks, including time-varying betas derived from GARCH models and state-varying betas implied by Markov-switching models, are employed and subjected to comparative analysis. The empirical findings of this work are consistent with the following notions. First, several types of beta distortions are demonstrated: the "beta smile" ("beta skew") curve for the Italian, U.S. and U.K. (Canadian, French and German) markets. That is, covariance risk among global stock markets in extremely bull and/or bear market states is significantly higher than that in stable period. Additionally, the Japanese market provides a special case, and its beta estimate at extremely bust state is significantly lower, not higher than that at the middle region. Second, this study hypothesizes two sorts of asset reallocation processes: "stock-to-stock" and "stock-to-bond", and employs them to explain these different types of beta distortions among various markets. Third, the quantile-varying betas are identified as possessing two key advantages. Specifically, the comparison of the system with quantile-varying betas against that with time-varying betas implied by GARCH models provides meaningful implications for correlation-volatility relationship among international stock markets. Furthermore, the quantile-varying beta design in this study releases a simple dual beta setting implied by Markov-switching models of Ramchand and Susmel (1998) and can identify dynamics of asymmetry in betas.

Chapter 9- In this chapter the authors look at the dynamic behavior of stock market volatility in the G-7 countries over a long term period which covers from 1960 to 2006. More generally, they ask whether there have been significant changes in the behavior of market volatility in the G-7 countries. They attempt to place the discussion of possible changes in this dynamic behavior in the context of the "Great Moderation": Has the volatility of the stock market gone down in a parallel manner to the volatility of real activity and inflation or are financial markets 'disconnected' from economic fundamentals? The authors data analyses and empirical results do not find evidence of a reduction in stock market volatility in most G-7 economies and, when these changes appear, they seem to have come years before the Great Moderation.

In: The Stock Market
Editor: Allison S. Wetherby

ISBN: 978-1-61122-545-7
© 2011 Nova Science Publishers, Inc.

Chapter 1

FEDERAL BUDGET DEFICITS, INTEREST RATES AND THE GENERAL STOCK MARKET

*Nikiforos T. Laopodis**

Department of Finance, School of Business,
Fairfield University, Fairfield, CT, USA

ABSTRACT

This paper examines the dynamic linkages among the federal budget deficit, interest rates and the stock market for the United States from 1960 to 2006 period. The empirical strategy is a structural VAR analysis. The results suggest that budget deficits negatively impact upon stock returns, which implies a violation of the Ricardian Equivalence Proposition. Further analysis shows a higher sensitivity of stock returns to corporate taxes relative to public spending. Finally, it is shown that although taxes are relevant for corporate profits in the short run, budget deficits are important for the stock market in the long run.

Keywords: federal budget deficit, stock market, VAR, taxes, Ricardian Equivalence Proposition

1. INTRODUCTION

The United States' (US) federal budget deficit is currently (in 2010) about $1.3 trillion or approximately 10% of the nation's gross domestic product (GDP), according to the Congressional Budget Office (CBO) estimates. The gross national debt (or the sum of past deficits) stands at an alarming 80% of GDP and is expected to reach 100% within two years, again according to CBO estimates. Figure 1 illustrates the federal deficit for the past 45 years (1965-2010) and Figure 2 the federal deficit as % of GDP. Many prominent individuals, ranging from the Federal Reserve (Fed), the government and the private sector, have been

---

* Telephone: (203) 254-4000 ext. 3272; Fax: (203) 254-4105; Email: nlaopodis@mail.fairfield.edu

issuing several warnings over the past decade or so about the growing size of the federal deficit. For example, the Fed's ex-chairman, Alan Greenspan, has said that the country's deficit must go down or risk a severe recession. The Fed's current chairman, Ben Bernanke, in recent speeches and testimonies before Congress also warned of the dangerous and unsustainable path of the deficit. The current administration's Secretary of the State, Timothy Geithner, also spoke of the dangerous effects of the growing budget deficit. Finally, Moody's, a leading credit-rating agency in the US, has warned of an impending downgrading of the country's debt because of its unsustainable path. Why are these people worried about the government's deficit? Let us trace the economic effects of federal deficits on various aspects of the economic activity.

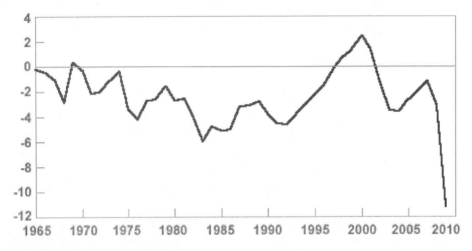

Source: Congressional Budget Office, 2010.

Figure 1. Total Budget Deficit (Surplus) as % of GDP, 1965-2010

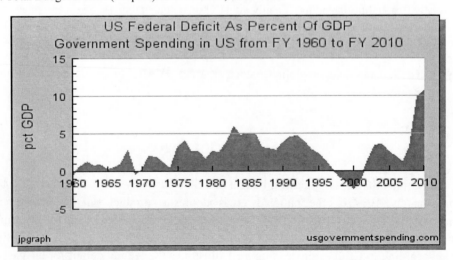

Source: usgovernmentspending.com

Figure 2. US Federal Deficit as % of GDP, 1960-2010.

On the Real Economy

Federal deficits have an important impact on how much the country saves. Since national saving is the sum of savings by the private and public sector, if private savings stay the same, then with a federal deficit the total saving falls. When national saving is reduced, persistent deficits lower the amount of resources dedicated to the production of goods and services in the economy. Domestic real and financial investment negatively affects both the growth rate of the economy and productivity. Further, the adverse impact of higher budget deficits on domestic investment is partly offset by foreign capital inflows (instead of domestic capital flows, if savings were higher at home). The latter increases U.S. foreign indebtedness meaning that future generations will have to pay more to foreigners (than to other domestic residents). The natural question to ask is: what would happen if one day, suddenly, foreigners (like the Chinese) wanted to withdraw their holdings from the U.S.?

On Financial Markets

When national saving, investment, productivity and capital flows change, federal deficits will impact the financial markets in various ways. First, higher deficits increase interest rates, exchange rates, and ultimately stock and bond market values. Second, higher interest rates attract more foreign capital thus financing domestic investment and further adding to the country's foreign indebtedness. Finally, these pressures strengthen the dollar presently but weaken it in the future and deteriorate the country's financial status in the world.

On Economic Policy

Fiscal imbalances create turbulence in financial markets with adverse implications on the potency of both fiscal (i.e., taxes and expenditures) and monetary (money supply, interest rates) policies.

Other Economic Effects

Other adverse effects include higher taxes for all residents (to pay for the service of the huge national debt, which is presently estimated to be $41,000 per household, according to some estimates), retirement entitlements, health care and so on. Here are some examples of the implications of soaring deficits on investors (see Gale and Orszag, 2003, 2004, Engen and Hubbard, 2005, and CBO, 2010).

- Investors' asset values decline with higher interest rates due to higher deficits
- Investor confidence is eroded when fiscal imbalances cause fluctuations in foreign exchange markets and international credit markets

- Loss of confidence of investors, both at home and abroad, also may cause them to avoid the US market in favor of foreign markets causing a depreciation of the US dollar
- Higher interest rates and a depreciation of the exchange rate will reduce total household wealth and raise the costs of financing and doing business thus reducing domestic spending and productive investment
- The government's inability to restore fiscal order may make the market susceptible to ongoing deficits and thus further undermine real economic activity.

2. IMPORTANCE OF THE STUDY AND RESEARCH QUESTIONS

Despite the above-mentioned consequences of high budget deficits on the stock market values, the relationship between fiscal policy actions and the stock market has not been adequately addressed in the empirical financial literature. An early study for the US case is that by Darrat and Brocato (1994), who investigated the efficiency of the stock market and the federal budget deficit and that past budget deficits exert a significant effect on current stock returns. By contrast, Lee [2004] re-examined the informational efficiencies of the U.S. stock and bond markets to fiscal policies for the 1969-1998 period and found support for them. Hancock (1989) tested the semi-strong form of market efficiency for the US stock market and established that the market is efficient with respect to anticipated and unanticipated (changes in) deficit measures. Finally, Laopodis (2009) examined the efficiency of the stock market to fiscal policy actions and concluded that the US stock market is not efficient with respect to information about federal deficits.

In view of the above mixed evidence on the relationship between budget deficits and the stock market, this study elicits the answering of several important questions. First, does the stock market offer an important channel for transmitting the impact of fiscal policy to the financial side of the economy and is the stock market efficient with respect to past fiscal policy moves? An implication of the latter is that if the market is not efficient then investor actions could exploit the stock market and profit from it, at least in the short-run. If market participants know of (or expect) in advance an increase in the deficit then they may expect future increases in taxes to cover the government spending gap. These actions might raise the risk premiums, associated with this deficit-generated market uncertainty, and may lead the market to change its expectations about future cash flows and/or interest (discount) rates (see Fama and French, 1988, and Shah, 1984).

The above questions are related to the public's perception of the role of deficits on stock returns, or to the well-known Ricardian Equivalence Proposition (REP), put forth by Barro (1974). This proposition states that rational individuals anticipate future tax liabilities, implied by current and expected deficits, and thus fully discount them currently. Consequently, they should not rebalance their portfolios since any future government debt would be cancelled out by future increases in taxation. This, in turn, suggests that government financing decisions should have no impact on stock (or asset) values. So, a finding that the federal deficits impact stock returns may imply a violation of REP.

A second question involves the nature and extent of the interactions between fiscal and monetary policies ultimately influencing the stock market. For example, if higher government borrowing raises interest rates, then future economic activity may be stifled and that might compel the Fed to step in to reverse this undesirable situation by lowering interest rates. Lower market interest rates, in turn, would force investors to value their equity holdings upward thus positively affecting the stock market (see Bordo and Wheelock, 2004, Laopodis, 2006, and Sinai, 2006). This scenario implies an interaction between fiscal and monetary policy and thus monetary policy needs to be studied in conjunction with fiscal policy within an empirical setting.

Another related question involves the examination of fiscal policy moves on the stock market from the perspective of government taxes and expenditures. In other words, do government tax and spending actions have a direct effect on the financial markets? Although it is well known that such actions affect a firm's expected cash flows, the empirical evidence is still varied (see also Tavares and Valkanov, 2003). For instance, while some authors, i.e., Cutler (1988) and Goolsbee (1998), found a limited asset price impact following a change in relative taxation (at the firm level), others, e.g., Lang and Shackelford (2000) and Sinai and Gyourko (2004), reported substantial effects of tax changes on share returns (again, at specific firm levels). Therefore, it is important to re-examine this issue within the context of dynamic interactions between budget deficits and stock returns.

All above issues will be empirically examined for the period from 1960 to 2007 for the US using the methodology of the vector autoregression (VAR) and examining some of its outputs. The sample data will be both quarterly and monthly when investigating the issue. Specifically, quarterly data is used when examining the main issue of the dynamic linkages among federal budget deficits, interest rates and the general stock market, and monthly data for the examination of the issue of stock market efficiency with respect to fiscal policy movements.

The remainder of the chapter is structured as follows. Section 3 considers the empirical methodological design of the study. Section 4 presents the empirical results, discusses them at length and presents some robustness tests. Section 5 extends the empirical analysis using alternative variable specifications for both the fiscal measure and stock returns. Finally, section 6 summarizes the study and concludes with some general observations.

3. METHODOLOGY AND DATA

The discussion henceforth follows that of Laopodis (2010) who examined in detail the dynamic linkages among federal budget deficits, interest rates and the equity market. The section is composed of the following subsections: Data and Preliminary Statistics, Model Specification, and The Endogeneity Problem Satisfied.

3.1 Data and Preliminary Statistics

We employ quarterly data on the variables to be described below for forty-seven years, from 1960:I to 2006:IV. The raw series are: GBD_t (the government budget deficit, cyclically adjusted, in millions of US dollars); GDP$_t$ (the gross domestic product, in billions of U.S. dollars (1984=100)); MS$_t$ (the money supply, in billions of US dollars, seasonally adjusted, proxied by M1); SP$_t$ (the S&P500 index); TB$_t$ (the 3-month Treasury Bill rate); and FFR$_t$ (the effective federal funds rate). The basic sources for all series are *DataStream* and the Fed's *FRED* online site.

Based on the series above, we construct the following basic variables to be included in the model estimation.

- BDY_t : federal budget deficit, as a percentage of GDP
- MSG_t : money supply growth {= log(MS$_t$/MS$_{t-1}$)*100}
- NSR_t : nominal stock returns {=log(SP$_t$/SP$_{t-1}$)*100}
- EMR_t : excess market returns {= NSR$_t$ – TB$_t$}

Table 1 contains some descriptive statistics on the deficit (as % of GDP), money supply growth, nominal stock returns, and the federal funds rate variables. From the table we can see that the government's budget was consistently negative, with the exception of the years of 1999 and 2000, and reached a record in 2004 (see first graph in Figure 3). We also observe that the growth rate of budget deficit has the smallest standard deviation, followed by the money supply growth. Notable is also the spike in the federal funds rate, as implied by the max value in 1981, which is evident in the second graph in Figure 3. The correlation matrix among the four variables indicates that most pairwise correlations are negative with the most notable correlation between the deficit and the stock returns (-0.2420). This is an important, but simple, result and implies that when federal deficits become larger and larger the stock market declines. The only positive correlation coefficient was between the money growth and the fed funds rate (0.100). However, these correlations are simple measures and do not fully reflect the underlying linkages among the variables and so a more robust approach is needed to which we now turn.

Table 1. Descriptive Statistics for Selected Variables

Statistics	BDY	FFR	NSR	MSG
Mean	-1.499850	6.184383	1.683771	1.255628
Median	-1.074185	5.586900	2.479662	1.145326
Maximum	2.344549	17.78690	19.54593	7.759145
Minimum	-4.518711	0.996700	-30.54775	-3.613204
Stand. Dev.	1.549810	3.309677	8.035652	2.608854
Skewness	-0.165349	1.113244	-0.915298	0.013738
Kurtosis	2.356522	4.418101	4.682105	2.112243
Jarque Bera	4.254547	48.55162	54.30996	6.086572
Probability	0.123271	0.000000	0.000007	0.071211
Correlation Matrix	**BDY**	**FFR**	**NSR**	**MSG**
	1	1	1	
	-0.19455	-0.184388	-0.10208	
	-0.24658	-0.11337		

Notes: time period is 1960:2 – 2006:4; BDY is the budget deficit as % of GDP; NSR is the nominal stock returns; MSG is the money supply growth rate, and FFR the federal funds rate; * test was done with up to 8 lags.

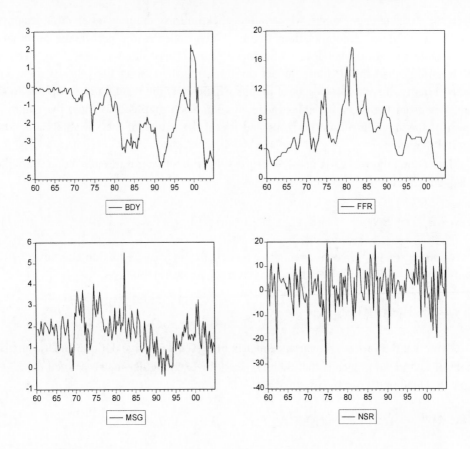

Figure 3. Plots of Budget Deficit (as % of GDP), BDY, Federal Funds Rate, FFR, Money Supply Growth, MSG, and Nominal Stock Returns, NSR, 1960:1 to 2006:4

3.2 Model Specification

Since the task here is to estimate the empirical relationship(s) between fiscal policy, monetary policy, and the stock market, while placing as few theoretical restrictions as possible on the system's variables, we will use the vector autoregression (VAR) framework.

VARs are attractive for three reasons. First, they impose very few a priori restrictions on explanatory variables or on the model's lag structure and this offers good protection from econometric problems in order to achieve identification. Second, the variables in a VAR model permit an efficient estimation over shorter periods of time, compared to large-scale structural models. And third, unrestricted VAR models examine the impact of policy by investigating the implication of a shock to the innovation of a variable rather than its predictable component. Thus VARs constitute a powerful vehicle for investigating policy transmission mechanisms or variable feedbacks, since they would make the estimation results more reliable for prediction when past changes in the underlying economic structure took place.

VAR models generate lots of outputs but in this study we will examine only three of them. First, the estimated (system) regression coefficients to see how one variable's change affects the variable under study, which is the stock returns, and how other variables impact it. Second, the variance decompositions output which indicates the percentage of variation in one variable to another variable within the system. This output is useful for determining which variable had the greatest impact on stock returns among the other variables in the system. Finally, the impulse response graphs which show the reaction of a variable to shocks emanating from the other variables in the system. Such graphs also show the nature of the impact of the shock in future horizons and reveal the nature of the variable's reaction over time has shaped.

More generally, the VAR involves regressing an $n \times 1$ vector of endogenous variables, y_t, on lagged values of itself as follows:

$$y_t = \Xi_1 y_{t-1} + \Xi_2 y_{t-3} + \ldots + \Xi_p y_{t-p} + e_t, \; E(e_t e'_t) = \Omega \qquad (1)$$

Assuming that y_t is covariance stationary, then the above equation can be inverted and represented by an (infinite) vector moving average process as follows:

$$y_t = e_t + \Pi_1 e_{t-1} + \Pi_2 e_{t-2} + \ldots \qquad (2)$$

Given that the variance-covariance matrix of e_t (Ω) is positive definite and symmetric, the Choleski factorization means that there exists a lower triangular matrix P such that $\Omega = PP'$. Using P, equation (2) can be rewritten as:

$$y_t = PP^{-1}e_t + \Pi_1 PP^{-1}e_{t-1} + \Pi_2 PP^{-1}e_{t-2} + \ldots \;\; = \Gamma_0 u_t + \Gamma_1 u_{t-1} + \Gamma_2 u_{t-2} + \ldots \qquad (3)$$

where $\Gamma_i = \Pi_i P$, $u_t = P^{-1}e_t$, and $E(u_t u'_t) = I$. So, equation (3) represents the endogenous variables as a function of the orthogonalized innovations (u_{t-i}).

More specifically, the 3-equation VAR system can be expressed in a matrix format as follows:

$$Z \begin{bmatrix} b_t \\ s_t \\ i_t \end{bmatrix} = C(L) \begin{bmatrix} b_{t-1} \\ s_{t-1} \\ i_{t-1} \end{bmatrix} + B \begin{bmatrix} \varepsilon_t \\ \eta_t \\ \upsilon_t \end{bmatrix} \qquad (4)$$

where b_t is the budget deficit (as % of GDP), s_t are nominal stock returns, i_t is the monetary policy instrument (the short-term interest rate), Z is a 3×3 matrix that describes the contemporaneous relations among the variables, $C(L)$ is a finite-order lag polynomial, B is a 3×3 matrix with non-zero off-diagonal elements that allow some shocks to affect all three endogenous variables, and ε_t, η_t and υ_t are structural disturbances.

If the above estimated coefficients are jointly found to be statistically significant, then past values of a given variable can explain variations in the other variable and the null hypothesis can be rejected. Finally, since determining the optimal lag structure of equation (4) is a concern that needs to be addressed, for if the lag structure is mis-specified the empirical results may be biased, the use of Akaike's (1976) Final Prediction Error (FPE) criterion will be employed.

Finally, the *atheoretical* nature of the VAR model and the presence of a large number of estimated parameters render the interpretability of these parameters difficult. This is further accentuated by the possibility of having coefficients with alternating signs across lags with not all of them being statistically significant (a possibility very real in our exercise). Therefore, one could not see the effect of a given variable on another variable within the VAR system. Fortunately, this problem can be partially mitigated by the use of a parameter block significance test (based on Wald's χ^2 statistic), the computation of variance decompositions, and the impulse response graphs.

3.3 Dealing with the Endogeneity Problem

The main objective here is to measure the reactions of the stock market to innovations emanating from changes in fiscal policy and, secondarily, monetary policy. Although changes in the stock market may affect the subsequent conduct of monetary policy, determining the monetary policy reaction to the stock market may be difficult. This arises because of the contemporaneous response of monetary policy to stock market movements and because of the possibility that the stock market and monetary authorities both may jointly react to any new information. This problem is known as the endogeneity (or simultaneity) problem and constitutes a violation of the assumption that the error term is orthogonal to the (changes in the) monetary policy tool.

Several researchers have proposed approaches to deal with this problem. For instance, Rigobon (2003) and Rigobon and Sack (2003) suggested an identification procedure based on the heteroscedasticity of stock returns. They argue that it is difficult to estimate the policy reaction because of the contemporaneous reactions of the stock market to policy changes. Further, they note that this problem cannot be adequately addressed using exclusion restrictions or instrumental variables due to the fact that almost all variables, i.e., instruments, are bound to correlate with interest rate movements. Craine and Martin (2003) also employed a similar approach in that their multivariate model allowed all asset returns to respond to common, unobservable shocks. Finally, Bernanke and Kuttner (2005) recommended the use of the 'event study' methodology and argued that either one of the above approaches would yield similar results to their approach.

In our case, the heteroscedasticity of returns is not an issue because our sample contains quarterly observations and not high-frequency data like daily or weekly where heteroscedasticity is usually present. Besides, the stock market - monetary policy linkage is not our main concern and any shocks emanating from the latter are not contemporaneous but with a lag. Finally, adopting the Bernanke and Kuttner (2005) approach it appears safe and appropriate to investigate the mutual effects of budget deficits and interest rates on the stock market.

4. EMPIRICAL FINDINGS AND DISCUSSION

This section is composed of the following subsections: 4.1 subsection on the dynamics among federal budget deficits, interest rates and stock prices, 4.2 on the efficiency of the stock market with respect to information coming from fiscal policies and 4.3 on the robustness tests.

4.1 Dynamic Linkages among Deficits, Interest Rates and Equity Prices

Preliminary statistical investigation on the three variables (budget deficit, money supply, and stock returns) included testing for unit roots in each variable and conducting a multivariate cointegration analysis. Although all three time series exhibited a unit root, the cointegration test did not show strong evidence of cointegration among them and thus we will proceed with the estimation of the basic VAR model with each of the variables expressed in first-difference form (these statistical results are available upon request). Since the ordering of the variables is an issue with VAR analyses, we used the Granger-causality test to determine which variable goes first and which one last.[1] In general, failure to detect a Granger-causal ordering scheme for the three variables may be consistent with the efficient market hypothesis or that past information on fiscal policy actions is fully incorporated into current stock pricing decisions. The results, however, showed an ordering scheme where the budget deficit variable, *BDY*, goes first, followed by the money supply growth variable, *MSG*, and the nominal stock returns, *NSR*.

Table 2 exhibits the results from the VAR analysis. The results indicate some significant, short-run, and reciprocal interactions between (changes in) the budget deficit, *ΔBDY*, and nominal stock returns. Specifically, for the first variable pair it is observed that the budget deficit positively affects the stock market with a one-quarter lag and negatively with a two-quarter lag. Also, movements in the stock market affect the deficit in a positive and a negative manner, with a one- and three-quarter lags, respectively. Finally, it is worth noting that the finding of the budget deficit affecting stock returns *may be* construed as evidence of market inefficiency.

What could possibly account for these findings? First of all, it is rather surprising that the financial/economic literature, as mentioned in the introduction, has not dealt much with the impact of fiscal deficits on the stock market despite the evidence that fiscal deficits lead to 'crowding-out' of real investment and higher interest rates, which would lower stock returns. Perhaps market participants are not aware of the full impacts of budget deficits and, as such, they do not consider it a relevant or fundamental macro variable for pricing/valuing stocks (or other assets). Alternatively, even if they recognize the full impact of deficits they may find it rather marginal (or unprofitable) to act upon this information (see Darrat, 1994, for further discussion on this). Another explanation could be offered by relating the results to the REP (Ricardian Equivalence Proposition). Recall that the REP states that rational individuals anticipate future tax liabilities, implied by current and expected deficits, and thus discount them fully at the present. This further implies that government financing decisions should not have an impact on the stock market. Thus, our finding that only two deficit lags are statistically significant in the stock returns equation perhaps implies a violation of the REP.

---

[1] The Granger causality test is used to determine if there exists a block recursive structure among the three variables expressed in first differences (via an F-test). Such a causal ordering is consistent with the Choleski decomposition. For instance, if BDY causes MSG and NSR, and MSG causes NSR (which means that NSR is caused by BDY and MSG), then the variable order should be BDY, MSG, NSR.

Contrary to the above findings, past changes in the money supply have no (short-run) impact on stock returns, a finding which suggests stock market efficiency with respect to monetary policy. In other words, it appears that participants in the U.S. market have incorporated all information pertaining to future Fed policy moves. This result is in line with Rozeff's (1974) model of pure efficient model and a similar finding by Darrat and Brocato (1994) for the U.S.

Table 2. Vector Autoregression Estimates, 1960-2006

	ΔBDY	MSG	NSR
ΔBDY(-1)	0.83241*	0.02348	0.02333*
	(2.49566)	(1.11982)	(1.92247)
ΔBDY(-2)	0.30462*	-0.01189	-0.01326*
	(2.89560)	(-1.01246)	(-1.97568)
ΔBDY(-3)	-0.19218*	-0.01443	-0.01154
	(-2.43743)	(-1.02415)	(-1.00123)
MSG(-1)	1.87845	1.02207*	0.43241
	(1.34243)	(2.12295)	(1.32222)
MSG(-2)	-1.83396	-0.33426*	0.33233
	(-1.52213)	(-2.13381)	(1.22259)
MSG(-3)	1.73328	-0.32217	-0.03364
	(1.12283)	(-1.23380)	(-1.03334)
NSR(-1)	0.84314*	-0.01152	0.85362*
	(2.32426)	(-0.11548)	(2.32257)
NSR(-2)	0.22220	0.01175	-0.12240
	(1.33297)	(0.12366)	(-1.11022)
NSR(-3)	-0.95229*	0.01345	0.12110
	(-2.22235)	(0.21193)	(1.11254)
Constant	0.45691	-0.02227	-0.02345
	(1.12310)	(-0.21009)	(-1.11867)
R-squared	0.86575	0.87657	0.86630
Adj. R-squared	0.80202	0.78343	0.82345
F-statistic	87.5593	435.603	543.271
Log likelihood	-556.431	-443.411	-223.616
FPE	1.37682		

Notes: *, ** mean statistically significant at the 5 and 10 percent levels, respectively; numbers in parentheses below estimates are t-ratios; negative numbers in parentheses next to variables denote a lag; FPE is the Final Prediction Error criterion.

Panel A of Table 3 depicts the variance decompositions (VD) results for each variable. The results for the deficit indicate that although changes in money supply account for a negligible amount, stock returns account for a larger and increasing amount over time that dies off extremely slowly (in fact, it takes more that three years to vanish). The VD results for the stock returns show that the explanatory portion attributable to the deficit increases initially but declines sharply after the third quarter.

Table 3. Variance Decompositions of Budget Deficit, Stock Returns, Money Supply Growth, and Federal Funds Rate

Period	Stand. Error	ΔBDY	NSR	MSG
Panel A: Variance Decompositions for ΔBDY, NSR and MSG				
Variance Decomposition of ΔBDY				
2	0.578947	98.45590	1.213531	0.330565
4	0.853918	94.26836	5.453285	0.278354
6	1.006390	92.33991	7.272972	0.387118
8	1.090329	90.94253	8.593468	0.464000
10	1.136987	89.89594	9.601834	0.502228
12	1.163600	89.05307	10.43412	0.512805
Variance Decomposition of NSR				
2	0.115658	7.507565	92.48983	0.002606
4	0.157959	8.701301	89.88036	1.418341
6	0.190226	7.299538	90.17286	2.527604
8	0.214615	6.027774	90.57910	3.393130
10	0.234460	5.090310	90.89804	4.011651
12	0.251214	4.435235	91.08744	4.477324
Variance Decomposition of MSG				
2	0.011925	1.254765	0.511220	98.23401
4	0.020814	1.019967	0.643815	98.33622
6	0.028197	0.663547	1.048767	98.28769
8	0.034672	1.622599	1.368048	97.00935
10	0.040733	3.984369	1.609343	94.40629
12	0.046603	7.203889	1.805958	90.99015
Panel B: Variance Decompositions for NSR, ΔBDY and FFR				
Variance Decomposition of NSR				
Period	Stand. Error	NSR	ΔBDY	FFR
2	0.117422	99.06509	0.933090	0.001822
4	0.160054	97.95146	2.339700	0.108839
6	0.192137	97.89297	3.000783	0.106242
8	0.216669	97.73972	3.055218	0.105062
10	0.236829	97.64662	3.045121	0.108258
12	0.254204	97.53820	3.031228	0.130576
Variance Decomposition of ΔBDY				
2	0.571160	7.018310	92.68124	0.010453
4	0.836429	3.681888	96.13056	0.050557
6	0.991534	5.593640	94.41625	0.647353
8	1.086227	15.75518	85.32731	0.917513
10	1.146359	16.92083	83.25940	1.019769
12	1.186861	17.72946	82.09059	1.179946
Variance Decomposition of FFR				
2	1.494608	2.528465	0.060879	97.41066
4	1.974128	6.253992	0.317816	93.42819
6	2.428109	5.713297	2.420605	92.86610
8	2.546720	4.288451	3.402848	92.30870
10	2.746896	3.601637	5.627099	91.77126
12	2.907999	3.109847	6.988678	90.90147

Finally, the money supply growth seems to account for most of its own variation, while stock returns are seen to explain a small but increasing portion (about 1%) of it, and the deficit seems to account for a greater and increasing portion in its error forecast variance. However, although the deficit's influence is initially negligible, it accounts for a large and rapidly increasing portion of the money supply's error forecast variance over time which extends well beyond three years.

It is important to note, at this point, that monetary policy can neutralize, at least in the short-run and to some extent, the effects of deficits via accommodation (that is, through an increase bank reserves) so as to keep short-term rates low. In the long run also monetary policy has an effect on deficits because continuing deficit-producing (fiscal) expenditures will raise inflationary expectations thus prompting the Fed to (proactively) act and apply a tight monetary policy.

Figure 4 displays the impulse response graphs for the three variables for up to 24 quarters (confidence bands are in dotted lines in each graph). From the first graph it is evident stock returns exert a mild, albeit persistent, and positive influence on the deficit which lasts for more than six years. A more interesting pattern emerges for the impulse response graph for the stock returns. Specifically, the effect of deficits on stock returns (see second graph horizontally) surfaces, initially, as positive and significant but after three quarters it becomes negative and remains negative for a much longer time. This behavior is consistent with the theoretically expected negative relationship between stock returns and the deficit, which implies market inefficiency. Since the negative impact of the deficit on the stock market does not surface immediately but after a year or so, it is quite plausible (to assume) that market participants overlook it or policy) has raised the interest rate. Note also that announcements regarding ignore it because they may believe that some other factors (including monetary upcoming monetary moves are much more (frequently) publicized than fiscal moves including increases or decreases in the deficit. Such announcements have only recently (i.e., the last few years) begun to be made publicly by the Fed's ex-Chairman Alan Greenspan.

As an alternative interpretation of the impulse response graphs above, the suggestion of market inefficiency could imply some indirect, long-term predictability of (time-varying) stock returns via budget deficits if the latter could affect some financial magnitude like dividends, returns or other variables. Under such circumstances, a permanent shock component on stock returns may not necessarily imply inefficiency of the stock market. Cash flows or dividend flows are known to be persistent and/or resemble the random walk. If the budget deficit (as a fraction of GDP) affects either cash flows, earnings or even the discount rate, then it would be consistent with the conventional rule for stock price determination. This conjecture (of long-run predictability) may be more convincing when we observe additional findings in later sections.

Notable is also the behavior of stock returns to changes in the money supply, which respond with a (two-quarter) lag to the monetary change, and the impact is then negative and persists for about two year (8 quarters). This lagged response of the stock returns is consistent with the general portfolio equilibrium approach explained above (see Hamburger and Kochin, 1972; Homa and Jaffee, 1971; and Rozeff, 1974). However, the negative and persistent response of the stock returns cannot be easily explained as other factors may be at play here such as an interest rate effect or a corporate earnings effect (both of which produce a positive sign), or a risk premium effect or an inflation effect (both of which produce a negative sign). We will, however, explicitly model some of these factors in subsequent sections.

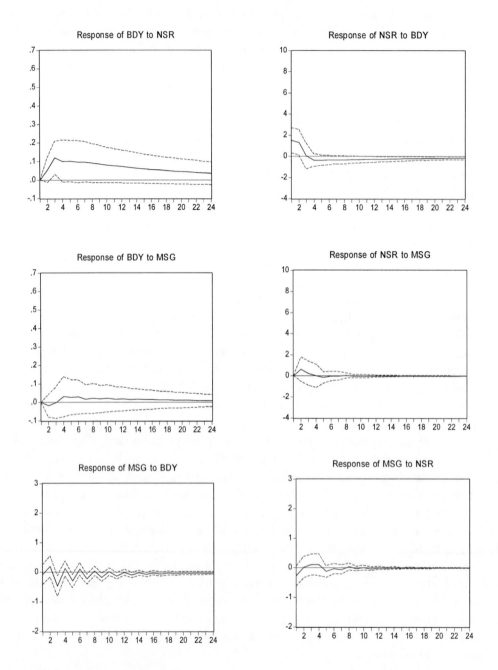

* dotted lines denote confidence bands

Figure 4. Impulse Response Graphs: Budget Deficit, BDY, Stock Returns, NSR and Money Supply Growth, MSG*

Finally, the graph for the money supply indicates a consistently alternating behavior, between positive and negative reactions, from the deficit (see first graph in last row) and a very mild, if any, reaction from the stock returns. These findings mean that there are no identifiable reactions to innovations to and from these magnitudes. Alternatively, it might be interpreted that the money supply does not significantly affect the deficit or stock returns and perhaps another monetary aggregate like the federal funds rate may be important. Better yet, it might be quite plausible to assume that the money supply impacts the stock market *indirectly* via its effects on the risk premium (magnitude not explicitly modeled here) or inflation (to be examined later). Nonetheless, it is well-known, after all, that the money supply or aggregates such as M1, M2 and so on, as meaningful and relevant measures of monetary policy, have broken down in the 1970s in favor of the federal funds rate henceforth.[2]

In view of the conclusions reached above that the money supply may not be a good indicator of the conduct of monetary policy, we decided to use the federal funds rate as the (more) appropriate tool for monetary policy. Consequently, Panel B of Table 3 exhibits the variance decomposition results for the stock returns, budget deficit, and the federal funds rate (we omitted the VAR coefficient results for the sake of space preservation but they are available upon request) for selected periods. In this specification (but not in the one with the money supply), we encountered a variable ordering problem. To this end, we again employed the Granger causality test to determine the order of the variables. It was revealed that stock returns Granger-cause the budget deficit which, in turn, causes the federal funds rate. So, the variable order will be as follows: stock returns, deficit, and federal funds rate. Finally, Akaike's FPE criterion suggested a three-lag optimal length for this VAR specification.

From the table, we observe that stock returns are rather 'exogenous' in the sense that shocks from neither the deficit nor the federal funds rate exert any significant impact on them. Almost all of its variation (97%) emanates from own innovations and only 3% from innovations in the deficit. The deficit's variance decomposition indicates a greater explanation from stock returns (about 17%) and a growing one from the federal funds rate (up to 2% after three years or beyond). Finally, the federal funds rate's decomposition results suggest an increasing fraction (about 7%) from the deficit and a decreasing one (from 6% to 3% or lower) from the stock returns account for its variability. These results imply that unexpected shocks from growing deficits seem to be more important than shocks from the stock market.

The impulse response graphs in Figure 5 highlight the following reactions by each variable. First, a shock to the deficit (that is, a reduction in the deficit, as measured here) has a positive impact on stock returns, initially, but a negative and a persistent one thereafter after about a year and a half (see second graph in 1st row). Second, the deficit responds in a significant, positive manner to innovations from stock returns but exhibits a weakening reaction over time, whereas it responds negatively and in a strengthening manner over time to innovations from the federal funds rate (see 1st graph in second row). Third, federal funds rate innovations do not impact stock returns at first but only with a lag of three quarters and then it dies out after two more quarters. Finally, the federal funds rate positively reacts to shocks from the deficit but negatively, initially, and positively after two years to shocks from the stock returns.

The response of the federal funds rate to fiscal shocks deserves some attention (2nd graph in last row). Recall that in Figure 4 we found an alternating pattern of responses by the money supply measure (to fiscal shocks) but a positive and perhaps expansive behavior with the federal funds rate. Although one can rationalize the second result, since higher deficits result

---

[2] We also did the analysis with M2 and M3 but did not find any qualitative difference in the results.

in increases in interest rates, the first is not easy to explain (with the current model specification). One thing that we can possibly say is that we observe a violation of the Ricardian Equivalence Proposition which postulates no relationship between the interest rate and the deficit(s). However, perhaps one needs to disaggregate fiscal policy (and hence, shocks) into its components (like taxes and expenditures) and see which one exerts such an impact on the interest rate. We plan to do these in the next section.

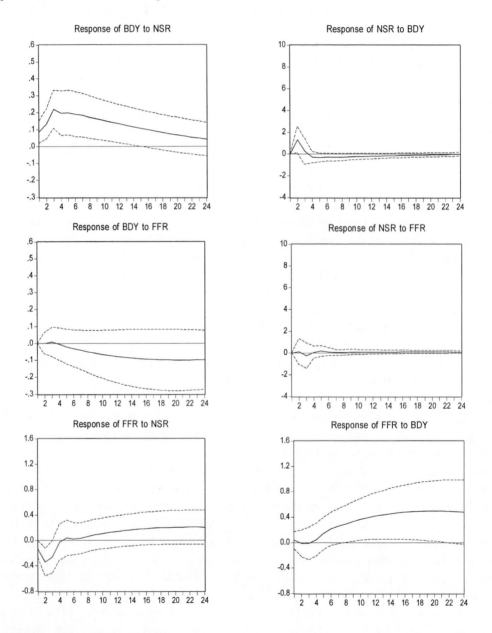

* dotted lines are confidence bands

Figure 5. Impulse Response Graphs: Budget Deficit, BDY, Stock Returns, NSR and Federal Funds Rate, FFR*

Finally, statistically speaking, the *atheoretical* nature of the VAR and the large number of parameters involved makes the estimated model (and its coefficients) difficult to interpret, as mentioned above. For that reason, we performed some block significance tests (or pairwise Granger causality tests) and the results from these tests are displayed in Table 4. In general, these results imply general significance of the tested variables (with the possible exception of the money supply in the stock returns equation in the first VAR specification, where the χ^2 statistic, 0.2712, is very low). The test statistic (*All*) in the last row of each tested equation tests the joint significance of all other lagged endogenous variables in that equation and its values always imply statistical significance overall. Note that the second set of these tests refers to the VAR specification with the deficit, stock returns and federal funds rate.

Table 4. Pairwise Granger causality tests for the VAR models

Block Exogeneity Test Results[1]			
Dependent Variable: ΔBDY			
Exclude	Chi-sq	df	Prob.
MSG	3.65458	3	0.2712
NSR	11.33566	3	0.1048
All	15.78348	6	0.0894
Dependent Variable: MSG			
Exclude	Chi-sq	df	Prob.
BDY	11.09002	3	0.0342
NSR	6.12379	3	0.1179
All	8.09839	6	0.2765
Dependent Variable: NSR			
Exclude	Chi-sq	df	Prob.
BDY	7.235476	3	0.0676
MSG	0.223412	3	0.9655
All	9.765503	6	0.0862
Block Exogeneity Test Results[2]			
Dependent Variable: ΔBDY			
Exclude	Chi-sq	df	Prob.
FFR	6.54349	3	0.2372
NSR	14.34505	3	0.1244
All	17.43313	6	0.1316
Dependent Variable: FFR			
Exclude	Chi-sq	df	Prob.
BDY	5.87649	3	0.1572
NSR	8.90803	3	0.0565
All	16.43312	6	0.0235
Dependent Variable: NSR			
Exclude	Chi-sq	df	Prob.
BDY	7.654864	3	0.0769
FFR	8.554875	3	0.0543
All	9.989060	6	0.0654

Notes: [1] tests refer to the VAR system with the deficit, money supply, and stock returns equation; [2] refers to the VAR system with the deficit, federal funds rate, and stock returns equation; sample: 1960:1 - 2006:4; included observations: 185; Chi-sq (χ^2) is a Wald statistic for the joint significance of each of the other lagged endogenous variables in that equation; the statistic in the last row of each test (All) is the χ^2 statistic of the joint significance of all other lagged endogenous variables in the equation; df denotes degrees of freedom.

4.2 Fiscal Policy and Stock Market Efficiency

This subsection follows closely Laopodis (2009) who investigated the degree of informational efficiency of the stock market to changes in the federal budget deficit. In this case, data gathered were monthly on the main three magnitudes and additional data was collected for short- and long-term interest rates, inflation rate and industrial production. The main model employed in this instance is as follows:

$$NSR_t = \alpha_0 + \beta_1 Z_t + \sum_{i=1}^{n1} \beta_{2,i} BDY_{t-i} + \sum_{j=1}^{n2} \beta_{3,j} M1G_{t-j} + \varepsilon_t \tag{5}$$

where NSR, BDY, and M1G are as defined above, Z is a vector of other macroeconomic variables serving as potential determinants of stock returns, and $n1$ and $n2$ are the lags on the fiscal and monetary variables, respectively. Finally, εt is a zero-mean, white noise error term. The vector of potential determinants of stock returns includes the following macro variables: two interest rates (one short-term, proxied by the 3-month Treasury bill, and one long-term, proxied by the 10-year Treasury note), inflation, and industrial production growth. The short term interest rate serves the purpose of having a proxy for the required rate of return of equity. If changes in fiscal and monetary policies affect the stock returns via the interest rate (or the required rate of return) then the fiscal and monetary measures should surface as insignificant in Eq. (5). Therefore, any correlation between the two measures and stock returns does not necessarily constitute rejection of market efficiency.

The final model surfaced with two monthly lags on the Treasury bill (TB), five lags for the nominal stock returns (NSR), up to twelve lags for the money supply growth (M1G), eight lags for the rate of inflation (INF), six lags for industrial production growth (IPG) and twelve lags for the budget deficit (as % of GDP, BDY). The results are shown in Table 5. From the findings, it can be seen that all of the variables surfaced as statistically significant, at varying degrees. For example, inflation is found to lower current nominal stock returns, despite its low explanatory power. The growth rate of industrial production, however, emerges as highly significant and is seen to either depress or enhance stock returns. This alternating behavior is consistent with the market's expectations in the sense that as economic activity picks up, inflationary expectations may be built up resulting in a corrective action by the Federal Reserve. Such action would take the form of an increase in the interest rate which, in turn, would lower stock returns. The short-term interest rate is also found to be statistically significant and appears to depress stock returns.

Regarding the evidence on the money supply growth, we observe that past monetary policy actions have had a marginally negative significance on current stock returns. This result for monetary policy is consistent with the semi-strong form of market efficiency which implies that participants in the US equity market appear to have included all available information about past and future monetary policy moves. Much more importantly, however, the results reveal that the lagged budget deficit exerts a significant effect on current nominal stock returns, perhaps a refutation of the (semi-strong form of the) efficient market hypothesis since the short-term interest rates surfaced as significant in the equation. This finding also reveals that the federal budget deficit has a consistently negative impact on current stock returns. Thus, one may tentatively conclude that fiscal movements are not incorporated into stock prices, rather monetary actions are more likely to be embedded in current stock prices (which is consistent with the efficient market hypothesis).

Table 5. Results on stock returns regressed on macro variables

Variable	Coefficient	T-Ratio	Probability
TB{1}	-6.04052	-1.9185	0.055726
TB{2}	6.38095	2.0437	0.041618
NSR{5}	0.08695	1.8707	0.062094
M1G{1}	-0.29017	-1.7156	0.086977
M1G{4}	0.19175	1.2953	0.195922
M1G{9}	-0.22895	-1.5247	0.128090
M1G{10}	-0.32126	-1.9968	0.091297
M1G{11}	-0.33877	-2.0454	0.101234
M1G{12}	-0.28052	-1.7237	0.085500
INF{6}	-1.05054	-1.8138	0.189639
INF{8}	-1.20609	-1.9446	0.149330
INF{10}	2.41022	2.9850	0.003004
IPG{2}	-0.78278	-2.4576	0.014395
IPG{3}	0.71869	2.2284	0.026388
IPG6}	-0.61810	-1.9849	0.047815
BDY{4}	-0.00953	-1.4390	0.150888
BDY{10}	-0.01773	-2.4412	0.015056
BDY{11}	-0.01891	-2.6589	0.008142
BDY{12}	-0.01133	-1.6510	0.099497

R-square = 0.1691; Standard Error of Estimate= 4.2732; $\log L$ = 239.083; Durbin-Watson = 2.0984.
Source: Laopodis (2009), p. 641.

4.3 Robustness tests

In this section we will perform several additional tests to see if our above results remain robust (stable) and not 'driven' by several events or alternative model specifications. Some events considered here are the Tax Reform Acts of 1986 and 1997, the market crashes of 1987 and 2000, and the stock market boom of mid 1990s. The two tax reform events called for the restructuring of the income tax code in the U.S. and reduced tax rates (on income and capital gains) significantly. The first stock market crash was short-lived but the second one lasted for a few years. Finally, the market boom of the mid 1990s (due to a tech sector bubble) gave rise to spectacular gains to the stock market. Because splitting the sample into subperiods would only leave us with a few observations, we reran the models for the entire period using dummy variables for each of these events.

The Tax Acts of 1986 and 1997 did not have any perceptible effects on stock market nominal returns since the dummy variable was statistically insignificant. This finding is justified because at the same time that the marginal tax rates were reduced (as in 1997), the U.S. economy experienced a boon in its stock market due to advances in technology and a sharp reduction in energy returns. As a result, tax revenues actually rose and the deficit was reduced. The same conclusion was reached with the inclusion of the dummy variable for the 1987 or 2000 market crashes. The aftermaths of the crash(es) did not impact upon the deficit and thus there was no significant influence of either crash dummies on either the stock market (measured by nominal or real returns) or the federal deficit.

Finally, the use of the dummy variable for the market boom of the mid to late 1990s revealed a positive and statistically significant coefficient for the dummy (for the budget deficit and stock returns equations only). Although the basic variance decomposition results were not significantly altered when we employed the three deficit measures, the impulse response graphs (in Figure 6) yielded the following conclusions (relative to Figure 4). First, and most important, the deficit's (BDY) responses to shocks from stock returns and the federal funds rate (FFR) have not been changed in nature. Second, the response of nominal stock returns (NSR) to shocks from the deficit remained the same but these from the federal funds rate emerged as more turbulent despite exhibiting a similar pattern as in Figure 5.[3] Finally, the reaction of the federal funds rate to shocks from the deficit becomes negative, at first, then positive and remaining positive until it dies out after four years. The same can be said to its response to shocks in the stock market which surfaces as swift(er) alternating between negative and positive values. Contrast these reactions of the federal funds rate to those which took much longer to materialize in this manner when the dummy variable was omitted in the specification that yielded the third graph in Figure 5.

Overall then, although the basic nature of the relationships among the variables has not been distorted, the speed of adjustment (or response) of each of these variables to shocks from the other variables has been shortened. For example, the reaction of the stock market to shocks from the federal funds rate surfaces immediately (within a quarter) as negative, relative to a year's time as seen in Figure 3, and the impact of the deficit on the stock market (regardless of the measure) emerges as stronger now than is evident in Figure 5. Therefore, we are very confident that the results from the earlier VAR specification were adequate in capturing the complex dynamics among the stock market, fiscal and monetary policies for the 1960:I to 2006:IV period.

Finally, given the marginal finding of cointegration among the three basic variables (BDY, NSR, and FFR) above, we decided to re-estimate a Vector Error-Correction Model (VECM) and contrast its findings with the basic VAR model estimated above. The impulse response graphs are depicted in Figure 7 in two panels: panel A shows selected results using a VAR (taken from Figure 5), whereas panel B shows the corresponding VECM results based on one cointegrating vector (no confidence band are available for a VEC specification) in order to facilitate a direct comparison between the two models. We note no difference in the results from the VECM which suggests that our VAR model was robust to an alternative model specification. In other words, even when assuming cointegration among the three variables the responses of a variable to shocks from the other variables were not changed.

---

[3] When we used the real stock returns, the results were very similar.

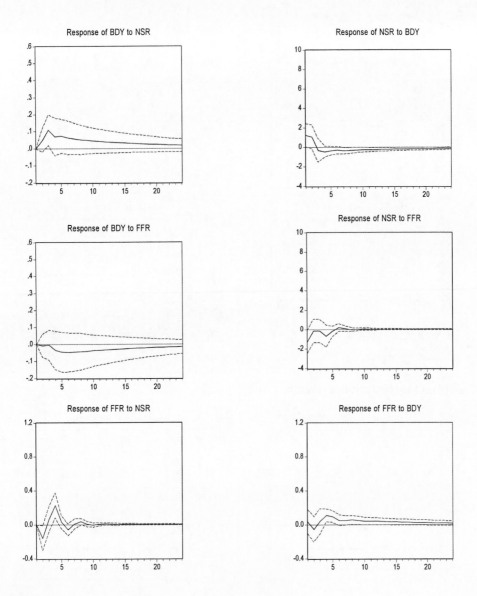

[1] VAR model graphs with 1995 boom market dummy
* dotted lines denote confidence bands

Figure 6. Impulse Response Graphs: Budget Deficit, BDY, Nominal Stock Returns, NSR, and Federal Funds Rate, FFR[1]*

5. ADDITIONAL EVIDENCE ON THE DEFICIT - STOCK RETURNS LINKAGE

In this section we will use different measures of fiscal policy and market returns in the VAR specifications to further shed light into the relationship.

Panel A: No cointegrating vector

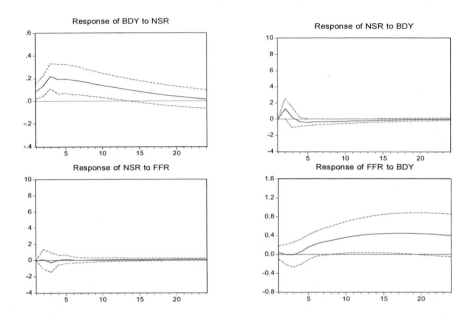

Panel B: One cointegrating vector

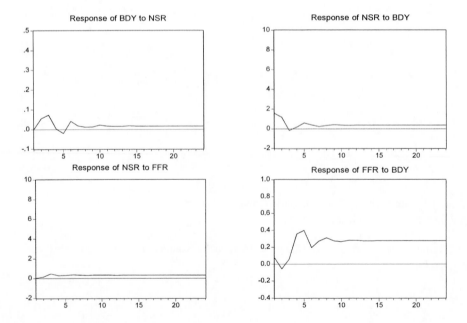

** no confidence bands are available in VECM

Figure 7. Impulse Response Graphs: Budget Deficit, BDY, Nominal Stock Returns, NSR, and Federal Funds Rate, FFR**

Specifically, we will decompose the fiscal measure (i.e., federal budget deficit) into taxes (or tax receipts, net of transfers) received by the government and general government expenditures (also net of transfers).[4] Both variables will be expressed as percentages of GDP. What is the rationale for this decomposition? As mentioned in the introduction, changes in government taxation and spending have an impact on the economy and the financial markets. Tax revenues depend on the state of the economy (that is, on the business cycle), while expenditures are less prone to economic fluctuations. What are the impacts of changes in taxation and expenditures by the government on stock prices?

Panel A

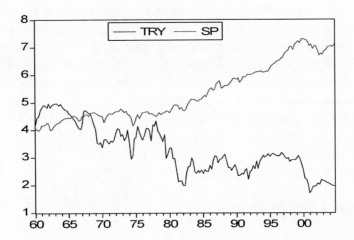

Panel B

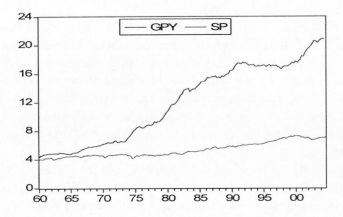

Figure 8. Tax Receipts (as % of GDP), TRY, Government Expenditures (as % of GDP), GPY, (log of) Stock Prices, SP*

In general, while higher taxes depress investment spending and thus affect the business cycle with a lag and, by extension, the stock market, higher (certain) government expenditures boost economic activity. Consequently, one should expect a negative sign

---

[4] The data were obtained from the NIPA (National Income and Product Accounts) site.

between taxation and stock returns since higher taxes present a disincentive to invest (see, for instance, Blanchard and Perotti, 1999). Other researchers have found exactly the opposite. For instance, Auerbach and Kotlikoff (1983) examined the impact of the government's Economic Recovery Tax Act (ERTA) and found that it induced a huge capital loss to the economy. Thus, the exact impact of tax changes is still an empirical issue.

The tax receipts as a fraction of GDP variable (denoted as *TRY*) can be considered as an aggregate tax rate imposed by the government on national output. Panel A of Figure 8 shows the (log of) stock returns and *TRY* for the 1960-2006 period. We see from this graph an inverse relationship between the two magnitudes seen as more pronounced after the Taxpayer Relief Act of 1997, which called for a reduction in the long-term capital gains tax from 28% to 20%. The second variable, the total government purchases (denoted as *GPY*), captures the government's demand on the national output. A priori, we should expect a positive sign for this variable as (certain categories of) government spending may stimulate the economy and thus the stock market via advances in productivity growth (see, Aschauer, 1989). Panel B of Figure 8 shows the (log of) stock returns and GPY for the same period. We observe from the graph a direct relationship between the two magnitudes despite a reduction in government expenditures in the mid 1990s. Finally, three alternative measures of market returns will be employed namely, the market excess returns and corporate profits (before and after taxes) along with the above fiscal measures and the federal funds rate.

5.1 Disaggregated Deficit Measures

Preliminary statistical investigation showed that tax receipts (as share of GDP), the federal funds rate, and the (log of) stock returns all contain a unit root, based on the Augmented Dickey-Fuller (Dickey and Fuller, 1987) test but become stationary when expressed in first-difference form. The next step would be to check if these variables are cointegrated. The Johansen (1995) cointegration test showed a mixed picture. Specifically, when assuming no trend in the data and the cointegrating relationship(s), cointegration was present, but when assuming a linear trend (with or without an intercept) or a quadratic trend (with an intercept), *no* cointegration was found. The conventional wisdom is to invoke the second assumption on the data because magnitudes are usually trending over time.[5] So, a VAR specification will be estimated, similar to the one in equation (4) above, with all three variables in levels.

Table 6 contains the VAR estimates, in Panel A, and the variance decompositions for selected lags, in Panel B. From the estimates, we see general absence of short-run linkages among the three variables. We see such linkages only in the cases of the taxes, *TRY*, and the federal funds rate, *FFR*, equations. Specifically, current tax receipts are positively and negatively affected by one- and three-quarter lags of stock returns, respectively, and by negative one- and a positive three-quarter lags of the federal funds rate. By contrast, the federal funds rate is negatively (and strongly) affected by lagged tax receipts but not by (much by any) movements in the stock market.

---

[5] We checked the robustness of the VAR with the vector error-correction model and found very little difference in the results (including the variance decompositions and impulse response graphs).

Table 6. VAR results for taxes (as share of GDP), TRY, federal funds rate, FFR, and stock returns, NSR, 1960-2006

Panel A: VAR Estimates			
Variable	NSR	TRY	FFR
NSR(-1)	0.11168*	0.08644	-2.54952*
	[10.1526]	[-0.65907]	[-3.09251]
NSR(-2)	-0.16848	-0.09730*	1.271781*
	[1.63211]	[2.87801]	[3.42473]
NSR(-3)	0.10598	-0.10894*	-0.89910
	[1.23017]	[-3.21725]	[-1.15190]
TRY(-1)	0.26320*	-0.27975*	-1.32172*
	[2.54166]	[-8.35180]	[-4.32860]
TRY(-2)	-0.16676	0.27866*	0.61154
	[-1.63605]	[3.43088]	[1.71247]
TRY(-3)	-0.12167*	-0.14782*	1.32129
	[-3.03271]	[-1.98887]	[2.28683]
FFR(-1)	0.00324	-0.00565*	0.11430
	[0.08590]	[-2.37708]	[11.5205]
FFR(-2)	-0.00324	-0.00565*	-0.32375*
	[-0.33291]	[-1.99322]	[-3.56364]
FFR(-3)	0.00436	0.00634	0.23584*
	[0.37053]	[0.89855]	[2.94611]
Constant	0.02665	0.43220	-0.07028
	[1.01266]	[1.45349]	[-1.11291]
Diagnostic Statistics			
R-squared	0.453204	0.234657	0.389739
Adj. R-squared	0.385034	0.217170	0.354247
F-statistic	3.012303	1.78992	8.908624
Log likelihood	-243.1272	-190.3239	-233.4413
FPE	1.1249		
Panel B: Variance Decompositions Results			
Variance Decomposition of NSR			
Period	Stand. Error	NSR	TRY	FFR
2	0.100301	96.28933	3.567824	0.142851
4	0.101087	95.43601	4.573251	0.090743
6	0.104342	94.40902	5.535057	0.140413
8	0.104102	93.48176	6.585561	0.162631
10	0.120762	92.36286	7.574269	0.164450
12	0.135194	90.29936	9.567803	0.122612
Variance Decomposition of TRY			
2	0.133483	0.039768	97.91187	2.048365
4	0.194289	0.670283	93.63466	6.695058
6	0.236347	1.549693	90.23508	8.615223
8	0.265101	1.851978	85.31070	17.37324
10	0.285269	1.314439	82.21500	17.00563
12	0.300502	2.512966	78.13613	21.30899
Variance Decomposition of FFR			
2	1.311268	2.58781	3.412792	95.28427
4	1.834198	2.45201	7.774760	90.73224
6	2.189409	2.06557	21.19604	76.14825
8	2.429415	1.19416	24.13671	74.84467
10	2.667660	1.26784	20.27112	79.89449
12	2.920588	1.23853	15.72708	82.88759

Notes: * denotes significance at the 5% level; t-ratios in parentheses; selected lags for variance decompositions.

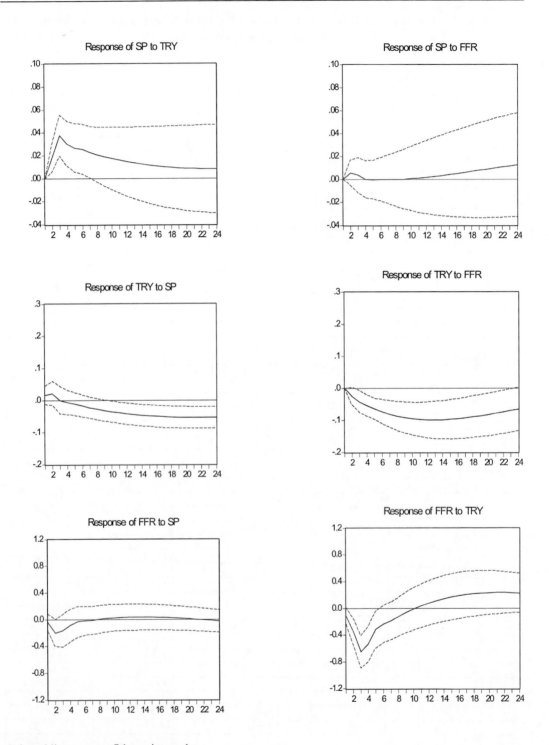

* dotted lines are confidence intervals

Figure 9. Impulse Response Graphs, Nominal Stock Returns, NSR, Tax Receipts (as % of GDP), TRY, and Federal Funds Rate, FFR*

These results merit some explanation. An increase in tax receipts by the government, *ceteris paribus*, implies a lower (future) government borrowing (or less debt) and thus a lower interest rate. This finding is consistent with evidence of substantial effects of a tax change on share prices as reported by Lang and Shackelford (2000) and Sinai and Gyourko (2004). Alternatively, stock market declines mean lower corporate profits and lower tax revenues, and this might necessitate higher government borrowing which would place an upward pressure on the interest rate in the future. In either case, this would constitute a violation of the Ricardian Equivalence Proposition again. In other words, the relationship between tax receipts and stock returns should not be statistically significant if market participants correctly expect future tax increases and price them fully currently.

The variance decomposition results (in Panel B) are more informative, however. For instance, tax receipts are seen to account for some significant portion of the stock returns error forecast variance and a high (and perhaps growing) fraction (above 20%) of the federal funds rate's variance. The federal funds rate accounts for a negligible percentage of stock returns' decomposition but a much larger portion of the taxes' decomposition (over 25% on average and rising). Finally, stock returns explain a small (and declining) portion of the federal funds rate's variance decomposition (ranging from 2% to 1%) but a similar one (about 2%) of the taxes' decomposition.

These findings are strongly reinforced by the impulse response graphs in Figure 9. Shocks from the stock market positively impact taxes initially, but negatively after four quarters and remain negative and persistent for several years ahead. A similar picture emerges with the shocks from the federal funds rate which negatively affect tax receipts and tend to only gradually die out well after six years. Shocks from taxes elicit a very strong and positive reaction, initially, by stock returns (for the first 3 quarters) but this reaction subsides thereafter and seems to decay very slowly and smoothly (after six years). Shocks from the federal funds rate appear to bring out a small positive or no response by the stock market subsequently by a year or so, but the response remains positive and rather persistent over time. Finally, shocks from the stock market and the taxes impact negatively the federal funds rate, in the short run, and positively thereafter but the impact of the taxes is much stronger than that of the stock returns. These results imply that tax receipts and the federal funds rate exert a lasting (and significant) impact on the stock market in the long run. Moreover, the initial (i.e., short run) behavior of the stock market to unanticipated tax revenue innovations is counterintuitive and perhaps this works through other concurrent changes in the tax code and/or the market (like reductions in the marginal tax rates or a booming stock market).

In general, the above evidence of a negative reaction of the federal funds rate to shocks from (an increase in) taxes is consistent with the argument that the Fed might feel compelled to step in the market should it deem necessary to offset the decline in the stock market due to higher taxes (and a possible future reduction in economic growth). Therefore, this result is in line with our hypothesis that monetary and fiscal policies should be examined simultaneously.

Finally, the results using the government expenditures magnitude (*GPY*) did not reveal any significant insights and that is why we are not presenting them. Perhaps the only finding of special mention was the observation that the reaction of the stock returns to a government expenditure shock surfaced as negative, at first, before turning into positive after more than two years. There are several explanations for this result. For instance, as the government increases its expenditures, the interest rate is raised because it issues more debt. A rise in the interest rate, in turn, is bad news for the stock market which retreats. As mentioned above and combining the roles of fiscal and monetary policy, to the extent that the Fed feels that a situation like this threatens economic health, it will be forced to counter this by accommodating the market (and lowering the federal funds rate). A reduction in the federal funds rate following a decrease in taxes (due to a repressed stock market) is borne out of our results above meaning that such a scenario is possible. Another plausible explanation is to assume that the initial market's reaction to such expenditures was not viewed as good news. However, after market participants realize that these expenditures are good for future economic growth and the stock market in the long run, the market moved in a positive manner. Nonetheless, the VAR output showed that the relationship is statistically insignificant.

5.2 Alternative Measures of Market Returns

We experiment in this subsection with various proxies for market returns namely, before- and after-tax corporate profits, *BTPROF* and *ATPROF* respectively, and excess market returns, *EMR*, in combination with the above two measures of the deficit and the federal funds rate. Preliminary statistical investigation indicated absence of cointegration in any combination of variables as they were included in each specification and, at times, the variable ordering issues were resolved via the use of Granger-causality tests. Below we will present only those results that revealed important insights concentrating on the interactions among the market returns, tax receipts, and the federal funds rate.

Only the following three-variable combinations yielded important results: taxes, *TRY*, after-tax corporate profits, *ATPROF*, and federal funds rate, *FFR*; *TRY, EMR, FFR*; and *BDY, EMR*, and *FFR*. For each of these groups, we will report their variance decomposition tables and the impulse response graphs. Selected variance decomposition results are shown in Panels A, B, and C of Table 7, which correspond to each of the three groups, while selected impulse response graphs are illustrated in Figure 10 in three panels, respectively.

Three observations can be made form the variance decomposition table. First, the tax receipts variable accounts for a significant portion of the variance decompositions of both the after-tax profits and the excess returns variables and perhaps are more pronounced for the after-tax profits. Second, the federal budget deficit explains a notable percentage of the variance decomposition of the excess market returns but much smaller than that of the tax receipts variable. And third, the federal funds rate does not appear to affect the error forecast variance of either measure of market returns.

The impulse response graphs from Panel A indicate that shocks to (after-tax) corporate profits elicit negative responses from the federal funds rate, a finding that economically makes sense. An unexpected increase, for instance, in the (short-term) interest rate (or the discount rate) lowers the firms' expected returns and thus corporate profits which, in turn, imply lower tax revenues for the government. A similar response is seen from the second graph in the figure. There, the reaction to an (unanticipated) increase in taxes results in lower corporate profits and this reaction remains negative for a long period (up to perhaps six years) before it is incorporated.[6] Essentially, the same finding is seen from panel B where the

---

[6] It is important to note that this reaction of the after-tax profits emerged as stronger than that of the before-tax corporate profits variable in an otherwise very similar reaction.

response of the market excess returns to shocks from taxes is negative but alternating between negative and positive reactions before the shock is fully absorbed (up to six years as in the case of the *ATPROF* variable above). By contrast, the response of the excess returns to innovations from the federal budget deficit (in Panel C) is positive and remains positive for a long time (well after six years). This behavior is consistent with the earlier findings that the deficit positively impacts upon the stock market (nominal stock returns). Also, the reactions of the budget deficit to shocks from *EMR* are positive initially, and become briefly negative at about a year before they turn positive again then negative and so on.

So, what is the message from these results? First, two conclusions are clear: corporate profits, in general, negatively react to shocks from taxes but excess stock returns positively react to higher deficits. Therefore, corporate profits are more sensitive to disaggregated deficit changes than aggregate deficit movements or that (shocks from) taxes have a strong and immediate impact on corporate profits than simply changes in the federal budget deficit. However, the long-run impact of the federal deficit is more persistent than that of taxes since the latter's impact tends to die out within five years but the former's goes well beyond seven years. So, taxes appear to have a strong short-run effect on corporate profits but deficits a strong long-run effect on the market as a whole. This implies that budget deficits are important determinants for the stock market for long horizons.

Table 7. Variance decomposition results from disaggregated returns

Panel A: Variance Decompositions with TRY, ATPROF, FFR			
Variance Decomposition ATPROF			
Period	Stand. Error	TRY	ATPROF	FFR
2	0.0792669	12.161448	87.55596	0.28258
4	0.0811420	15.750704	83.85128	0.39801
6	0.0824403	15.943621	83.59728	0.45909
8	0.0831791	17.104132	82.26640	0.62946
10	0.0843019	19.229510	80.11675	0.65373
12	0.0844099	19.424316	79.92256	0.65311
Panel B: Variance Decompositions with TRY, EMR, FFR			
Variance Decomposition of EMR			
Period	Stand. Error	TRY	EMR	FFR
2	7.977897	0.4511312	99.15070	0.39816
4	8.497422	10.870776	87.75856	1.37066
6	8.543214	11.050363	87.21844	1.73119
8	8.747286	12.166771	83.80154	4.03168
10	8.786571	12.385784	83.18402	4.43019
12	8.818623	12.790081	82.71399	4.49592
Panel C: Variance Decompositions with BDY, EMR, FFR			
Variance Decomposition of EMR			
Period	Stand. Error	BDY	EMR	FFR
2	0.123291	0.788253	99.137743	0.07399
4	0.167720	3.373758	96.098278	0.52796
6	0.213087	5.504963	93.809632	0.68540
8	0.241029	5.615384	93.837023	0.54759
10	0.265423	5.229342	94.292068	0.47858
12	0.285683	5.048014	94.535240	0.41674

Panel A: TRY, ATPROF, FFR

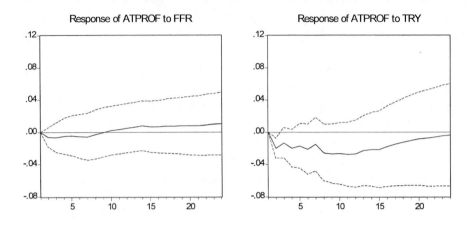

Panel B: TRY, EMR, FFR

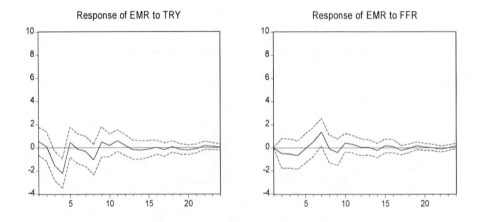

Panel C: EMR, BDY, FFR

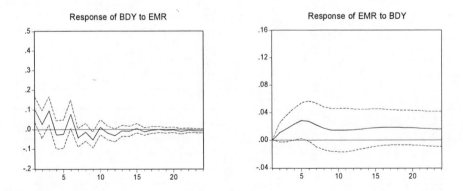

* dotted lines are confidence bands

Figure 10. Impulse Response Graphs with Disaggregated Returns Measures*

So, what is the message from these results? First, two conclusions are clear: corporate profits, in general, negatively react to shocks from taxes but excess stock returns positively react to higher deficits. Therefore, corporate profits are more sensitive to disaggregated deficit changes than aggregate deficit movements or that (shocks from) taxes have a strong and immediate impact on corporate profits than simply changes in the federal budget deficit. However, the long-run impact of the federal deficit is more persistent than that of taxes since the latter's impact tends to die out within five years but the former's goes well beyond seven years. So, taxes appear to have a strong short-run effect on corporate profits but deficits a strong long-run effect on the market as a whole. This implies that budget deficits are important determinants for the stock market for long horizons.

6. SUMMARY AND CONCLUSIONS

This paper examined the dynamic linkages among the federal budget deficit, monetary policy and the stock market for the 1960-2006 period using quarterly data. The empirical results among the federal budget deficit (as % of GDP), nominal stock returns, and money supply magnitudes reveal reciprocal, short-run linkages between deficits and stock returns but not with the money supply. The first finding suggests that deficits matter for the stock market and imply a violation of the Ricardian Equivalence Proposition, which states that current government deficits become irrelevant for current portfolio substitution decisions by rational investors if they correctly anticipate increased future taxation. Upon replacing the money supply with the federal funds rate, in view of the relative exogeneity of the money supply as a measure of monetary policy, we see that higher deficits increase the short-term interest rate due to higher government borrowing, *ceteris paribus*.

Further analyses, using decompositions of the federal deficit (into taxes and government spending, both as fractions of GDP), show a higher sensitivity of the stock market to them and especially to taxes relative to spending and/or the general deficit measures. When employing variations of market returns such as before- and after-tax corporate profits and excess market returns, we observe several economically significant results. For instance, corporate profits are more sensitive to disaggregated deficit changes than to aggregate deficit movements, meaning that taxes have a strong and immediate impact on corporate profits than changes in the federal budget deficit. However, the impact of the federal deficit is more relevant for the stock market for the long run while that of taxes for the short run.

Overall then, we conclude that U.S. federal deficits do matter for the stock market and are becoming more important over time. It should not come as a surprise that the Fed's ex-chairman made (and still makes) it a routine in his public speeches to include information and/or warnings on the growing size of the federal deficit and its potential financial implications. A useful exercise would be to see if deficits are becoming more and more important in the eyes of investors using different methodologies and additional data/variables. Moreover, that study could be extended to draw inferences about market efficiency with respect to government deficits and the further determination of validation or violation of the Ricardian Equivalence Proposition and its policy implications.

REFERENCES

Akaike, H., 1976, Canonical Correlation Analysis of Time Series and the Use of an Information Criterion, in System Identification: Advances and Case Studies, R.K. Mehra and D.G. Lainiotis, eds., New York: Academic Press, 27-96.

Allen, S. D. and M.D. Smith, 1983, Government borrowing and monetary accommodation, *Journal of Monetary Economics* 12, 605-16.

Ali, S.M. and Hasan, M.A, 2003, Is the Canadian stock market efficient with respect to fiscal policy? Some vector autoregression results, *Journal of Economics and Business* 45(1), pp. 45-59.

Aschauer, David, 1989, Is public expenditure productive? *Journal of Monetary Economics* 23, 177-200.

Auerbach, A. and L. Kotlikoff, Investment versus savings incentives: the size of the bang for the buck and the potential for self-financing business tax cuts, in L.H. Meyer, eds., The Economic Consequences of Government Deficits, USA: Kluwer-Nijihof, 1983, 121-149.

Barnhart, S.W., and A. F. Darrat, 1989, Federal deficits and money growth in the United States: a vector autoregressive analysis, *Journal of Banking and Finance* 13, 137-49.

Barro, R.J., 1974, Are government bonds net wealth? *Journal of Political Economy* 82, 1095-1117.

Bernanke, B.S. and Kuttner, K.N., 2005. What explains the stock market's reaction to Federal Reserve policy? *Journal of Finance* 3, 1221-1257.

Blanchard, Olivier, J, 1981, Output, the stock market and interest rates, *American Economic Review* 71, 132-43.

Bordo, M. and D.C., Wheelock, 2004, Monetary Policy and Asset Returns: A Look Back at Past U.S. Stock Market Booms. Federal Reserve Bank of St. Louis *Review* 86 (6), November/ December 2004, pp. 19-44.

Long-term economic effects of chronically large federal deficits, 2005, *Congressional Budget Office,* October 13.

Cooper, R.B.L, 1974. Efficient capital markets and the quantity theory of money, *Journal of Finance* 29, 383-403.

Craine, R. and V. Martin. 2004.Monetary policy shocks and security market responses. Working Paper (July), University of California, Berkeley.

Cutler, D., 1988. Tax reform and the stock market: an asset price approach. *American Economic Review* 78, 1107-1117.

Darrat, Ali F., 1987. Money and stock prices in West Germany and the UK: is the stock market efficient? *Quarterly Journal of Business and Economics* 26.

_____, 1988. On fiscal policy and the stock market, *Journal of Money, Credit and Banking* 20(3), 353-363.

_____, 1990, Stock returns, money and fiscal deficits, *Journal of Financial and Quantitative Analysis* 25(3), 387-398.

_____, and J., Brocato, 1994. Stock market efficiency and the federal budget deficit: another anomaly, *The Financial Review* 29, 49-75.

DeLeeuw, F. and T.M. Holloway, 1985, The measurement and significance of the cyclicaly-adjusted federal budget and debt, *Journal of Money, Credit and Banking* 17, 232-42.

Dickey, D.A., and W.A., Fuller, 1987. Distribution of the Estimators for Autoregressive Time Series with a Unit Root. *Journal of the American Statistical Association* 74, pp. 427-431.

Engen, E., and R. G. Hubbard, 2005, Federal government debt and interest rates, *National Bureau of Economic Research Macroeconomics Annual.*

Ewing, B.T., 1998. The impact of federal budget deficits on movements in the stock market: evidence from Australia and France. *Applied Economics Letters* 5, 649-651.

Fama, E.F., and G.W. Schwert, 1977, Asset returns and inflation, *Journal of Financial Economics* 5, 115-46.

Fama, E.F. and French, K. R. (1988). Permanent and temporary components of stock returns. *Journal of political Economy* 96, 246-273.

Gale, William G. and Peter R. Orszag, 2003. The economic effects of long-term fiscal discipline, Urban-Brookings Tax Policy Center *Discussion Paper* No. 8, April.

_____, 2004, Budget deficits, national saving, and interest rates, *Brookings Papers on Economic Activity* No. 2, 101-187.

Geske, R., and R. Roll, 1983, The fiscal and monetary linkage between stock returns and inflation, *Journal of Finance* 38, 7-33.

Goolsbee, A., 1998. Investment tax incentives, prices, and the supply of capital goods. *Quarterly Journal of Economics* 113(1), 121-148.

Hamburger, J., and L. Kochin, 1971, Money and stock prices: the channels of influence, *Journal of Finance* 26, 1056-66.

Hancock, D.G., 1989, Fiscal policy, monetary policy and the efficiency of the stock market, *Economics Letters* 31, 65-69.

Hoelscher, G.P., 1986, New evidence on deficits and interest rates, *Journal of Money, Credit and Banking* 18, 1-17.

Homa, K.E., and D.M. Jaffee, 1971, The supply of money and common stock prices, *Journal of Finance* 26, 1056-66.

James, C, S. Koreisha, and M. Partch, 1985, A VARMA analysis of the causal relations among stock returns, real output, and nominal interest rates, *Journal of Finance* 40, 1375-84.

Johansen, S., 1995. Likelihood-based inference in cointegrated vector autoregressive models. Oxford University Press.

Lang, M.H. and D.A. Shackelford, 2000. Capitalization of capital gains taxes: evidence from stock price reactions to the 1997 rate reduction. *Journal of Public Economics* 76, 69-85.

Laopodis, Nikiforos T., 2006, Dynamic linkages among the stock market, inflation, monetary policy and real activity, *The Financial Review* 41, 513-545.

_____, 2009, Fiscal Policy and Stock Market Efficiency: Evidence from the USA, *Quarterly Review of Economics and Finance* 49, 633-650.

_____, 2010, Fiscal policy, Monetary Policy and the Equity Market, Working paper.

Lee, Bong-Soo, 1992, Causal relations among stock returns, interest rates, inflation, and real activity, *Journal of Finance* 42(4), 1591-1603.

Lee, Unro, 1997, Stock market and macroeconomic policies: new evidence from Pacific Basin countries, *Multinational Finance Journal* 1(2), 273-289.

_____, 2004. U.S. Asset Returns and Fiscal Policy: New Empirical Investigation. *Quarterly Journal of Economics and Business* 3 and 4, Summer/Autumn.

McCarthy, J., M. Najand, and B. Seifert, 1990, Empirical tests of the proxy hypothesis, *Financial Review* 25, 251-64.

Park, Sangkyun, 1997, Rationality of Negative Stock-Price Responses to Strong Economic Activity. *Financial Analysts Journal* 53(5), 52-56.

Patelis, A.D., 1997, Stock return predictability and the role of monetary policy, *Journal of Finance* 52(5), 1951-1972.

Rezessy, A. (2005). Estimating the immediate impact of monetary policy shocks on the exchange rate and other asset prices in Hungary, Magyar Nemzeti Bank (Economics department) Occasional Paper no. 38.

Rigobon, R., 2003. Identification through heteroskedasticity. *The Review of Economics and Statistics* 85(4), 777-792.

Rigobon, R. and Sack, B., 2003. Measuring the reaction of monetary policy to the stock market. *Quarterly Journal of Economics* 118, 639-670.

Rozeff, M.S., 1974, Money and stock prices. *Journal of Financial Economics* 1, 243-302.

Shah, A., 1984, Crowding out, capital accumulation, the stock market, and money-financed fiscal policy. *Journal of Money, Credit, and Banking* 16(part 1), 461-473.

Siklos, P., and B. Kwok, 1999, Stock Returns and Inflation: A New Test of Competing Hypotheses, *Applied Financial Economics* 9, 567-81.

Sinai, Allen, 2006. Deficits, expected deficits, financial markets, and the economy. *North American Journal of Economics and Finance* 17, 79-101.

Sinai, T. and J. Gyourko, 2004. The asset price incidence of capital gains taxes: evidence from the Taxpayer Relief Act of 1997 and publicly-traded real estate firms. *Journal of Public Economics* 88, 1543-1565.

Tavares, J. and Valkanov, R., 2003. Fiscal policy and asset returns. Working Paper (August), UCLA.

Thorbecke, W., 1997, On stock market returns and monetary policy, *Journal of Finance* 52(2), 635-654.

Tobin, James, 1969, A general equilibrium approach to monetary theory, *Journal of Money, Credit and Banking* 1, 15-29.

Wei, K.C. John and K. Matthew Wong, 1992, Tests of inflation and industry portfolio stock returns, *Journal of Economics and Business* 44, 77-94.

In: The Stock Market
Editor: Allison S. Wetherby

ISBN: 978-1-61122-545-7
© 2011 Nova Science Publishers, Inc.

Chapter 2

STRATEGIC STOCK MARKETS RISK ASSESSMENT IN EMERGING ECONOMIES[*]

Mazin A. M. Al Janabi
Department of Economics and Finance,
United Arab Emirates University
Al-Ain, United Arab Emirates

ABSTRACT

The aim of this study is to fill a gap in modern risk management literature and especially from the perspective of stock markets in emerging economies. This paper provides pioneering strategic risk assessment techniques that can be applied to investment and trading portfolios in emerging financial markets, such as in the context of the Gulf Cooperation Council (GCC) stock markets. In this work, key equity price risk assessment methods and modeling techniques that financial entities, regulators and policymakers should consider in developing their daily price risk management objectives are examined and tailored to the particular needs of emerging markets. This is with the intent of setting-up the basis of a modeling technique for the measurement of strategic equity price exposures in the day-to-day financial trading operations. While extensive literatures have reviewed the statistical and economic proposition of Value at Risk (VaR) models, this paper provides real-world modeling techniques that can be applied to financial trading portfolios under the notion of illiquid and adverse financial market circumstances. In this paper, we demonstrate a practical modeling approach for the measurement of stock markets risk exposure for financial trading portfolios that contain several illiquid equity asset positions. This approach is based on the renowned concept of liquidity-adjusted VaR (LVaR) along with the innovation of a simulation tool utilizing matrix-algebra technique. To this end, a matrix-algebra modeling technique is used to create the necessary quantitative infrastructures and trading risk simulations. This tactic is a useful form to avoid mathematical complexity, as more and more securities are added to the portfolio of assets. In addition, it can simplify the financial modeling and programming process and can allow as well a clear-cut incorporation of short (sell) and long (buy) positions in the daily risk management process. As such, our broad risk model

---

[*] e-mail: mazinaljanabi@gmail.com and m.aljanabi@uaeu.ac.ae

can simultaneously handle LVaR appraisal under normal and severe market conditions besides it takes into account the effects of liquidity of the traded equity securities. In order to illustrate the proper use of LVaR and stress-testing methods, real-world paradigms of trading risk assessment are presented for the GCC stock markets. To this end, simulation case studies are attained with the aspiration of bringing about a reasonable framework for the measurement of equity trading risk exposures. The modeling techniques discussed in this paper will aid financial markets' participants, regulators and policymakers in the instigation of meticulous and up to date simulation algorithms to handle equity price risk exposure. The suggested analytical methods and procedures can be put into practice in virtually all emerging economies, if they are bespoke to correspond to every market's preliminary level of intricacy.

JEL Classifications: C10, C13, G20, and G28

Keywords: Asset Management; Emerging Economies; Emerging Markets; Financial Engineering; Financial Modeling; Financial Risk Management; GARCH Model; GCC Financial Markets; Liquidity Risk; Portfolio Management; Stress Testing; Value at Risk.

INTRODUCTION AND OVERVIEW

The global deregulation of financial markets has created new investment opportunities, which in turn require the development of new instruments, regulations and efficient risk assessment and modeling techniques to cope with the increased risks. Nonetheless, many disastrous financial crises have hit several financial and non-financial corporations in emerging economies; even so, the developments and innovations in equity cash-markets instruments and derivative securities are on continuous growth. Indeed, emerging countries and markets, since the early nineties, have started to play an important role in the trading of standardized and over-the-counter (OTC) equity derivatives and cash-markets securities.

Yet while emerging economies share some similarities in development patterns, it is often their individual differences that create unique opportunities and risks that may be addressed through derivative structures and sound risk assessment practices. Consequently, while these emerging economies are characterized with weak regulations and financial infrastructure, the volatility component gives an important ingredient for the creation and trading of equity cash-markets instruments and derivative products. However, the management of the inherited risks must be dealt with by exercising both art and science techniques. Accordingly, the task and duties of risk managers, treasurers and CFOs in any emerging market environment will, of course, be multiplied several-fold. As such, the role of strategic risk assessment and its proper implementations are essential factors in the success of emerging markets' financial trading activities.

Today, emerging markets of cash instruments and derivative products service a huge number of investors—all of whom have different capabilities, needs, and constraints, as well as different perspectives on the market and different attitudes toward risk. The variety of instruments (both cash and derivative markets) now available means that each of these investors should be able to implement a risk/return strategy that corresponds to their needs and expectations. At this time in several emerging economies, major commercial banks, investment banking firms and insurance companies have established new units of specialized traders and financial engineers to design and structure tailor-made risk management products for corporate and retail customers. The continued success of these new emerging markets, as well as the satisfaction of each user, depends on a clear understanding of what these markets can offer of diverse product-lines and consequently the tradeoff between expected returns and their uncertainties (risks).

Trading consists of proprietary positions in financial instruments which are held for resale (available for sale) and/or which are taken on by the financial entity with the intention of benefiting from actual and/or expected differences between purchase and sale prices or from other price variations (such as spread differentials). By and large, market (or trading) risk is defined as the risk at which trading income will decrease due to an adverse price change in traded financial instruments.

To quantify the risks involved in their trading operations, major financial institutions are increasingly exploiting Value at Risk (VaR) models. Since financial institutions differ in their individual characteristics, a tailor-made internal risk models are more appropriate. Fortunately, and in accordance with the latest Basel II capital accord, financial institutions are permitted to develop their own internal risk models for the purposes of providing for adequate risk measures. Furthermore, internal risk models can be used in the determination of economic-capital (or risk- capital) that banks must hold to endorse their trading of securities. The benefit of such an approach is that it takes into account the relationship between various asset types and can accurately assess the overall risk for a whole combination of trading assets (Al Janabi, 2009a).

A number of Arab countries are voluntarily joining the implementation of modified versions of Basel II accord. In fact, the Gulf Cooperation Council (GCC) financial markets, in general, are in progressive stages of implementing advanced risk management regulations and techniques. Moreover, in recent years outstanding progress has been done in cultivating the culture of risk management among local financial entities and regulatory institutions. In the Middle East, the majority of banking assets is expected to be covered by Basel II regulations during 2008-2012. Generally speaking, capital ratios are fairly strong in the GCC, though they have fallen lately as banks have expanded their products and operations. Within the GCC, there have been negotiations for common application of Basel II rules, though with different timeframes. This is due to the fact that some GCC countries are more diverse, for instance, in terms of the presence of foreign banks than others.

The financial industry in GCC countries is generally sound, and the six countries continue to develop their financial system to attract more foreign portfolio investors, and to expand the opening of its financial system to the exterior world. Consequently, several local financial institutions are in a consolidation route; and some others have already followed a process of convergence of their financial operations and have started the procedure of modernizing their internal risk management capabilities. By the standards of emerging market countries, the quality of banking supervision in the six GCC states is well above average. Despite the latest progress in the GCC financial markets to become Basel-compliant countries, recently it has been deemed necessary (by local regulatory authorities) to adapt proper internal risk models, rules and procedures that financial entities, regulators and policymakers should consider in setting-up their daily trading risk management objectives (Al Janabi, 2009b).

Set against this background, equity risk assessment has become an important theme in emerging and illiquid markets, such as in the case of GCC financial markets. Accordingly, the goals of this work are to demonstrate the necessary analytical modeling steps and internal risk management simulation techniques that a market's participant (dealer or market-maker) will need in his day-to-day positions' taking. To this end, this paper provides real-world risk assessment techniques and strategies (drawn from a practitioner viewpoint) that can be applied to equity trading portfolios in emerging markets, such as the GCC financial markets. This is with the objective of developing the basis of a modeling tactic for the assessment of risk exposures in day-to-day trading operations. Financial modeling procedures that are discussed in this work will aid financial markets' participants, regulators and policymakers in founding sound and up to date modeling techniques to handle equity trading risk exposures.

To this end, in this paper the parameters required for the construction of appropriate and simplified Liquidity-Adjusted VaR (LVaR) and stress-testing methods are reviewed from previous works and adapted to the specific applications of these methods to emerging GCC financial markets. The theoretical mathematical algorithms and financial modeling structure applied herein are based on a matrix-algebra approach. The latter tactic can simplify the financial modeling and the algorithms' programming process and can consent as well a straightforward incorporation of short-sales of assets in the daily equity trading process. Moreover, a simplified modeling technique for the incorporation of illiquid asset, in daily trading risk management practices, is defined and is appropriately integrated into LVaR and stress-testing models.

LITERATURE REVIEW, SCOPE AND OBJECTIVE OF THIS STUDY

Risk assessment and management have become of paramount importance in the financial industry and a major endeavor by academics, practitioners, and regulators, and a cornerstone of recent interest is a class of models called Value at Risk (VaR) techniques. The concepts of VaR and other advanced risk management techniques are not new and are based—with some modifications—on modern portfolio theory. Albeit VaR is one of many—both quantitative and qualitative—factors that should be integrated into a cohesive risk management approach, it is remarkably a vital one. In fact, VaR is not the maximum loss that will occur, but rather a loss level threshold that will be pierced some percentage of the time. The actual loss that occurs could be much higher than VaR estimations. As such, VaR should be used in conjunction with other risk measures such as stress-testing, scenario analysis, and other asset/business specific risk measures. The most common VaR models estimate variance/covariance matrices of asset returns using historical time series, under the assumption that asset returns are normally distributed and that portfolio risk is a function of the risk of each asset and the correlation factors among the returns of all trading assets within the portfolio. The VaR is then calculated from the standard deviation of the portfolio, given the appropriate investment/liquidation horizon, and the specified confidence interval (Al Janabi, 2009a).

In the 1950s Markowitz (1959) describes the theoretical framework for modern portfolio theory and the creation of efficient portfolios. Markowitz's mean-variance portfolio optimization methodology is a landmark in the development of modern portfolio theory. The solution to the Markowitz theoretical models revolves around the portfolio weights, or the percentage of asset allocated to be invested in each instrument. In a similar vein, Sharpe (1963), develops the single-index model, which relates returns on each security to the returns on a common index—abroad market index of common stock returns such as S&P 500 is generally used for this purpose.

Despite many criticisms and limitations of the VaR method, it has proven to be a very useful measure of market risk, and is widely used in financial and non-financial markets. The *RiskMetrics*^{TM} system (1994), developed and popularized by *J. P. Morgan*, has provided a tremendous impetus to the growth in the use of VaR concept and other modern risk management modeling techniques. Since then the VaR concept is well-known and scores of specific applications are adapted to credit risk management and mutual funds investments. The general recognition and use of large scale VaR models has initiated a considerable literature including statistical descriptions of VaR and assessments of different modeling techniques. For a comprehensive survey, and the different VaR analysis and techniques, one can refer to Jorion (2001).

On another front, Berkowitz and O'Brien (2001) question how accurate VaR models are at commercial banks. Due to the fact that trading accounts at large commercial banks have considerably grown and become increasingly diverse and complex, the authors presented statistics on the trading revenues from such activities and on the associated VaR forecasts internally estimated by banks. Several other authors have attempted to tackle the issues of extreme events and fat tails phenomena in the distribution of returns. Nonetheless, most of their approaches and techniques are good exercises for academic purposes they do lack evidence of real-world applications with actual market portfolios.

On the other hand, Garcia et al. (2007) tackle a specific issue within the VaR and that is the subadditivity property required for the VaR to be a coherent measure of risk. The authors argue that, in the context of decentralized portfolio management, central management possesses only a fraction of information that belongs to each specialist (trader). In such a context, a distribution appears always thicker to the central unit than to the specialist. Therefore, because of a lack of information, VaR may appear fallaciously nonsubadditive to the central management unit. Despite evidence to the contrary, the authors show that decentralized portfolio management with a VaR allocation to each specialist will work, and furthermore VaR remains subadditive in many situations of practical interest.

In his research papers, Al Janabi (2007a and 2007b) establishes a practical framework for the measurement, management and control of trading risk. The effects of illiquid assets, that are dominant characteristics of emerging markets, are also incorporated in his models. The established models and the general framework of risk calculations are mainly based on matrix-algebra techniques. A rigorous analytical risk management study of the Mexican Stock Market (BMV) is performed by Al Janabi (2007c). The parameters of a practical framework for the management of market risk are illustrated and a case study is carried out on 11 well-known Mexican stocks in addition to a number of sectors indices and main market indicators. Moreover, in his research paper, Al Janabi (2008b), the robust quantitative measurements and procedures of market risk are applied to emerging markets' equity trading portfolios that are combined with foreign exchange trading portfolios. Market risk management models, which are implemented in his latest work, are applied to both, the Mexican foreign exchange and stock markets.

In a similar vein, lately in his research papers, Al Janabi (2010), (2009b) and (2008a) establishes a practical framework for the measurement, management and control of trading risk under illiquid and adverse market conditions. The effects of illiquid assets, that are dominant characteristics of emerging markets, are also incorporated in the risk models. These literatures provide real-world risk management techniques and strategies (drawn from a practitioner viewpoint) that can be applied to trading portfolios in emerging markets. The intent is to propose a simple approach for including of liquidation trading risk in standard VaR analysis and to capture the liquidity risk arising due to illiquid trading positions by obtaining LVaR estimation. The key methodological contribution is a different and less conservative liquidity scaling factor than the conventional root-time multiplier. The proposed add-on is a function of a predetermined liquidity threshold defined as the maximum position which can be unwound without disturbing market prices during one trading day. In addition, the re-engineered model is quite simple to implement even by very large financial institutions with multiple assets and risk factors.

Set against this background, the objective of this research study is to provide practical and robust guidelines, modeling techniques and assessments of market risk for equity trading portfolios (frequently it can be called, trading, investment or price risk). As such, the aim is to create a pragmatic approach to assist in the establishment of sound risk assessment practices and within a prudential framework of rules and policies. To this end, the parameters required for the construction of appropriate and simplified LVaR and stress-testing methods are reviewed from previous works and refined to the specific applications of these methods to equity trading portfolios of the GCC stock markets. Furthermore, a simplified approach for the incorporation of illiquid assets is defined and is appropriately integrated into LVaR and stress-testing models. For this purpose, a risk-engine algorithm has been developed to assess market risk exposure under illiquid and adverse market conditions.

The remainder of the paper is organized as follows. The following section lays out the financial mathematical technique and the quantitative modeling infrastructure of VaR method, its limitations, and a model that incorporates the effects of illiquid assets in daily market risk assessment. Results of the empirical tests and simulations of structured case studies for the GCC financial markets are drawn in the fourth section. The final section provides a summary along with concluding remarks. Further details for the derivation of the Liquidity-Adjusted Value at Risk (LVaR) formula are illustrated in Appendix I. Finally, exhibits of the risk-engine's simulation outcomes along with the two structured case studies for the GCC stock markets are included in Appendix II.

ESTIMATION OF LIQUIDITY-ADJUSTED VALUE AT RISK (LVaR) WITH A CLOSED–FORM PARAMETRIC SCHEME

Major Limitations and Pitfalls of Value at Risk Method:

Value at Risk is a method of assessing market risk that uses standard statistical techniques routinely used in other technical fields. Formally, VaR measures the worst expected loss over a given time interval under normal market conditions at a given confidence level. Assuming the return of a financial product follows a normal distribution, linear pay-off profile and a direct relationship between the underlying product and the income, the VaR is to measure the standard deviation of the income for a certain confidence level. Although the method relies on many assumptions, it has gained wide acceptance for the quantification of financial risks. As a result of the generalization of this method, economic-capital allocations for trading and active investment activities tend to be calculated and adjusted with the VaR method.

So far, there is no industry consensus on the best method for calculating VaR. As with any statistical model, VaR depends on certain assumptions. The choice of which method of calculation is used is normally dictated by the user's aversion to unrealistic or over-simplistic assumptions. There are three popular methods: the parametric method (it is also known as the variance/covariance, correlation and delta-neutral method), the historical simulation method and the Monte-Carlo simulation method. Each of these methods has its own set of assumptions and each is a simplification of reality.

The parametric method is the simplest one in terms of application to financial practices and computer time consumption. This method assumes that the returns of the risk factors are normally distributed and the correlations between risk factors are constant. For risk assessment purposes using the normal distribution assumption is generally considered to be acceptable. Deviation from normality usually does not significantly alter the results of the VaR calculations under normal market conditions. Within this method a bell-shaped curve (Gaussian distribution) is essentially assumed and it also assumes that extreme price swings, such as market crashes, occur too rarely to contribute to an accurate picture of the likelihood of future events.

Although the VaR method has gained wide acceptance and it is currently used by both financial and non-financial firms, there are some common limitations and pitfalls to applying the method adequately, and thus they need to be highlighted in conjunction with the benefits, detailed as follows:

- VaR is now one of the essential tools of risk management but it is not the whole story. Its purpose is to give an estimate of losses over a short period under normal market conditions. It is not going to tell you what might happen during a market crash. VaR estimations cannot be taken as a panacea, since they are typically based on historical patterns that are not always a good guide to the future—especially in times of turmoil. For that reason most entities supplement the analysis of VaR with other tools such as stress-testing and scenario analysis (under severe market conditions) to grasp a better picture of hidden unexpected events.

- The main assumption underpinning VaR, which is also one of the concept's main drawbacks, is that the distribution of future price (or rate) changes will be similar to that of past price variations. That is, the potential portfolio loss calculations for VaR are worked out using distributions or parameters from historic price data in the observation period.

- The assumption that asset returns are normally distributed may underestimate potential risk due to *"fat tails"* in the distribution of returns. For this reason it will be useful to check the validity of the normality assumption on different assets throughout other parameters such as skewness (a measure of asymmetry), kurtosis (a measure of flatness/ peakedness) and Jarque-Bera non-normality statistical test, and to carry out scenario analysis to fully understand the impact of extreme moves.

- The VaR methodology is more appropriate for measuring the risk of cash instruments (with linear payoffs) such as foreign exchange rates, equities and bonds. In dealing with complex instruments (with nonlinear payoffs) such as derivative securities, the method might not give reasonable answers and may misstate non-linear risks as in the case of options contracts or other financial instruments with embedded option features.

- Correlation assumptions in emerging markets must be taken seriously as correlation can break down or even change signs under extreme or crises circumstances. Correlation assumptions can be either explicit or implicit. In some ways the implicit assumptions are more dangerous in that they are more easily overlooked. A typical implicit assumption is a correlation of either zero or one. For example, some emerging-markets' currencies are pegged to the US dollar and one can assume the correlation is very close to one. This in not really a statistical fact, but rather reflects a policy decision that could change abruptly.

- As VaR is not calculating standard deviations but rather estimating what they may be in the immediate future. The impact of market volatility and how to forecast its effects is a crucial issue for emerging markets that are characterized with low level of liquidity. The estimation of statistical parameters, such as the volatility of a particular common stock, requires a time series of market data. This can be particularly troublesome in markets in which the underlying common stock experiences only sporadic bursts of trading volume. While techniques have been developed to account for this, the net result is that a lack of liquidity reduces confidence in the forecasted volatility, which is an essential tool for the pricing of options contracts.

Appraisal of Liquidity-Adjusted Value at Risk (LVaR) Technique:

To calculate VaR using the parametric method, the volatility of each risk factor is extracted from a pre-defined historical observation period. The potential effect of each component of the portfolio on the overall portfolio value is then worked out. These effects are then aggregated across the whole portfolio using the correlations between the risk factors (which are, again, extracted from the historical observation period) to give the overall VaR value of the portfolio with a given confidence level.

Many financial service institutions have chosen a confidence interval of 95% (or 97.5% if we only look at the loss side [one-tailed]) to calculate VaR. This means that once every 40 trading days a loss larger than indicated is expected to occur. Some entities use a 99% (one-tailed) confidence interval, which would theoretically lead to larger loss once every 100 trading days. Due to fat tails in the distribution of probability, such a loss will occur more often and can cause problems in calculating VaR at higher confidence levels. Some financial institutions feel that the use of a 99% confidence interval would place too much trust on the statistical model and, hence, some confidence level should be assigned to the "art–side" of the risk measurement process.

Really, the choice of the confidence level also depends on its use. If the resulting VaRs are directly used for the choice of an economic-capital cushion, then the choice of the confidence level is crucial, as it should reflect the degree of risk aversion of the firm and the cost of a loss of exceeding the calculated VaR numbers. The higher the risk aversion or the greater the costs, implies that a big amount of economic-capital should be set a side to cover possible losses and this consequently will lead to a higher confidence level. In contrast, if VaR numbers are only used to provide a firm-wide yardstick to compare risks among different portfolios and markets, then the choice of confidence level is not that relevant.

To this end, a simplified calculation process of the estimation of VaR risk factors (using the parametric method), for a single and multiple assets' positions, is illustrated (Al Janabi, 2007a) as follows:

From elementary statistics it is well known that for a normal distribution, 68% of the observations will lie within 1σ (standard deviation) from the expected value, 95% within 2σ and 99% within 3σ from the expected value. As such, for a single trading position the absolute value of VaR can be defined in monetary terms as follows (Al Janabi, 2010):

$$VaR_i = \left| (\mu_i - \alpha * \sigma_i)[EquityAsset_i * Fx_i] \right| \approx \left| \alpha * \sigma_i [EquityAsset_i * Fx_i] \right| \quad (1)$$

where μ_i is the expected return of the asset, α is the confidence level (or in other words, the standard normal variant at confidence level α) and σ_i is the forecasted standard deviation (or conditional volatility) of the return of the security that constitutes the single position. The *Equity Asset_i* is the mark-to-market value of the trading asset and indicates the monetary amount of equity position in asset i and Fx_i denotes the unit foreign exchange rate of asset i. Without a loss of generality, we can assume that the expected value of daily returns μ_i is close to zero. As such, though equation (1) includes some simplifying assumptions, yet it is routinely used by researchers and practitioners in the financial markets for the estimation of VaR for a single trading position.

Trading risk in the presence of multiple risk factors is determined by the combined effect of individual risks. A magnitude of the total risk is determined not only by the magnitudes of the individual risks but also by their correlations. Portfolio effects are crucial in risk management not only for large diversified portfolios but also for individual instruments that depends on several risk factors.

For multiple assets or portfolio of assets, VaR is a function of each individual security's risk and the correlation factor $[\rho_{i,j}]$ between the returns on the individual securities, detailed as follows:

$$VaR_i = \sqrt{\sum_{i=1}^{n}\sum_{j=1}^{n} VaR_i VaR_j \rho_{i,j}} = \sqrt{\left| VaR \right|^{T} \left| \rho \right| \left| VaR \right|} \qquad (2)$$

This formula is a general one for the calculation of VaR for any portfolio regardless of the number of securities. It should be noted that the second term of this formula is presented in terms of a matrix-algebra technique—a useful form to avoid mathematical complexity, as more and more securities are added. This approach can simplify the algorithmic programming process and can permit a straightforward incorporation of short-sales positions in the market risk assessment process. As such, in order to calculate the VaR (of a portfolio of any number of securities), one needs first to create a vector $\left| VaR \right|$ of the individual VaR positions—explicitly n rows and one column ($n*1$) matrix—a transpose vector $\left| VaR \right|^{T}$ of the individual VaR positions—an ($1*n$) vector, and hence the superscript "T" indicates transpose of the vector—and finally a matrix, $\left| \rho \right|$, of all correlation factors (ρ)—an ($n*n$) matrix. Consequently, as one multiplies the two vectors and the correlation matrix and then takes the square root of the result, one ends up with the VaR_P of any portfolio with any n-number of securities. This simple number summarizes the portfolio's exposure to market risk. Investors and senior mangers can then decide whether they feel comfortable with this level of risk. If the answer is no, then the process that led to the estimation of VaR can be used to decide where to reduce redundant risk. For instance, the riskiest securities can be sold, or one can use derivative securities such as futures and options to hedge undesirable risk.

Illiquid securities such as foreign exchange rates and equities are very common in emerging markets. Customarily these securities are traded infrequently (at very low volume). Their quoted prices should not be regarded as a representative of the traders' consensus vis-à-vis their real value but rather as the transaction price that arrived at by two counterparties under special market conditions. This of course represents a real dilemma to anybody who seeks to measure the market risk of these securities with a methodology which is based on volatilities and correlation matrices. The main problem arises when the historical price series are not available for some securities or, when they are available, they are not fully reliable due to the lack of liquidity.

Given that institutional investors usually have longer time horizons, the liquidity of their positions will be lower. The investment horizon of the investor as well as the liquidity characteristics of the mutual fund need to be integrated into the risk quantification process. For instance, portfolios with long investment horizons and/or low liquidity need distinct risk measures than those that have shorter horizons and are very liquid. The choice of time horizon or number of days to liquidate (unwind) a position is very important factor and has big impact on VaR numbers, and it depends upon the objectives of the portfolio, the liquidity of its positions and the expected holding period. Typically for a bank's trading portfolio invested in highly liquid currencies, a one-day horizon may be acceptable. For an investment manager with a monthly re-balancing and reporting focus, a 30–day period may be more appropriate. Ideally, the holding period should correspond to the longest period for orderly portfolio liquidation.

In fact, if returns are independent and they can have any elliptical multivariate distribution, then it is possible to convert the VaR horizon parameter from daily to any t–day horizon. The variance of a t–day return should be t times the variance of a 1–day return or σ^2 = $f(t)$. Thus, in terms of standard deviation (or volatility), $\sigma = f(\sqrt{t})$ and the daily VaR number [VaR (1-day)] can be adjusted for any t horizon as:

$$VaR(t-day) = VaR(1-day)\sqrt{t} \qquad (3)$$

The above formula was proposed and used by *J.P. Morgan* in their earlier *RiskMetrics*[TM] method (1994). This methodology implicitly assumes that liquidation occurs in one block sale at the end of the holding period and that there is one holding period for all assets, regardless of their inherent trading liquidity structure. Unfortunately, the latter approach does not consider real-life-trading situations, where traders can liquidate (or re-balance) small portions of their trading portfolios on a daily basis. Moreover, this could generate unreliable risk assessments and can lead to considerable overestimates of VaR figures, especially for the purposes of economic-capital allocation between trading and/or investment units.

The assumption of a given holding period for orderly liquidation inevitably implies that assets' liquidation occurs during the holding period. Accordingly, scaling the holding period to account for orderly liquidation can be justified if one allows the assets to be liquidated throughout the holding period. In order to perform the calculation of VaR under more realistic illiquid market conditions, we can define the following[1]:

$$LVaR_{adj} = VaR\sqrt{\frac{(2t+1)(t+1)}{6t}} \qquad (4)$$

where, VaR = Value at Risk under liquid market conditions (as presented formerly in equation [1]) and $LVaR_{adj}$ = Value at Risk under illiquid market conditions. The latter equation indicates that $LVaR_{adj} > VaR$, and for the special case when the number of days to liquidate the entire assets is one trading day, then $LVaR_{adj} = VaR$. Consequently, the difference between $LVaR_{adj} - VaR$ should be equal to the residual market risk due to the illiquidity of any asset under illiquid markets conditions. As a matter of fact, the number of liquidation days (t) necessary to liquidate the entire assets fully is related to the choice of the liquidity threshold; however the size of this threshold is likely to change under severe market conditions. Indeed, the choice of the liquidation horizon can be estimated from the total trading position size and the daily trading volume that can be unwound into the market without significantly disrupting market prices.

Essentially, LVaR method is only one approach of measuring market risk and is mainly concerned with maximum expected losses under normal market conditions. In extreme situations, LVaR models do not function very well. As a result, for prudent risk management and as an extra management tool, firms should augment LVaR analysis with stress-testing and scenario procedures. From a risk management perspective, however, it is desirable to have an estimate for what potential losses could be under severely adverse conditions where statistical tools do not apply.

---

[1] For further details on the mathematical derivation and rational usefulness of this formula one can refer to Appendix I or Al Janabi, (2010), (2009b) and (2008a) research papers.

As a result, stress-testing estimates the impact of unusual and severe events on the entity's value and should be reported on a daily basis as part of the risk reporting process. For emerging economies with extreme volatility, the use of stress-testing should be highly emphasized and full description of the process is to be included in any financial service entity's policy and procedure manual. In general terms, stress-testing usually takes the form of subjectively specifying scenarios of interest to assess changes in the value of a portfolio and it can involve examining the effect of past large market moves on today's portfolio.

The advantage of this method is that it may cover situations that are completely absent from historical data and therefore forces management to consider events that might have otherwise ignored. Albeit stress-testing may provide a better idea for potential losses under worst-case events, like the devaluation of an emerging market's currency, politically upheavals events etc., it gives little indication of the prospect of such extreme events. It also handles correlations very flimsily, which can be an indispensable component of risk in a portfolio of securities. However, it can be a very robust tool when used to complement the statistical LVaR analysis. Subsequent to exploring the bulk of value distribution through LVaR methodology, stress-testing might provide key insights by drawing a few situations from the furthest tails.

In this paper, risk management procedure is developed to assess potential exposure due to an event risk (severe crisis) that is associated with large movements of the GCC stock markets indices, under the assumption that certain GCC markets have typical 6%-12% leap during periods of financial turmoil. The task here is to measure the potential trading risk exposure that is associated with a pre-defined leap and under the presumption of several correlation factors.

Certain stocks and stock market indices are highly exposed to event risk. As such, event risk is used to describe the risk that the financial entity runs into under unusual situations and that is not captured by day-to-day risk management tools. In essence, event risk will be evident in situations where prices are heavily dependent on certain structural factors (e.g. a political restructuring) or where price behavior is manipulated due to the lack of reinforcement of adequate regulations. Moreover, event risk will usually coincide with relative illiquidity of financial markets.

For trading risk management it is essential to draw a distinction between developed stock markets and emerging markets. In general, emerging-economies' stock markets are more prone to event risk, thus it is necessary to establish separate LVaR limit-setting for trading in these securities. Volume based limits or a combination of LVaR limits and volume based limits are applied in markets which are prone to event risk and where liquidity is not sufficient at all times (Al Janabi, 2007a).

In most professional trading and asset management units (such as commercial banks, foreign exchange dealers, institutional investors, etc.), LVaR limit-setting (or risk budgeting) is based on the concept of risk appetite. The risk appetite is defined as the maximum loss potential that management is willing to accept when an adverse move, in stocks or stock market indices, occurs within a specified time horizon. In general risk appetite will be dependent upon:

- The performance track-record in trading/investing equity securities.
- The strategic importance of equity trading by the trading/investment unit in question.

- The quality of trading/investment unit's infrastructure in handling traded products.
- The overall exposure that trading/investment unit wants to have to proprietary trading and/or active investment risks in general and equity risks in particular.
- The volatilities of the stocks/indices (as determined by the risk manager) and the correlation factors between all assets within the trading portfolio.
- The forecasted liquidation horizons (unwinding, or close-out periods) of the equity assets.
- The forecasted unwinding period of the entire trading portfolio(s) that consists of varied equity assets.
- Local and/or global regulatory constraints for the operations of equity securities.

In general, LVaR limits are allocated to each trading desk and the head of a particular trading unit is responsible for the delegation of limits to individual traders and books within the overall guidelines as specified by the trading risk management unit. In general, global and main trading units (within commercial banks) should have higher risk appetite percentage than local trading units in emerging countries. This will enables them to focus more on proprietary trading than solely on customer-driven businesses.

RISK ASSESSMENT IN EMERGING ECONOMIES—SIMULATION OF TWO STRUCTURED CASE STUDIES FOR THE GCC STOCK MARKETS

The market risk of a trading position is the risk of experiencing unexpected changes in the value of the position due to unexpected changes in the market variables or factors that affect the valuation of the position. Such market factors may be the level of equity markets or individual foreign exchange security. These market variables that affect the value of a trading position are customarily called market-risk-factors. Specifically, a trading risk manager is interested in the likelihood of unexpected losses (rather than gains) and their magnitude for a trading position over a given time horizon. The interest in possible future losses in a trading operation is obvious as every trading house has only limited economic or risk-capital. In order to continue operating as a going concern even in the most adverse conditions, the allocated trading capital must be able to absorb the *"maximum"* loss at any given time. As a result, the important parameters in equity trading risk assessment are:

- The composition of the equity trading position and its mark-to-market (MTM) value.
- The impact of changes in the market risk factors on its MTM value.
- The time horizon (or unwinding period) for the liquidation of equity trading positions.
- The magnitude of the maximum loss that may be experienced and the likelihood of such a loss.

In measuring the market risk of a trading position the first step is to identify the market risk factors that affect its mark-to-market value. For certain trading positions, the identification of market risk factors is quite straightforward. For instance, for a trading position in cash equities, prices of individual stocks determine the value of the position and, therefore, equity prices could be taken as the market risk factors. There is, however, a problem with this approach: for a large and diversified trading book the number of risk factors becomes very large and the risk measurement and aggregation becomes unmanageable. Fortunately, financial theory and related empirical research provide ways of simplifying the number of market risk factors for equity positions.

Description of the Dataset:

In the study reported herein, database of daily price returns of the GCC stock markets' main indicators (indices) are assembled, filtered and adequately adapted for the creation of relevant inputs for the calculation of all risk factors. The total numbers of indices that are considered in this work are nine indices; seven local indices for the GCC region (including two indices for the UAE markets) and two benchmark indices, detailed as follows:

1. DFM General Index (United Arab Emirates, Dubai Financial Market General Index)
2. ADX Index (United Arab Emirates, Abu Dhabi Stock Market Index)
3. BA All Share Index (Bahrain, All Share Stock Market Index)
4. KSE General Index (Kuwait, Stock Exchange General Index)
5. MSM30 Index (Oman, Muscat Stock Market Index)
6. DSM20 Index (Qatar, Doha Stock Market General Index)
7. SE All Share Index (Saudi Arabia, All Share Stock Market Index)
8. Shuaa GCC Index (Shuaa Capital, GCC Stock Markets Benchmark Index)
9. Shuaa Arab Index (Shuaa Capital, Arab Stock Markets Benchmark Index)

For this particular study we have chosen a confidence interval of 95% (or 97.5% with *"one-tailed"* loss side) and several liquidation time horizons to compute LVaR. Historical database (of more than six years) of daily closing index levels, for the period 17/10/2004-22/05/2009, are assembled for the purpose of carrying out this research and further for the construction of market risk assessment parameters. The analysis of data and discussions of relevant findings and results of this research are organized and explained as follows:

Statistical Inference of Correlation Patterns

Three matrices of correlations are created in this study, namely $\rho = 1$, 0, and empirical correlations. The objectives here are to establish the necessary financial modeling infrastructure for cutting-edge risk assessment that will follow shortly. For the empirical correlation case, the assembled correlation matrix is depicted in Exhibit (1) for the nine GCC stock markets indices. The latter correlation matrix is an essential element along with conditional volatilities matrices for the simulation of LVaR and stress-testing. Contrary to general belief, our analysis indicates that for long-run period in general there are relatively small correlations (relationships) between the GCC stock markets. Nonetheless, in the short-run period (or on a daily crisis basis), however, we found that correlations tend to increase in value (although not on a large scale) and it could even switch signs under certain circumstances.

These long-run low correlation relationships are advantageous information for investors who would like to hold a diversified equity portfolio in GCC countries and particularly for medium/long investment horizon. On the whole, it seems that the Saudi market, with correlation factors of 62% and 60% respectively, presides over the scenery of actions and therefore has the principal effect (and correlation relationship) on both the Shuaa GCC and Shuaa Arab indices. The Dubai and Abu Dhabi financial markets have indicated a relatively low relationship of 56%, albeit both markets are operating and regulated in the same country. Likewise, and in accordance with general expectation, the Shuaa GCC and Shuaa Arab indices have shown a strong relationship of 93%.

Simulation of Trading Risk Exposure for Structured Equity Portfolios:

To examine the relationship between stock market indices' expected returns and volatility, we implement a conditional volatility approach to determine the risk parameters that are needed for the LVaR's engine and thereafter for the estimation of daily market risk exposure. To this end, a generalized autoregressive conditional heteroskedasticity (GARCH) in Mean model [that is, GARCH-M (1,1) model] is used for the estimation of expected return and conditional volatility for each of the time series variables. As a result, Exhibit (2) illustrates the daily conditional volatility and expected return of each of the sample indices under normal market and severe (crisis) market conditions[2]. Crisis market volatilities are calculated by implementing an empirical distribution of past returns for all stock market indices' time series and, hence, the maximum negative returns (losses), which are observed in the historical time series, are selected for this purpose. This approach can aid in overcoming some of the limitations of normality assumption and can provide a better analysis of LVaR and particularly under severe and illiquid market circumstances.

In order to emphasize the importance of simulating different portfolios under varied market settings, two full case studies are performed on the GCC stock markets. This is with the intention of setting-up a financial modeling tool for proactive daily equity risk taking practices and for assessing trading risk properly under extreme market circumstances. In the calculations reported herein, the effects of different combinations of structured portfolios, various liquidation periods (or unwinding horizons of assets holdings) are investigated. Furthermore, all risk modeling and analyses are performed at the one-tailed 97.5% level of confidence over different liquidation periods.

---

[2] In this paper, severe or crisis market conditions refer to unexpected extreme adverse market situations at which losses could be several-fold larger than losses under normal market situation. Stress-testing technique is usually used to estimate the impact of unusual and severe events.

The LVaR results are calculated under normal and severe market conditions by taking into account different correlation factors (+1, 0, and empirical correlations between the various risk factors). Under correlation +1, one is assuming 100% positive relationships between all risk factors (risk positions) all the times, whereas for the zero-correlation case, there are no relationships between all positions at all times. The last correlation case takes into account the empirical correlation factors between all positions and is calculated via a variance/covariance matrix as indicated in Exhibit (1).

Exhibit (2) illustrates a hands-on simulation report for the modeling of trading risk assessment of a hypothetical equity portfolio consisting of several indices of the GCC stock markets. Asset allocation and LVaR analysis are performed under the assumption that local indices represent exact replicas of diversified portfolios of local stocks for each GCC stock market respectively. In the first case study, total portfolio value is AED 120 millions (UAE Dirham), with varied asset allocation ratios and with a liquidity horizon of one trading day— that is, one day to unwind all equity trading positions. Furthermore, Exhibit (2) demonstrates the effects of stress-testing (that is, LVaR under severe market conditions) and different correlation factors on daily LVaR assessments. The LVaR simulation report also depicts the overnight conditional volatilities and expected returns calculated via the means of a GARCH-M (1,1) model, in addition to their respective sensitivity factors vis-à-vis the benchmark Shuaa Arab index[3]. Severe market daily volatilities are calculated and illustrated in the simulation report too. As discussed earlier, these daily volatilities, under severe market settings, represent the maximum negative returns (losses), which are perceived in the historical time series, for all stock market indices.) As a result, we can observe from Exhibit (2) that the index with the highest volatility is the SE All Share Index (under normal market condition) whereas the DFM General Index demonstrates the highest volatility under severe market situations. An interesting outcome of the study of beta factors for systematic risk is the manner in which the results are varied across the sample indices as indicated in Exhibit (2). SE All Share Index appears to have the highest sensitivity factor (0.98) vis-à-vis the Shuaa Arab Index (that is the highest systematic risk) and the BA All Share Index seems to have the lowest beta factor (0.06). Likewise, and in accordance with general belief, Shuaa GCC Index (with a sensitivity factor of 1.05) is the best contender of the entire sample indices that appears to move very closely with respect to the benchmark Shuaa Arab Index (with a beta factor of 1.0).

Additionally, Exhibit (2) points out the individual risk factors for each equity index in terms of AED and under the perception of normal and severe market specifications. These individual risk factors are in fact a reflection of a non-diversified LVaR figures. As such, the LVaR-engine's simulation report depicts the overnight conditional undiversified LVaRs (or undiversified risk factors) for each GCC stock market. These undiversified risk factors (under normal and severe market conditions) are calculated also with the aid of the conditional volatilities estimated via a GARCH-M (1,1) model. Expected returns and risk-adjusted expected returns (under normal and severe market situations) are also included in the LVaR's simulation report. Consequently, with 97.5% confidence, the actual equity trading portfolio should expect to realize no greater than AED 2,013,541 decrease in the value over a one-day

---

[3] The sensitivity factors are indeed the common beta factors for the measurement of systematic risk. These factors assess the relationship of each GCC stock market index against the benchmark index (Shuaa Arab Index).

time frame[4]. In other words, the loss of AED 2,013,541 is one that an equity portfolio should realize only 2.5% of the time. If the actual loss exceeds the LVaR estimation, then this would be considered a violation of the assessment. From a risk management perspective, the LVaR estimate of AED 2,013,541 is a valuable piece of information. Since every equity trading business has different characteristics and tolerances toward risk, the trading risk manager must examine the LVaR estimation relative to the overall position of the entire business. Simply put, can the firm tolerate or even survive such a rare event—a loss of AED 2,013,541 (or a 1.68% of total portfolio value)? This question is not only important to the equity trading unit, but also to financial institutions (or other funding units such as treasury unit within the same hierarchy and organizational structure of the trading unit) who lend money to these trading units. The inability of a trading unit to absorb large losses may jeopardize their ability to make principal and interest payments. Therefore, various risk management strategies could be examined in the context of how they might affect the LVaR estimation. Presumably, risk management strategies, such as the use of futures and options contracts in hedging possible fluctuation in equity prices, should reduce the LVaR appraisal. In other words, those extreme losses in equity trading, that would normally occur only 2.5% of the time, should be smaller with the incorporation of some type of risk management strategy.

Furthermore, the analysis of LVaR under illiquid market conditions is performed with three different correlation factors: empirical, zero and unity correlations respectively. Indeed, it is essential to include different correlation factors in any LVaR and stress-testing exercises. This is because existing trends in correlation factors may break down (or change signs) under adverse and severe market movements, caused by unforeseen financial or political crises. As one might expect, the case with correlation +1 gives the highest LVaR numbers (AED 3,306,106 and AED 20,958,156), owing to the fact that under these circumstances the total LVaR is the weighted average of the individual LVaRs of each equity trading position. It is essential to include various correlation factors in any stress-testing exercise, based on the fact that current trends in correlations may break down with severe market movements, caused by unexpected financial or political crises. The degree of diversification of this hypothetical equity trading portfolio can also be displayed as the difference in the value of the two greatest LVaRs, that is the LVaR of correlation +1 case versus the LVaR of empirical correlation case (that is, AED 1,292,566 or 64.19% for normal market conditions case). The overall sensitivity factor (beta factor) of this portfolio is also indicated in this report as 0.459, or in other words, the total equity portfolio value, with actual asset allocation percentage, moves distantly from the benchmark index (Shuaa Arab Index).

Finally, since the variations in daily LVaR are mainly related to the ways in which trading assets are allocated in addition to the liquidation periods of each trading position, it is instructive to examine the way in which LVaR figures are influenced by changes in such parameters. All else equal, Exhibit (3) illustrates the changes to LVaR figures when the liquidation periods (or holding horizons) of each trading position are increased from 1-day to 2-days, 3-days, 4-days, and 5-days for all indices within the trading portfolio. As such, for the empirical correlation case, the LVaR figures increased to AED 2,325,177 (1.94%) and AED 14,739, 257 (12.28%) under normal and severe markets conditions respectively.

---

[4] It should be noted that under severe or crisis market conditions the actual equity trading portfolio can expect to realize greater decrease in value and major losses of approximately six-fold the normal market conditions simulation case. As depicted in the simulation report, the losses could amass to a total of AED 12,602,514 (10.50% of total portfolio value) over a one-day time horizon.

SUMMARY AND CONCLUDING REMARKS

There are many methods and ways to identify, to assess and to control market risk, and trading risk managers have the task to ascertain the identity of the one that suits their needs. In fact, there is no right or wrong way to assess and to manage trading risk; it all depends on each entity's objectives, lines of business, risk appetite and the availability of funds for investment in trading risk management projects. Regardless of the methodology chosen, the most important factors to consider are the establishment of sound risk modeling techniques, standard policies & procedures and the consistency in the implementation process across all lines of businesses and risks.

Under special conditions when changes in market risk factors are normally distributed, the Liquidity-Adjusted Value at Risk (LVaR) can be calculated using a closed-form parametric approach. However, for emerging economies environments, one needs to supplement the closed-form parametric approach with other analysis such as stress-testing and simulation analysis. This is done with the objective of estimating the impact of assumptions that are made under LVaR approach. Likewise, the effects of illiquidity of trading assets, in emerging economies, must be dealt with more wisely and should be brought into existence within the LVaR framework.

In this document, a simplified and practical method for calculating portfolios' market risk is presented and analyzed. To this end, matrix-algebra approach is used to derive the necessary mathematical modeling and quantitative market risk assessment methods. This approach has several advantages owing to the fact that it can facilitate the algorithmic programming process and can permit easy incorporation of short-sales of trading assets into the equity trading process. In addition, the effects of illiquidity of trading assets are incorporated into our LVaR quantitative approach. For that purpose a simplified and practical model for the assessment of the effects of illiquid assets (unwinding of trading assets), in daily market risk management practices, is defined and is appropriately integrated into LVaR and stress-testing models.

For this particular study, LVaR simulations are assessed for normal and severe market conditions and under the notion of different correlation factors and unwinding periods. To this end, case studies are performed with different asset allocations and liquidation horizons with the aim of setting-up a hands-on framework for the appraisal of market risk exposure of an equity trading unit. As such, a meaningful financial modeling procedure for constructing a structured risk-engine with a robust simulation algorithm is developed. This is with the ultimate aim of instigating a no-nonsense approach for the estimation of LVaR under varied market circumstances.

Trading risk management models, which are adopted in this work, are applied to the GCC stock markets. Thus, our analyses are carried out for main market indicators in the GCC stock markets, in addition to two benchmark GCC indices. To this end, databases of daily indices settlement levels are obtained, filtered and matched. Two full simulation case studies are carried out with the objectives of calculating LVaR numbers under various scenarios and market conditions. The different scenarios are performed with distinct asset allocation percentages in addition to analyzing the effects of illiquidity of trading assets by imposing different unwinding horizons for each trading asset. All simulations and quantitative analyses are carried out under the assumption of normal and severe (crisis) market conditions. The appealing outcome of this study suggests the inevitability of combining LVaR calculations with other methods such as stress-testing and scenario analysis to grasp a thorough picture of other remaining risks (such as, fat-tails in the probability distribution) that cannot be revealed with the plain assumption of normality. In conclusion, proper assessment of LVaR is an important element for daily risk management process and for strategic risk-decision-making under adverse and illiquid market circumstances and particularly for emerging economies.

ACKNOWLEDGMENT

This work has benefited from a financial support in the form of a summer-grant (for the summer semester of the academic year 2009-2010) from the Faculty of Business and Economics (FBE), United Arab Emirates University, Al-Ain, UAE. The usual disclaimer applies.

APPENDIX I: DERIVATION OF LIQUIDITY-ADJUSTED VALUE AT RISK (LVAR) FORMULA

In this Appendix we present a simple re-engineered modeling approach for calculating a closed-form parametric LVaR. The proposed model and liquidity scaling factor is more realistic and less conservative than the conventional root-t multiplier. In essence the suggested multiplier is a function of a predetermined liquidity threshold defined as the maximum position which can be unwound without disturbing market prices during one trading day. The essence of the model relies on the assumption of a stochastic stationary process and some rules of thumb, which can be of crucial value for more accurate overall trading risk assessment during market stress periods when liquidity dries up. To this end, a practical framework of a modeling technique (within a simplified financial mathematical approach) is proposed below with the purpose of incorporating and calculating illiquid assets' daily LVaR, detailed as follows (Al Janabi, 2010, 2009b, and 2008a):

The market risk of an illiquid trading position is larger than the risk of an otherwise identical liquid position. This is because unwinding the illiquid position takes longer than unwinding the liquid position, and, as a result, the illiquid position is more exposed to the volatility of the market for a longer period of time. In this approach, a trading position will be considered illiquid if its size surpasses a certain liquidity threshold. The threshold (which is determined by each trader) and defined as the maximum position which can be unwound, without disrupting market prices, in normal market conditions and during one trading day. Consequently, the size of the trading position relative to the threshold plays an important role in determining the number of days that are required to close the entire position. This effect can be translated into a liquidity increment (or an additional liquidity risk factor) that can be incorporated into VaR analysis. If for instance, the par value of a position is $10,000 and the liquidity threshold is $5,000, then it will take two days to sell out the entire trading position. Therefore, the initial position will be exposed to market variation for one day, and the rest of the position (that is $5,000) is subject to market variation for an additional day. If it assumed that daily changes of market values follow a stationary stochastic process, the risk exposure due to illiquidity effects is given by the following illustration, detailed along these lines:

In order to take into account the full illiquidity of assets (that is, the required unwinding period to liquidate an asset) we define the following:

t = number of liquidation days (t–days to liquidate the entire asset fully)
σ_{adj}^2 = overnight (daily) variance of the illiquid position; and
σ_{adj} = liquidity risk factor or overnight (daily) standard deviation of the illiquid position.

The proposed approach assumes that the trading position is closed out linearly over t-days and hence it uses the logical assumption that the losses due to illiquid trading positions over t-days are the sum of losses over the individual trading days. Moreover, we can assume with reasonable accuracy that asset returns and losses due to illiquid trading positions are independent and identically distributed (*iid*) and serially uncorrelated day–to–day along the liquidation horizon and that the variance of losses due to liquidity risk over t-days is the sum of the variance (σ_i^2, for all $i = 1,2...,t$) of losses on the individual days, thus:

$$\sigma_{adj}^2 = \left(\sigma_1^2 + \sigma_2^2 + \sigma_3^2 + \cdots + \sigma_{t-2}^2 + \sigma_{t-1}^2 + \sigma_t^2\right) \tag{A1}$$

In fact, the square root-t approach (equation [3]) is a simplified special case of equation (A.1) under the assumption that the daily variances of losses throughout the holding period are all the same as first day variance, σ_1^2, thus, $\sigma_{adj}^2 = \left(\sigma_1^2 + \sigma_1^2 + \sigma_1^2 + \cdots + \sigma_1^2\right) = t\,\sigma_1^2$.
Basically, the square root-t equation overestimates asset liquidity risk since it does not consider that traders can liquidate small portions of their trading portfolios on a daily basis and then the whole trading position can be sold completely on the last trading day. Undeniably, in real financial markets operations, liquidation occurs during the holding period and thus scaling the holding period to account for orderly liquidation can be justified if one allows the assets to be liquidated throughout the holding period. As such, for this special linear liquidation case and under the assumption that the variance of losses of the first trading day decreases linearly each day (as a function of t) we can derive from equation (A.1) the following:

$$\sigma_{adj}^2 = \left(\left(\frac{t}{t}\right)^2\sigma_1^2 + \left(\frac{t-1}{t}\right)^2\sigma_1^2 + \left(\frac{t-2}{t}\right)^2\sigma_1^2 + \cdots + \left(\frac{3}{t}\right)^2\sigma_1^2 + \left(\frac{2}{t}\right)^2\sigma_1^2 + \left(\frac{1}{t}\right)^2\sigma_1^2\right) \tag{A2}$$

Evidently, the additional liquidity risk factor depends only on the number of days needed to sell an illiquid equity position linearly. In the general case of t-days, the variance of the liquidity risk factor is given by the following mathematical functional expression of t:

$$\sigma_{adj}^2 = \sigma_1^2\left(\left(\frac{t}{t}\right)^2 + \left(\frac{t-1}{t}\right)^2 + \left(\frac{t-2}{t}\right)^2 + \cdots + \left(\frac{3}{t}\right)^2 + \left(\frac{2}{t}\right)^2 + \left(\frac{1}{t}\right)^2\right) \tag{A3}$$

To calculate the sum of the squares, it is convenient to use a short-cut approach. From mathematical series the following relationship can be obtained:

$$(t)^2 + (t-1)^2 + (t-2)^2 + \cdots + (3)^2 + (2)^2 + (1)^2 = \frac{t(t+1)(2t+1)}{6} \qquad (A.4)$$

Accordingly, from equations (A.4) and (A.5) the liquidity risk factor can be expressed in terms of volatility (or standard deviation) as:

$$\sigma_{adj} = \sigma_1 \left(\sqrt{\frac{1}{t^2}[(t)^2 + (t-1)^2 + (t-2)^2 + \cdots + (3)^2 + (2)^2 + (1)^2]} \right)$$

$$\text{or } \sigma_{adj} = \sigma_1 \left(\sqrt{\frac{(2t+1)(t+1)}{6t}} \right) \qquad (A.5)$$

The final result is of course a function of time and not the square root of time as employed by some financial market's participants based on the $RiskMetrics^{TM}$ methodologies.

The above approach can also be used to calculate the LVaR for any time horizon. In order to perform the calculation of LVaR under illiquid market conditions, the liquidity risk factor of equation (A.5) can be implemented in LVaR modeling, hence, one can define the following:

$$LVaR_{adj} = VaR \sqrt{\frac{(2t+1)(t+1)}{6t}} \qquad (A.6)$$

where, VaR = Value at Risk under liquid market conditions (as presented formerly in equation [1]) and $LVaR_{adj}$ = Value at Risk under illiquid market conditions. The latter equation indicates that $LVaR_{adj} > VaR$, and for the special case when the number of days to liquidate the entire assets is one trading day, then $LVaR_{adj} = VaR$. Consequently, the difference between $LVaR_{adj} - VaR$ should be equal to the residual market risk due to the illiquidity of any asset under illiquid markets conditions. As a matter of fact, the number of liquidation days (t) necessary to liquidate the entire assets fully is related to the choice of the liquidity threshold; however the size of this threshold is likely to change under severe market conditions. Indeed, the choice of the liquidation horizon can be estimated from the total trading position size and the daily trading volume that can be unwound into the market without significantly disrupting market prices; and in actual practices it is generally estimated as:

t = *Total Trading Position Size of Equity Asset$_i$ / Daily Trading Volume of Equity Asset$_i$* (A.7)

APPENDIX II: EXHIBITS OF THE RISK-ENGINES SIMULATION OUTCOMES AND STRUCTURED CASE STUDIES OF THE GCC FINANCIAL MARKETS

Exhibit (1) Risk Simulation Data: Correlation Matrix of GCC Stock Markets Indices

	DFM General Index	ADX Index	BA All Share Index	KSE General Index	MSM30 Index	DSM20 Index	SE All Share Index	Shuaa GCC Index	Shuaa Arab Index
DFM General Index	100%								
ADX Index	56%	100%							
BA All Share Index	12%	8%	100%						
KSE General Index	17%	16%	12%	100%					
MSM30 Index	12%	17%	11%	11%	100%				
DSM20 Index	18%	23%	12%	12%	20%	100%			
SE All Share Index	20%	20%	7%	16%	11%	10%	100%		
Shuaa GCC Index	37%	35%	13%	19%	13%	26%	62%	100%	
Shuaa Arab Index	39%	36%	12%	24%	15%	26%	60%	93%	100%

Exhibit (2) Simulation of Liquidity Trading Risk Management and Asset Allocation (Full Case LVaR Analysis)

Stock Market Indices	Market Value in AED	Asset Allocation	Liquidity Holding Horizon	Daily Volatility (Normal)	Daily Volatility (severe)	Sensitivity Factor	Expected Return	Undiversified LVaR in AED (Normal)	Undiversified LVaR in AED (Severe)
DFM General Index	$ 25,000,000	20.8%	1	1.81%	12.16%	0.53	0.14%	453,411	3,039,316
ADX Index	$ 20,000,000	16.7%	1	1.32%	7.08%	0.40	0.07%	261,942	1,415,107
BA All Share Index	$ 10,000,000	8.3%	1	0.58%	3.77%	0.06	0.04%	58,084	376,816
KSE General Index	$ 10,000,000	8.3%	1	0.71%	3.74%	0.14	0.08%	71,249	373,646
MSM30 Index	$ 15,000,000	12.5%	1	0.79%	8.70%	0.10	0.10%	118,901	1,304,848
DSM20 Index	$ 15,000,000	12.5%	1	1.48%	8.07%	0.31	0.07%	222,049	1,211,120
SE All Share Index	$ 25,000,000	20.8%	1	1.86%	11.03%	0.98	0.01%	464,418	2,758,224
Shuaa GCC Index	$ -	0.0%	1	1.30%	8.10%	1.05	0.08%	-	-
Shuaa Arab Index	$ -	0.0%	1	1.15%	7.57%	1.00	0.10%	-	-
Total Portfolio Value in AED	$ 120,000,000	100%					0.07%		

Daily Liquidity-Adjusted Value at Risk (LVaR) in AED [Normal Market Conditions]

ρ = Empirical	ρ = 1	ρ = 0
2,013,541	3,306,106	1,501,137
1.68%	2.76%	1.25%

Diversification Benefits

$ 1,292,566	64.19%

Daily Liquidity-Adjusted Value at Risk (LVaR) in AED [Severe (Crisis) Market Conditions]

ρ = Empirical	ρ = 1	ρ = 0
12,602,514	20,958,156	9,444,324
10.50%	17.47%	7.87%

Diversification Benefits

$ 8,355,642	66.30%

Overall Sensitivity Factor: Portfolio of Stock Indices
0.459

Expected Return and Risk-Adjusted Return

Trading Portfolio Expected Return	0.07%
Risk-Adjusted Expected Return (Normal)	4.39%
Risk-Adjusted Expected Return (Severe)	0.70%

Exhibit (3) Simulation of Liquidity Trading Risk Management and Asset Allocation (Full Case LVaR Analysis)

Stock Market Indices	Market Value in AED	Asset Allocation	Liquidity Holding Horizon	Daily Volatility (Normal)	Daily Volatility (severe)	Sensitivity Factor	Expected Return	Undiversified LVaR in AED (Normal)	Undiversified LVaR in AED (Severe)
DFM General Index	$ 25,000,000	20.8%	2	1.81%	12.16%	0.58	0.14%	506,929	3,398,059
ADX Index	$ 20,000,000	16.7%	2	1.32%	7.08%	0.40	0.07%	296,214	1,582,138
BA All Share Index	$ 10,000,000	8.3%	4	0.58%	3.77%	0.06	0.04%	79,535	515,976
KSE General Index	$ 10,000,000	8.3%	4	0.71%	3.74%	0.14	0.08%	97,561	511,636
MSM30 Index	$ 15,000,000	12.5%	5	0.79%	8.70%	0.10	0.10%	176,359	1,935,403
DSM20 Index	$ 15,000,000	12.5%	3	1.48%	8.07%	0.31	0.07%	276,944	1,510,532
SE All Share Index	$ 25,000,000	20.8%	2	1.86%	11.03%	0.98	0.01%	519,235	3,083,788
Shuaa GCC Index	$ -	0.0%	1	1.30%	8.10%	1.05	0.08%	-	-
Shuaa Arab Index	$ -	0.0%	1	1.15%	7.57%	1.00	0.10%	-	-
Total Portfolio Value in AED	$ 120,000,000	100%					0.07%		

Daily Liquidity-Adjusted Value at Risk (LVaR) in AED [Normal Market Conditions]

ρ = Empirical	ρ = 1	ρ = 0
2,325,177	3,905,552	1,718,102
1.94%	3.25%	1.43%

Diversification Benefits

$ 1,580,376	67.97%

Daily Liquidity-Adjusted Value at Risk (LVaR) in AED [Severe (Crisis) Market Conditions]

ρ = Empirical	ρ = 1	ρ = 0
14,739,257	25,075,065	10,975,465
12.28%	20.90%	9.15%

Diversification Benefits

$ 10,335,808	70.12%

Overall Sensitivity Factor: Portfolio of Stock Indices

0.459

Expected Return and Risk-Adjusted Return

Trading Portfolio Expected Return	0.07%
Risk-Adjusted Expected Return (Normal)	3.80%
Risk-Adjusted Expected Return (Severe)	0.69%

REFERENCES

Al Janabi, M. A. M. (2010), "Incorporating Asset Liquidity Effects in Risk-Capital Modeling," *Review of Middle East*, Vol. 6, No. 1, Article 3.

Al Janabi, M. A. M. (2009a), "Corporate Treasury Market Price Risk Management: Practical Approach for Strategic Decision-Making," *Journal of Corporate Treasury Management*, Vol. 3, No. 1, pp. 55-63.

Al Janabi, M. A. M. (2009b), "Market Liquidity and Strategic Asset Allocation: Applications to GCC Stock Exchanges," *Middle East Development Journal*, Vol. 1, No. 2, pp. 227-254.

Al Janabi, M. A. M. (2008a), "Integrating Liquidity Risk factor into a Parametric Value at Risk Method," *Journal of Trading,* summer issue, pp. 76-87.

Al Janabi, M. A. M. (2008b), "A Practical Approach to Market Risk Analysis and Control: Empirical Test of the Mexican Foreign Exchange and Stock Markets," *Int. J. Risk Assessment and Management*, Vol. 9, Nos. 1 & 2, pp. 70-103.

Al Janabi, M. A. M. (2007a), "On the Use of Value at Risk for Managing Foreign Exchange Exposure in Large Portfolios," *Journal of Risk Finance*, Vol. 8, No. 3, pp. 260-287.

Al Janabi, M. A. M. (2007b), "Equity Trading Risk Management: The Case of Casablanca Stock Exchange," *Int. J. of Risk Assessment and Management*, Vol. 7, No. 4, pp. 535-568.

Al Janabi, M. A. M. (2007c), "Risk Analysis, Reporting and Control of Equity Exposure: Viable Applications to the Mexican Financial Market," *Journal of Derivatives & Hedge Funds,* Vol. 13, No. 1, pp. 33-58.

Berkowitz, J and O'Brien, J. (2001), "How Accurate are Value-at-Risk Models at Commercial Banks?" working paper, US Federal Reserve Board's Finance & Economic.

Garcia, R., Renault, E., and Tsafack, G. (2007), "Proper Conditioning for Coherent VaR in Portfolio Management," *Management Science*, Vol. 53, No. 3, pp 483-494.

Jorion, P. (2001), *"Value-at-Risk: The New benchmark for Controlling Market Risk,"* Chicago: McGraw-Hill.

Markowitz, H. (1959), *"Portfolio Selection: Efficient Diversification of Investments,"* John Wiley, New York.

Morgan Guaranty Trust Company (1994), *"RiskMetrics-Technical Document,"* New York: Morgan Guaranty Trust Company, Global Research.

Sharpe, W. (1963), "A simplified Model for Portfolio Analysis," *Management Science*, Vol. 9, No. 2, pp. 277-293.

FURTHER READING

Al Janabi, M. A. M. (2009), "Commodity Price Risk Management: Valuation of Large Trading Portfolios under Adverse and Illiquid Market Settings," *Journal of Derivatives & Hedge Funds*, Vol. 15, No. 1, pp. 15-50.

Al Janabi, M. A. M. (2008a), "On the Appropriate Function of Trading Risk Management Units: Principal Objectives and Adequate Use of Internal Models," *Journal of Banking Regulation*, Vol. 10, No. 1, pp. 68-87.

Al Janabi, M. A. M. (2008b), "Internal Regulations and Procedures for Financial Trading Units," *Journal of Banking Regulation*, Vol. 9, No. 2, pp. 116-130.

Al Janabi, M. A. M. (2006). Foreign Exchange Trading Risk Management with Value at Risk: Case Analysis of the Moroccan Market. *Journal of Risk Finance,* Vol. 7, No. 3, pp. 273-291.

Al Janabi, M. A. M. (2005), "Trading Risk Management: Practical Applications to Emerging-Markets," in Motamen-Samadian S. (Ed.), *Risk Management in Emerging Markets*, Palgrave/MacMillan, UK, pp.91-136.

Almgren, R. and Chriss, N. (1999), "Optimal Execution of Portfolio Transaction," Working Paper, Department of Mathematics, The University of Chicago.

Angelidis, T. and Degiannakis, S. (2005), "Modeling risk for long and short trading positions," *The Journal of Risk Finance*, Vol.6, No.3, pp 226-238.

Bangia, A., Diebold, F., Schuermann, T. and Stroughair, J. (1999), "Modeling Liquidity Risk with Implications for Traditional Market Risk Measurement and Management," Working Paper, The Wharton School, University of Pennsylvania.

Berkowitz, J. (2000), "Incorporating Liquidity Risk into VaR Models," Working Paper, Graduate School of Management, University of California, Irvine.

Bredin, D. and Hyde, S. (2004), "FOREX Risk: Measurement and Evaluation Using Value-at-Risk," *Journal of Business Finance & Accounting*, 31(9) & (10), pp. 1389-1417, November/December.

Culp, C., Mensink, R. and Neves, A. (1998), "Value at Risk for Asset Managers," *Derivatives Quarterly*, Winter Issue, pp. 21-33.

Danielsson, J., and Zigrand, J-P. (2006), "On time-scaling of risk and the square-root-of-time rule," *Journal of Banking & Finance*, Vol. 30, No. 10, pp. 2701-2713.

Dowd, K., Blake, D., and Cairns, A. (2004), "Long-Term Value at Risk," The *Journal of Risk Finance*, Winter/Spring Issue, pp. 52-57.

Embrechts, P., Hoeing, A. and Juri, A. (2003), "Using Copulae to Bound the Value at Risk for Functions of Dependent Risks," *Finance & Stochastics*, 7(2), 145-167.

Hendricks, D. (1996), "Evaluation of Value-at-Risk Models Using Historical Data," *Economic Policy Review*, Federal Reserve Bank of New York, April, 39-69.

Hisata, Y. and Yamai, Y. (2000), "Research Toward the Practical Application of Liquidity Risk Evaluation Methods," Discussion Paper, Institute for Monetary and Economic Studies, Bank of Japan.

Hull, J.C. (2009), "Risk Management and Financial Institutions," 2nd Edition, Prentice Hall, Pearson Education, Inc., USA

Jarrow, R. and Subramanian, A. (1997), "Mopping up Liquidity," *Risk*, Vol. 10, No. 12, pp. 170-173.

Le Saout, E. (2002), "Incorporating Liquidity Risk in VaR Models," Working Paper, Paris 1 University.

Marshall, C. and Siegel, M. (1997), "Value-at-Risk: Implementing a Risk Measurement Standard," *Journal of Derivatives*, 1, 91-111.

Neftci, Salih F. (2000), "Value at Risk Calculations, Extreme Events and Tail Estimations," *Journal of Derivatives*, Spring Issue, pp. 23-37.

Pritsker, M. (1997), "Evaluating Value at Risk Methodologies: Accuracy versus Computational Time," *Journal of Financial Services Research*, 12, 201-242

Saunders, A. and Cornett, M. (2008), "Financial Institutions Management," 6th Edition, McGraw Hill International Edition, Singapore.

BIOGRAPHICAL NOTES

Mazin A. M. Al Janabi is associate professor of finance and banking at the Faculty of Business and Economics (FBE), United Arab Emirates University, Al-Ain, UAE. He has several years of real-world experience in financial markets and banking sector where he held a number of senior positions, such as Head of Trading of Financial Derivative Products, Head of Trading Risk Management, Director of Asset and Liability Management and Director of Global Market Risk Management. He has written extensively, in leading scholarly journals, on finance & banking and contemporary topics in trading, market and credit risk management as well as on strategic asset allocation and modern portfolio management. His research and consulting activities address practitioner and regulatory issues in finance & banking, financial risk management, derivative securities and portfolio management.

In: The Stock Market
Editor: Allison S. Wetherby

ISBN: 978-1-61122-545-7
© 2011 Nova Science Publishers, Inc.

Chapter 3

AFRICA'S EMERGING CAPITAL MARKETS AND THE FINANCIAL CRISIS

*Paul Alagidede**

Division of Economics, Stirling Management School,
University of Stirling, Stirling, Scotland, U.K.

ABSTRACT

The past two decades alone has witnessed four major shocks to the global financial system: the collapse of the European exchange rate mechanism in 1992-1993, the peso crisis in 1994-1995 and the Asian turmoil in 1997-1998. The most recent, the subprime crisis, started in the summer of 2007 in the United States and intensified in 2008 and 2009 and has since changed the face of global finance and economics. As developed economies emerge from the recession, the contagion has spilled over from Wall Street to Main Street, engulfing hitherto resilient emerging market economies. For African countries, two notions of the financial crisis have become prominent: (a) the transmission mechanism between the financial systems in Africa and the rest of the world are weak and this has moderated, if not averted a catastrophic consequence of the spillover and (b) the main effect of the financial crisis is that of a second round effect.

So far the argument has been on the real sector effects of the crisis, and the analysis, more anecdotal than empirical. However, under alternative channels of transmission, both second and first round effects are significant. We show with extensive analysis of recent data from various indicators of stock market, bank and real economy variables that Africa's emerging and frontier markets have suffered as much as other markets from the spill over of the 2007 slow down: plummeting equity prices, deteriorating bank balance sheets, capital flow reversals, and reduction in remittances. We offer important policy conundrums, including but not limited to financial market reform, improving efficiency of Africa's emerging equity markets and regional integration to exploit the benefits of scale economics.

Keywords: Financial crisis, contagion, African stock markets
JEL Classification: G21, F2

---

* Email: paul.alagidede@stir.ac.uk; Tel:+44(0)1786467483; Fax: +44(0)1786467469

INTRODUCTION AND BACKGROUND

Financial development, liberalisation, economic growth and poverty reduction are inextricably linked. Several studies have suggested that sound financial development is good for growth. Contributions to the endogenous growth literature, typified by Greenwood and Jovanovic (1990) and Bencivenga and Smith (1991) argue that financial intermediaries gather and analyse information and facilitate better risk sharing among individuals, thus allowing credit to be allocated more efficiently. Innovative financial technologies tend to ameliorate informational asymmetries and lead to better project selection and monitoring (see King and Levine, 1993)[1]. This reasoning is even more plausible when a market becomes financially integrated, as this allows companies to access a large new pool of investors. Levine (2001) suggests that liberalising restrictions on international portfolio flows tends to enhance stock price liquidity, which in turn accelerates economic growth by increasing productivity growth. Kim and Singal (2000), and Levine and Zervos (1998) posit that liberalisation of financial markets in general, and stock markets in particular increases the scale and scope of financial transactions through intermediaries.

Thus, over the past three decades, financial sector reforms in emerging market economies have become a centrepiece in the debate on how to foster growth, and reduce stark poverty levels. This has led to policies aimed at improving the functioning of financial systems in general, dismantling existing impediments to growth, widening the availability of financial products, attracting external sources of finance and establishing new financial institutions such as stock and bond markets.

Stock markets have become an important for long-term finance. This is particularly true for well functioning and efficient markets, for they allow agents to diversify their sources of investment capital and to spread investment risk (Caprio and Demirguc-Kunt, 1998). Also, efficient stock prices and yields provide benchmarks against which the cost of capital for, and returns on, investment projects can be judged (Green et al, 2005). Furthermore, since stock prices are forward looking, they provide a unique record of shifts in investor's views about the future prospects of companies as well as the economy. Judging from the role of the stock market, it is thus not surprising that a number of African countries have embraced the stock market culture.

This chapter examines the impact of the financial crisis on African captial markets. So far the consensus drawn from the media and most policy circles indicate that the financial crisis have had only second round effects on African countries. This is founded on the observation that the transmission mechanism between the financial systems in Africa and the rest of the world are weak and this has moderated, if not averted a catastrophic consequence of the spill over since African financial systems, with small interbank markets and relying mostly on deposits to fund loan portfolios are not exposed to risks emanating from the complex derivative instruments in international financial markets. While this observation may be plausible, especially on account of the limited or even non-existent bailout of African institutions, we take the view that in the morning after the crisis, events have changed, and that the effects of the crisis have been both direct and severe. Using a multivariate generalised autoregressive conditional heteroscedasticity model we showed that volatility spill over from developed stock markets has both direct and immediate impact on African markets. We show that higher market correlations are seen in periods of crisis compared to tranquil times. We document through extensive data from various indicators of stock market, bank and real economy sector indicators that through their financial links with other regions in the world, Africa's emerging and frontier markets have suffered as much as other markets from the spill over of the subprime burst: plummeting equity values, deteriorating bank balance sheets, capital flow reversals, and reduction in remittances, which until the financial crisis replaced official development assistance in most developing countries. For instance, the Nairobi Stock Exchange (NSE) 20 Share Index declined by 46% in February 2009. In Sudan, portfolio investment fell from $30.5 million in 2007 to -$33.4 million in 2008. Net flows in Zambia turned negative in 2008 and remained so until at least September 2009. The weakening state of affairs means that stock market capitalisation as a percentage of GDP dropped from 293% in 2008 to 177% in 2009 for South Africa, and 106% to 52% for Egypt during the same period.

The rest of the chapter is organised as follows: section two gives an overview of African capital markets. Over the past two decades the number of stock markets have grown rapidly, reaching 24 at the end of 2009. The institutional set up, trading environment and structure of the markets and their role in long term capital mobilization is presented and discussed in this section. Section three examines the current financial crisis, focusing particularly on the factors that gave birth to the asset bubble and the subsequent burst. The effect of the crisis on African markets is analysed formally in section four. The channels of transmission are examined in section five and section six concludes and offers some thoughts on capital market reform.

OVERVIEW OF AFRICAN CAPITAL MARKETS

Africa's emerging stock markets

At the turn of the 20th century Africa had just 4 stock markets: South Africa, Egypt, Zimbabwe and Namibia. The initial impetus to stock market development in southern Africa was the discovery of large mineral deposits. The Johannesburg stock exchange (JSE) was established in 1887 to enable the new mines and their financiers to raise funds for the development of the fledgling mining industry. Zimbabwe's exchange opened in 1896 in response to mineral discovery, operated for only six years, submerged and re-emerged in 1946, and started trading again in 1974. The upsurge of diamonds led to the establishment of the Ludertzbucht stock exchange in 1910 in Namibia with a range of companies mostly in diamond mining. However, the Ludertzbucht stock exchange was a nine-day wonder. It submerged within few years of the end of the diamond rush. For almost a century investors lost interest and there was little activity regarding a capital market in Namibia. The present Namibian stock exchange only re-emerged in 1992. The Cairo stock exchange is the oldest in Africa, established in 1883. The second Egyptian exchange in Alexandria was founded in 1903. Both exchanges were very active in the 1940s. However, central planning in the mid 1950s and large scale nationalisation of many of the listed firms stifled the market until the dawn of privatisation and market reforms in the 1990s.

Since the dawn of structural adjustment programmes with its attendant financial sector reforms, and with donor support, Africa has expanded its domestic stock exchanges to 24 currently, some newly established, and others revitalised. As Ducker (1996) rightly put it, 'stock exchanges had become the 1990s equivalent of national anthems and flags in Africa'. Swaziland, Namibia and Uganda established stock markets in 1990, 1992 and 1997 respectively. Mozambique's market was opened in 1999. If the 1990s was an era of stock market activism, the 2000s can be described as an era of expansion and consolidation. The Economic and Monetary Community of Central Africa (CEMAC) created the Doula stock exchange (DSX) in Cameroon in 2001 and intends to establish another one in Gabon, in line with the regional stock exchange experiment of West Africa[2]. The DSX had only one listed stock at its founding in 2001, Société des Eaux Minérales du Cameroun (SEMC), and only had its second issue in May 2008, Société Africaine Forestière et Agricole du Cameroun (SAFACAM). The exchange trades government bonds which are unlisted. Cape Verde Stock Exchange was opened in 2005 with 44 treasury bonds and three corporate equities. The current four listed stocks are made up of three banks and one tobacco company. The Libyan stock exchange was opened in 2007 and currently has 10 listed stocks; 99% of the listed companies are in the financial sector (six of the listed stocks are banks and three insurance companies). Rwanda has an over the counter market which opened in 2008 and originally traded only bonds: one by the Central Bank of Rwanda, and the other by the Commercial Bank of Rwanda. There are currently two listed stocks, Kenya Commercial Bank, a cross listed stock in Dare Salem, and Bralirwa, a brewery company. Angola is one of the few countries in the southern African region that still does not have its own stock market. However, plans are far advanced to establish one in the last quarter of 2010[3].

Table 1 summarises the regional locations of the markets: West Africa (Cape Verde, Cote d'Ivoire, Ghana and Nigeria); East Africa (Kenya, Rwanda, Tanzania and Uganda); and North Africa (Algeria, Egypt, Morocco, Libya, Sudan and Tunisia). In southern Africa, there are thriving exchanges in Botswana, Malawi, Mauritius, Mozambique, Namibia, South Africa, Swaziland, Zambia and Zimbabwe. Cameroon in central Africa.

The antecedents to the proliferation of stock markets in Africa stems from the fact that most African countries in the immediate post-independence era chose a state-sponsored route to development. The emphasis on state-led growth meant a relatively insignificant role assigned to private enterprise. This phenomenon was compounded by the East-West confrontation, with most development aid flowing from the eastern bloc to Africa, largely to secure ideological partners. Following the end of the Cold War however, this door to economic development was shut, thus prompting a shift to market capitalism. With the increasing shrinking of the state and liberalisation and financial sector reforms, stock markets became common place.

Additionally, most long-term finance was initially channeled through development finance institutions (DFIs). However, evidence indicates that a significant amount of World Bank lending to these institutions reversed in the 1980s because of the debt and portfolio crisis faced by the DFIs (see Murinde and Kariisa-Kasa, 1997; and Caprio and Demirgüç-Kunt, 1998). In the 1980s World Bank loans to DFI's dropped dramatically from 11% of new credits in 1989 to only 2.4% in 1993. The 1980s debt crisis also made it difficult for developing countries to attract debt capital. Attention thus turned to setting up and revitalising stock markets to raise capital domestically, often with the assistance of the World Bank and International Finance Corporation (IFC). The revitalisation of these markets has also been motivated by the growing need to promote the role of the private sector in stimulating growth (Khambata, 2000). In addition, the markets are expected to enhance international risk sharing through global diversification, improve resource allocation, and generate large steady state welfare gains (Kim and Singal, 2000). And this is supported both in the theoretical and empirical literature. For instance, Levine and Zervos (1995) argue that the two main channels of financial intermediation—banks and stock markets— complement each other, while, Cho (1986) posits that credit markets need to be supplemented by well functioning equity markets since equity finance does not experience adverse selection and moral hazard problems to the same extent as debt finance. The existence of equity markets would thus enhance market mechanisms for raising and distributing scarce financial resources. More specifically, stock markets are expected to affect economic growth through raising the domestic saving rate, and the quantity and quality of investments.

Stock market development in many African countries is inextricably linked to the widespread financial sector reform, which is in turn a key component of wider economic restructuring efforts to encourage greater economic activity and generate higher levels of wealth. Many countries have been undergoing economic reform programmes that have involved a reduction in the role of the state in the economy and a strengthening of the role of the private sector. This has been accompanied by a greater role for market forces in price determination and the allocation of both real and financial resources. Financial sector reforms have often included the establishment of new stock markets, or improving the environment in which existing stock markets operate. The Swaziland, Uganda, Namibia, Mozambique, Cameroon, Malawi, Botswana, Ghana, Algeria and Sudan stock markets owe their establishment to the financial sector reforms of the late 1980s following the implementation of World Bank and IMF sponsored structural adjustment programmes. In Cameroon, Uganda and Zambia, for instance, the stock markets were set up mainly to divest state interest in economic activities. Privatisation has received greater attention during the 1980s and 1990s. Although privatisation has primarily been pursued as a means of improving economic efficiency in public enterprises, a secondary objective has been capital market development. Privatisation programmes have involved the listing/or offloading of shares in formerly nationalised firms, which are often very large in relation to the size of national economies, thus providing a supply of new shares and a further boost to stock market development. Furthermore, it has been shown that privatisation is easier to implement and more effective at wider participation in the ownership of privatised enterprises if an effective capital market is in existence.

The low interest rates and high industrial country liquidity may have also accounted for the flight of capital to emerging markets looking for high yielding investments. Most studies suggest that the rise in capital flows in the early 1990s was primarily due to the decline in global, and especially, US interest rates and the cyclical downturn in industrial countries (see Calvo, et al. 1993). Low international interest rates were particularly important in encouraging inflows into emerging market bonds and high-yielding currencies.

Stock markets have also become important because, the international finance institutions see their growth as a natural progression in the economic development of a nation. As a country begins to industrialise, it needs more sophisticated markets including stock markets.

The stock markets in Africa present institutional and regulatory circumstances that set them apart from markets in other regions. With the exception of South Africa, they are small by global standards, highly illiquid, and are not well regulated. Empirical evidence suggests that emerging stock markets in Africa and elsewhere tend to have low correlation with the more advanced markets. We address these stylized facts next.

Stylized Facts of African Stock Markets

Table 1 presents a survey of the key themes in African stock markets, including the date of establishment, trading environment, and delivery and settlement procedures. The trading environment and trading system, volatility and liquidity are critical to the price discovery process and hence for stock market efficiency (see Green et al, 2005, for a survey of key microstructure issues in emerging markets). With the exception of the well established markets, trading in African markets takes place in a few days during the trading week and, in some cases, a few hours during the trading day. For instance, the Ivory Coast exchange trades only three days a week. Until July 2006, the Ghana stock exchange traded just three days a week. In Malawi, Tanzania and Swaziland trading time is less than two hours of most trading days. The evidence from Table 1 shows that the trading system varies, from the call over system in Ghana and Botswana to the continuous or fixed order driven systems in Tunisia and Kenya.

The frequency of trade and the trading system are key components in the price discovery process, since market inefficiency can be induced by factors such as infrequent trading, market over and under reaction, bid-as-spread bounce and risk premia (see Lang and Lee, 1999). The last column of Table 1 reveals the major instruments traded in African stock markets. Evidence suggests that equities and bonds dominate. The issue of bonds, in particular, suggests that most of the exchanges exist as vehicles for issuing government debt, chiefly to finance trade deficits. With the exception of South Africa, where derivatives are traded, none of the African countries has a derivative market (there are plans to open one in Kenya and Mauritius). The sustenance of markets such as Cameroon, Malawi, Tanzania, Sudan and Uganda, and to some extent Zambia, rest on the continued supply of new shares from formerly state owned enterprises.

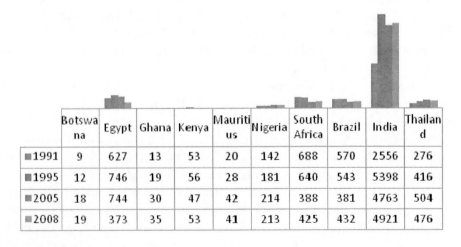

	Botswana	Egypt	Ghana	Kenya	Mauritius	Nigeria	South Africa	Brazil	India	Thailand
■1991	9	627	13	53	20	142	688	570	2556	276
■1995	12	746	19	56	28	181	640	543	5398	416
■2005	18	744	30	47	42	214	388	381	4763	504
■2008	19	373	35	53	41	213	425	432	4921	476

Figure 1: Listed companies[4]

Table 1. Snap Shot of African Stock Markets

COUNTRY	DATE EST.	TRADING, CLEARING & SETTLEMENT	TAX STRUCTURE	MARKET SEGMENTS
Algeria	1993	ATS. No CDS. C&S done electronically= T+4	No taxes	OS,CB
Botswana	1989; 1990	Call over with presiding officer. C&S is manual. SC= T+5 cycle. No CDS	DD= 15%, INT= 15%. CG= 0%	Equity Market, Bond Market
Cameroon	2001	Inactive	-	EQTS
Cape Verde	2005	Quote Driven systems	Capital gains: 15%; Corporate-Bonds are taxed at a rate of 5%	EQTS, CB
Cot d'Ivoire	1998	Computerised trading system with T+3 settlement cycle.	DD=10%	EQTS and CB
Egypt	1883&1903	T+2. Computer based screen trading with automated matching. CDS	No taxes	OS, MF, Tbonds, DB.
Ghana	1989;1990	Manual continuous auction trading system. SC= T+3. CDS	"Withholding taxes on dividend 8%.	Cash and Bond Market
Kenya	1954;1990	Automated Trading System. T+5. CDS. Intra-day Trading	Dividends 5% (domestic investors) 10% (foreign investors); interest 15%; capital gains suspended	Cash and Bond Market
Libya	2007			
Malawi	1994;1996	Manual Trading System. T+5. Intra-day Trading	10% on Dividends. No Capital Gains tax after 12 months of holding the shares	Cash Market
Mauritius	1989	ATS. T+3. Electronic trading system. CDS	No taxes.	Cash and Bond Market
Morocco	1929;1995	ATS. T+3. CDS	INT= 10%	EQTS, GB and other securities.
Mozambique	1999	Online Trading. T+3	10% for listed securities and 20% for non listed	Bond Market
Namibia	1900s: 1992	Computerized screen trading. T+5 Intra-day Trading, Margin Trading		Cash and Bond Market
Nigeria	1960	Screen based ATS. T+3. CDS. Intra-day Trading, Online Trading	10% on dividend, no capital gains tax	Cash and Bond Market
Rwanda	2008	-		Bond Market
South Africa	1887	Electronic trading system- JET Electronic central scrip depository- STRATE.T+5 cycle. Margin Trading, Intra-day Trading, Online Trading, Short Selling & Borrowing	No taxes on dividends for Non Residents, Interest = 12% Royalties,Visiting Entertainers = 15%	Cash and Derivative Market
Sudan	1994	Manual System trading system. T+0. Intra-day Trading	No Tax Rates	Cash Market
Swaziland	1990	Manual C&S.SC=T+5. Call over floor based trading. No CDS	DD= 15%; INT= 10%	Cash and Bond Market
Tanzania	1996	Automated Trading System. T+5 settlement cycle.	DD= 5%; INT= 5%	Cash and Bond Market
Tunisia	1969:1994	ATS. Electronic on a continuous or fixed quoting system depending on company size. SC=T+5. CDS	No taxes	OS, CB,Unit Trusts, CB
Uganda	1997: 1998	Manual continuous open outcry auction system. T+5.	10% tax on dividend and interest income.	Cash and Bond Market
Zambia	1994	Automated Trading System. T+3. Intra-day Trading	-	Bond Market
Zimbabwe	1896;1946	C&S is transaction by transaction. Call over, floor based. SC=T+7. No CDS	Dividends 15%	Cash and Bond Market

Source: Author's survey (2010); UNDP African Stock Market Handbook (2003) and African Securities Exchanges Association Yearbook (2008)
Notes: CDS is central depository system; ATS is automated trading system; T+ indicates the number of days it takes for trades to be settled. DD, INT, CG represent taxes on dividend, interest and capital gains respectively; OS, PS CB stands for ordinary shares, preference shares and corporate bonds respectively. EQTS is equities; GB is government bonds and MF stands for mutual funds. Note that under column 2 the second dates indicate the date the market either started operation or was revitalised. For instance the Botswana, Ghana, Malawi and Ugandan exchanges started operation a year after they were established. Zimbabwe and Kenya were revitalised in 1946 and 1990 respectively. Morocco and Tunisia were privatised in 1994 and 1995 respectively and Namibia re-emerged in 1992.

On the one hand, a process of shrinking states has been taking place in which some state shareholders have sold their controlling stakes in listed firms to private investors. Moreover, a number of privately controlled firms have also been listed in African markets through IPOs, however, vestiges of the socialist mentality remain and equity finance is usually last in the perking order for corporate financing in many countries. This leaves the typical African enterprise small scale, family owned, starved of funds and short lived.

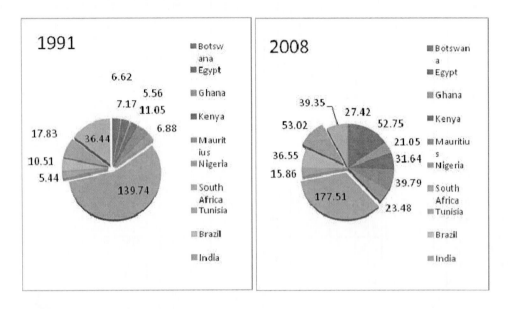

Figure 2: Market Capitalisation (% GDP)

With many enterprises run as family owned or one man businesses, the fear of dilution through listing in the stock market is endemic. Yet another major problem is the fear of discipline that the securities market imposes on their operation. For shares to be publicly traded, regulatory authorities will have to dig into the financial records of the company to ensure that only shares of credible companies are placed on the stock exchange. Thus many local entrepreneurs shy away from the stock market. Needless to say many small scale companies cannot maintain the services of professional accountants and auditors to meet the requirements of public placement. Privatisation provides a channel for keeping the stock market afloat in the presence of these hurdles. Listing/or offloading of shares in formerly nationalised firms provide the supply of new shares to the market. However, the evidence indicates that after the first wave of privatisations, the most recent sale of government stakes in many countries are concluded without floating in the stock market. A typical example is the sale of 70% stake of governments' shares in Ghana Telecom, the huge state telecom operator in Ghana in 2008.

African stock markets are also small in comparison with their national economies, with the ratio of market capitalisation to GDP averaging 17.3%. Apart from the JSE, all the stock markets in Africa are small in comparison to other emerging markets in Asia and Latin America.

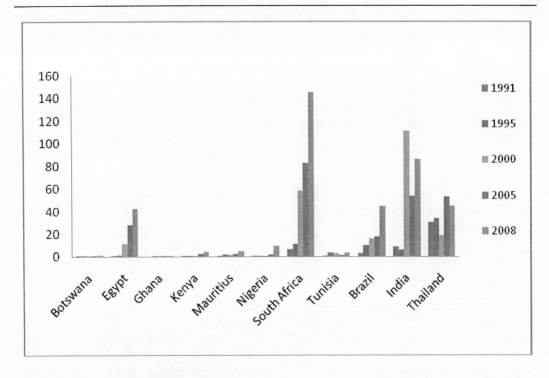

Figure 3: Total Value of Stocks traded (% GDP)

Figure 3 shows total value of stocks traded as a percentage of GDP. This ratio captures trading relative to the size of the economy. South Africa is clearly dominant in Figure 3. Total value traded as percentage of GDP is 145% for South Africa in 2008, down from 153% in 2007, compared with 0.93% for Botswana and 4% and 5% for Mauritius and Kenya respectively. The turnover ratio is the value of total shares traded divided by market capitalisation. In theory, the turnover ratio proxies the liquidity of the market; high turnover is often used as an indicator of low transaction costs. With the exception of South Africa, turnover averages less than 10% in African markets. Turnover averaged 2.6% for Botswana for the decade 1996-2006. For the same period, the average turnover ratio for Kenya and Mauritius was 4.7% and 5.3% respectively. Thus, ranked by liquidity, South Africa dominates with a high turnover ratio of 79% in 2002, dropping to 55% in 2007. However, the relative importance of Africa's markets diminishes when compared with medium size European stock markets or similar emerging markets elsewhere. For instance the turnover ratio for Korea, Taiwan and Turkey is 172.5%, 156.9% and 140.5% respectively. Thus the combined turnover ratio of all African stock markets in 2006 is less than that of Korea alone, and even more so for Pakistan (288.4%).

The low capitalisation, low trading volume and turnover would suggest the embryonic nature of African stock markets. There are other features that set African stock markets apart from their emerging markets counterparts in Asia and Latin America. These issues range from information dissemination/or disclosure, the legal and regulatory environment, capital controls, tax structure, and investment climate, as well as the economic environment in which the stock exchanges operate.

Foreign participation in developing countries stock markets is central for improvements in performance and efficiency. This, in turn, requires openness to foreign investments. Almost all African markets are now opened to foreign investors. In Botswana, Kenya and Zimbabwe, foreigners may not own over 40% of the shares in a single company. Egypt and Morocco are totally free to enter, while restrictions in Mauritius, Nigeria and South Africa are applied to specific sectors of the economy. In Ghana restriction that 74% of the shares in a single company cannot be owned by foreign investors has been lifted. Stock market openness and liberalisation in general, has been argued, both theoretically and empirically, to boost economic growth. Kim and Singal (2000) find that foreign investors will demand transparency and improved disclosure rules. They will also demand accountability of management and shareholder rights in order to protect themselves against expropriation of wealth by controlling investors. A convincing and satisfactory response to these demands will decrease the risk of holding stocks which, in turn, will lower the cost of capital (Rajan and Zingales, 1998).

Banking Sector

Although there have been a number of policy reforms over the decades, and financial deepening has taken place in several countries, the pace of progress has been sluggish. African financial systems are shallow and with a few exceptions—such as Mauritius, South Africa, and a handful of offshore financial centres— African financial systems are among the smallest across the globe, relative to economic activity (see Beck et al, 2009). Many African financial systems are smaller than a mid-sized bank in continental Europe, with total assets often less than US$1 billion. Small size is connected to low productivity and skill shortages, and prevents banks from exploiting scale economies; in addition, it might deter them from undertaking large investments in technology. Africa's financial systems are characterized by very limited outreach, with less than one in five households having access to any formal banking service—savings, payments, or credit .

We use three main indicators to measure banking sector development: domestic credit to the banking sector, domestic credit to the private sector and the ratio of liquid liabilities to GDP. Figures 4 and 5 shows these indicators of banking sector development[7]. Egypt, Mauritius, South Africa and Tunisia stand out using this indicator. However, there is some intra-regional variation, with banking penetration surpassing 40% in South Africa but remaining below 20 % in most of East Africa. Banking is also very expensive in Africa. This is typically reflected by high interest spreads and margins. This spread between deposit and lending interest rates provides disincentives for both savings and lending, as it depresses the returns for savers and pushes lending interest rates up. (Beck et al, 2009).

Bond markets

Bond markets in Africa are extremely thin, highly underdeveloped and very illiquid. This in turn related to a number of factors, including but not limited to the absence of a sound market infrastructure, a paucity of institutional investors, low domestic savings rates, and lack of interest from international investors resulting in a small, highly homogeneous investor group, contrary to the heterogeneity needed for an efficient bond market. Furthermore, economic instability, often fed by high fiscal deficits, rapid growth of the money supply, and a deteriorating exchange rate, more often than not weakens investor confidence and increase the risks associated with development of a market for government bonds. Without the benchmark yield curve provided by a large public debt market, weak balance sheets, poor disclosure, opaque corporate structures and governance means limited or completely non-existent bond markets for most African countries. South Africa is the only country with a well-developed local bond market and almost its entire debt is held by private creditors, mostly in the form of bonds. For the rest of sub-Saharan Africa, excluding South Africa, the debt is split largely between multilateral (45%) and bilateral (43%) debt with the minority as private (12%). In theory only the privately held debt is tradeable, i.e. less than 12% of sub-Saharan Africa's debt. In the context of the global market, Africa is insignificant. In 2001, Africa as a whole only accounted for 7% of the total tradeable debt of emerging markets or less than 0.4% of the total world bond market. Of Africa's total tradeable debt, sub-Saharan Africa, excluding South Africa, only accounted for 15%. Yet, it is Africa that need bond markets the most.

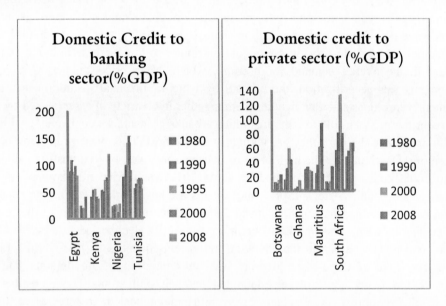

Figure 4: Domestic credit (%GDP)

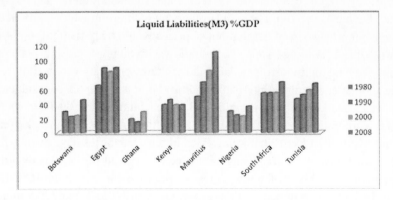

Figure 5: Ratio of Liquid Liabilities to GDP

3. THE SUBPRIME BUBBLE: BACKDROP

According to the National Bureau of Economic Research Business Cycle Dating Committee (NBERBC) the US officially entered recession in December 2007. Several of the developments during this time were reminiscent of events during the 1930s, making the 2007 recession the severest since the great depression. By early 2008 the slowdown in US growth had spread to both emerging and developed countries. The story of 2008 crisis begins a few years earlier with a substantial boom in the housing market. The boom had several sources. In part, it was fuelled by low interest rates. The FED lowered interest rates to historical low levels in the aftermath of the 2001 recession. Low interest rates and large inflows of foreign funds (into the U.S. from fast-growing economies in Asia and oil-producing countries) created easy credit conditions for a number of years prior to the crisis, fueling a housing market boom and encouraging debt-financed consumption. The US home ownership rate increased from 64% in 1994 to an all-time high of 69.2% in 2004. Loans of various types (e.g., mortgage, credit card, and auto) were easy to obtain and consumers assumed an unprecedented debt load. Subprime lending (borrowers with higher risk of default based on their income and credit history) was a major contributor to this increase in home ownership rates and in the overall demand for housing, which drove prices higher. One of these developments was securitization, the process by which a financial institution (a mortgage originator) makes loans and then bundles them together into variety of asset backed securities. These securities are then sold to other institutions (banks or insurance companies), which may not fully appreciate the risks they are taking. From 1995 to 2006, average housing prices in the US more than doubled. The high price of housing, however, proved unsustainable. From 2006 to 2008, housing prices declined by about 20%. Such price fluctuations should not necessarily cause panic. After all, price movements are how markets equilibrate supply and demand. Moreover, the price of housing in 2008 was merely a correction to the level that prevailed in 2004. But this time is different, and the price decline led to a series of chain reactions and reverberations in the US with untold consequences for the world's financial system. The first of these repercussions was substantial mortgage defaults and home foreclosures, as many home owners defaulted on their obligations. By September 2009, 14.4% of all US mortgages outstanding were either delinquent or in foreclosure, up from 9.2% in August 2008. Failed banks in the US were about 130 in 2009 as the banking industry suffered under the weight of deteriorating loans, and financial giants such as Merril Lynch, Freddie Mac, Fannie Mae, AIG, Lehman Brothers and Citigroup which borrowed large sums to buy high risk mortgages, and bet that house prices would keep rising, found themselves in bad light when the bets turned sour. The meltdown involving these big players meant that confidence in the banking industry was affected to the extent that even healthy banks stopped trusting one another and avoided interbank lending. These bankruptcies introduced substantial volatility in stock markets around the globe. Between January and October 2008, owners of stocks in U.S. corporations had suffered about $8 trillion in losses, as their holdings declined in value from $20 trillion to $12 trillion. Losses in other countries have averaged about 40%. Losses in the stock markets and housing value declines placed further downward pressure on consumer spending. As this book goes to press unemployment was above 10% in the US, and growth in 2010 had just returned to France and Germany. Stock markets around the world rebounded in 2009 after a dismal performance in 2008, even though confidence had not been completely restored.

4. THE FINANCIAL CRISIS AND AFRICAN CAPITAL MARKETS

There was an initial optimism that the crisis will not impact negatively on African countries, and if at all the effects would only be second round. Such optimism has its roots in a number of conjectures: Africa's financial systems are not as closely integrated in the global financial system as other regions of the developing world; African banks tend to hold most of their assets and commitments on, rather than off the balance sheet; Africa's financial institutions are not exposed to risks emanating from complex instruments in international financial markets, instead African banks have typically low loan-deposit ratios and high liquidity reserves. Unlike in several European countries—and with the notable exception of South Africa—there is also very limited household lending, at the core of the subprime crisis in developed economies (see Beck et al, 2009). The net effect of this is that the financial crisis will only have indirect effects on the real economy through reduced private capital inflows caused by reduced risk appetite, and trade channels, given that majority of sub-Saharan African countries exports mainly primary commodities.

While this stand point may be true two decades ago and indeed for the much closed economies, the evidence till date suggests that the most liquid stock markets have so far borne the direct brunt of the crisis. This is not necessarily surprising since stock prices are leading indicators. We take the stance that the effects of the financial crisis on Africa have been direct, particularly through the stock market channel and to the real economy. We concentrate on the transmission of shocks from global stock markets to African stock markets. Evaluating the extent to which shocks elsewhere affect African countries is important for a variety of reasons. A critical tenet of investment strategy is that most economic disturbances are country specific, so stock markets in different countries should display relatively low correlations. International diversification would therefore substantially reduce portfolio risk and increase expected returns. If spill over occurs after a negative shock, however, then market correlations would increase in bad states, which would undermine much of the rational for international diversification. In addition asset pricing models tend to assume that investors react differently after a large negative shock. Understanding how individual behaviour changes in good and bad states are key to understanding how shocks are transmitted across markets. Moreover, many international institutions and policy makers worry that a negative shock to one country can have a negative impact on financial flows to another country—even if the fundamentals of the second economy are strong and there is little real connection between the two countries. Even if this effect is temporary, it could lead to a financial crisis in the second country—a crisis completely unwarranted by the country's fundamentals and policies. If this sort of contagion exists, it could justify intervention by multilateral agencies such as the IMF and the dedication of massive amounts of money to stabilization funds (see Forbes and Rigobon, 2002). In the sections that follow we establish the spillover of the crisis and then trace the channels of the contagion on various indicators.

The Subprime Contagion

Contagion is a difficult term to define and measure. We generally define contagion in our context as the spread of disturbances from one market to another, particularly during crisis. Crisis can erupt from currency, bond, stock or the real estate sectors of an economy which tend to cause a significant increase in cross-market linkages between one country and its trading / or regional partners. How is the volatility of one country related to the volatility or co-volatility of several countries? Is the volatility of an asset transmitted to another asset directly (through its conditional variance) or indirectly (through its conditional covariance)? Does a shock in one market increase the volatility on another market, and by how much? A related issue is whether the correlations between asset returns change over time. Are they higher during periods of higher volatility (sometimes associated with financial crisis)? The autoregressive conditional heteroscedasticity (ARCH) model of Engle (1982) and later generalized by Bollerslev (1986), and the multivariate GARCH provide answers to these questions. The analyses here focus on Egypt, South Africa and Morocco and how shocks from US and UK impact on these markets[8]. By abstracting this way we are essentially focusing on the most liquid African markets where spillover matters most. Moreover MGARCH models are computationally extensive and given the many parameters involved and the large number of possible markets we can analyse the work becomes more daunting, hence the need to deliberately restrict the analysis. The mean equation for each return series is

$$R_{i,t} = \mu_i + \alpha R_{i,t-1} + \varepsilon_{it} \tag{1}$$

where $R_{i,t}$ is the return on index i between time $t-1$ and t, μ_i is a long term drift coefficient, and $\varepsilon_{i,t}$ is the error term for the return on index i at time t. We tested this for ARCH effects in line with Engle (1982)[9]. All estimated series exhibited evidence of ARCH effects. Volatiltity transimission is carried out through a multivariate GARCH model, following the BEKK[10] representation of Engle and Kroner (1995)

$$H_{t+1} = C'C + A'\varepsilon_t\varepsilon_t'A + B'H_tB \tag{2}$$

C is a 3*3 lower triangular matrix with six paprameter. A is a 3*3 square matrix of parameters and shows how conditional variancess are correlated with past squared erros. The elements of matrix A measure the effects of shocks or 'news' on conditional variances. B is also a 3*3 square matrix of parameters and shows how past conditional variances affect current levels of conditional variances. The total number of estimated elements for the variance equations for our trivariate case is 24.

The conditional variance for each equation, ignoring constant terms, can be expanded for the trivariate GARCH(1,1) as:

$$h_{11,t+1} = a_{11}^2\varepsilon_{1,t}^2 + 2a_{11}a_{12}\varepsilon_{1,t}\varepsilon_{2,t} + 2a_{11}a_{31}\varepsilon_{1,t}\varepsilon_{3,t} + a_{21}^2\varepsilon_{2,t}^2 + 2a_{21}a_{31}\varepsilon_{2,t}\varepsilon_{3,t}$$

$$+ a_{31}^2 \varepsilon_{3,t}^2 + b_{11}^2 h_{11,t} + 2b_{11}b_{12}h_{12,t} + 2b_{11}b_{31}h_{13,t} + b_{21}^2 h_{22,t} + 2b_{21}b_{31}h_{23,t} + b_{31}^2 h_{33,t} \quad (3)$$

$$h_{22,t+1} = a_{12}^2 \varepsilon_{1,t}^2 + 2a_{12}a_{22}\varepsilon_{1,t}\varepsilon_{2,t} + 2a_{12}a_{32}\varepsilon_{1,t}\varepsilon_{3,t} + a_{22}^2 \varepsilon_{2,t}^2 + 2a_{22}a_{32}\varepsilon_{2,t}\varepsilon_{3,t}$$

$$+ a_{32}^2 \varepsilon_{3,t}^2 + b_{12}^2 h_{11,t} + 2b_{12}b_{22}h_{12,t} + 2b_{12}b_{32}h_{13,t} + b_{22}^2 h_{22,t} + 2b_{22}b_{32}h_{23,t} + b_{32}^2 h_{33,t}$$

$$(4)$$

$$h_{33,t+1} = a_{13}^2 \varepsilon_{1,t}^2 + 2a_{13}a_{23}\varepsilon_{1,t}\varepsilon_{2,t} + 2a_{13}a_{33}\varepsilon_{1,t}\varepsilon_{3,t} + a_{23}^2 \varepsilon_{2,t}^2 + 2a_{23}a_{33}\varepsilon_{2,t}\varepsilon_{3,t}$$

$$+ a_{33}^2 \varepsilon_{3,t}^2 + b_{13}^2 h_{11,t} + 2b_{13}b_{23}h_{12,t} + 2b_{13}b_{33}h_{13,t} + b_{23}^2 h_{22,t} + 2b_{23}b_{33}h_{23,t} + b_{33}^2 h_{33,t}$$

$$(5)$$

Equations (3), (4), and (5) show how shocks and volatility are transmitted across markets and over time. We maximized the following likelihood function assuming the errors are normally distributed

$$L(\theta) = -T\ln(2\pi) - \frac{1}{2}\sum_{t=1}^{T}\left(\ln|H_t| + \varepsilon'_t H_t^{-1}\varepsilon_t\right)$$

The estimation results of the multivariate GARCH model with BEKK parameterisation for each variance equation are reported in Table 2.

The conditional variance is determined by own past variance, own past squared shock and external innovations. Sticking with column 1 of Table 2 our first trivariate system has UK, US and South Africa. The conditional variances, $h_{11,t}$ is the own shocks while $h_{12,t}$ and $h_{13,t}$ measures the volatility spill over from UK to US and from UK to South Africa respectively. We must emphasize that the volatility spill over coefficient $h_{12,t}$ and $h_{13,t}$ is also a reflection of the degree of volatility co-movement between the markets. Statistically significant spill over coefficients imply that significant volatility shocks are imported from one country to another through the variances. As volatility spill over from one market to another becomes pronounced, volatility co-movement between the two markets increases. The spill over coefficients by no means implies causality. Rather, it reflects the degree of correlation and co-movement. The ε represents the effect of 'news', such that $\varepsilon_{1,t}^2, \varepsilon_{2,t}^2, \varepsilon_{3,t}^2$ represent unanticipated news in UK, US and South Africa respectively. The cross terms, $\varepsilon_{1,t}\varepsilon_{2,t}$, represents the effect of news in UK and US and in that order for any subsequent combinations.

Table 2. Volatility Spillover and Comovement

	UK, US, South Africa	South Africa, Egypt, Morocco	South Africa, Egypt, UK
$\varepsilon^2_{1,t}$	0.0003*** (3.95)	0.001** (2.807)	0.0006** (2.879)
$\varepsilon^2_{2,t}$	0.0003*** (4.522)	0.000 (1.44)	0.0004** (2.089)
$\varepsilon^2_{3,t}$	0.0006*** (3.445)	0.000* (1.884)	0.0003*** (3.06)
$\varepsilon_{1,t}\varepsilon_{2,t}$	0.225*** (8.805)	0.265*** (7.367)	0.242*** (5.768)
$\varepsilon_{1,t}\varepsilon_{3,t}$	0.234*** (9.621)	0.362*** (5.729)	0.347*** (4.216)
$\varepsilon_{2,t}\varepsilon_{3,t}$	0.258*** (5.105)	0.358*** (3.657)	0.227*** (7.301)
$h_{11,t}$	0.0004*** (3.97)	0.001*** (4.471)	0.0013*** (4.791)
$h_{12,t}$	0.0002** (2.996)	0.000 (1.102)	0.00017 (1.212)
$h_{13,t}$	0.0006** (2.672)	0.001 (1.416)	0.0002*** (3.468)
$h_{22,t}$	0.0003*** (3.302)	0.001*** (3.176)	0.001** (2.959)
$h_{23,t}$	0.0003** (2.175)	0.001 (1.339)	0.00006 (1.031)
$h_{33,t}$	0.0012*** (4.672)	0.001 (1.645)	0.0004*** (3.86)

Note: *,**,*** denotes significance at the 10%, 5% and 1% levels respectively.

Volatility can be transmitted directly through the variance of asset returns or indirectly through the covariances. Own market volatility is statistically significant for our specification. Volatility in UK, US and South Africa tend to be affected directly by volatility in each market. This is true for the significant $h_{11,t}$. A critical look at the results indicate that not only is volatility in each market directly affected by own volatility, but also that the volatility of other markets matter for each market. For instance UK volatility indirectly affects South African volatility. The effect of unanticipated news on each market and other markets is also shown to be important in Table 2. Unanticipated news for South Africa, UK and US matter for each country. So is the effect of news from other countries as shown by the significant $\varepsilon_{1,t}\varepsilon_{2,t}$. To throw more light on the spillover effects we plot the conditional correlations and covariances between the markets in Figures 6 and 7.

Looked at in this way, contagion is driven largely by changes in economic fundamentals which increases the extent of cross market correlations and interdependence through technological and financial links, trade flows and regional and historical linkages. However, contagion can also spread through pure fads and noise. This is particularly relevant for emerging markets, where information asymmetry can set off a chain reaction. For instance declines in asset prices cause large capital losses, which induce investors to sell off securities in other markets to raise cash for redemptions. Similarly, investors who manage portfolios based on benchmark weightings will keep their weightings the same by selling off assets that have increased in value and thus hold too great a proportion of the portfolio. It is this type of behaviour that penalizes more liquid markets. It may also be that investors are imperfectly informed and they might assume (correctly or not) that one country has the same problems as another in crisis. They may take the actions of other investors to make this conclusion. These information asymmetries, particularly in circumstances of high fixed costs in gathering and processing country-specific information, could lead to "herd behaviour".

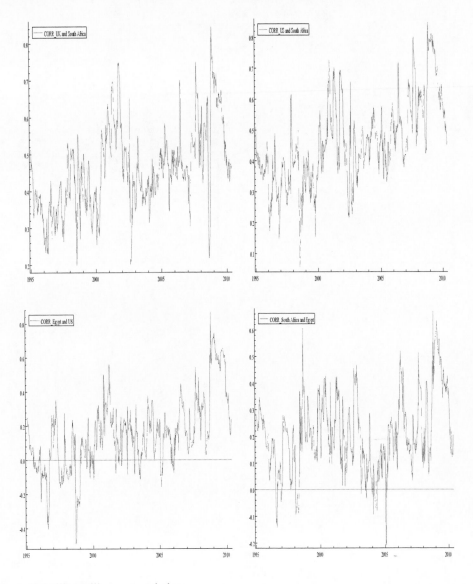

Figure 6: Volatility spillover: correlations

As can be seen from Figure 6 the correlations tend to change over time. Higher market correlations are seen in periods of crisis compared to tranquil times. Egypt and US and South Africa and Egypt depict this in Figure 6. The covariances in Figure 7 tell the story of the most recent crisis better. There is a huge spike between 2007-2009 in the sample depicting the effect of the subprime crisis and its spillover effect on African countries. Thus the increase in the correlation suggests that the transmission mechanism between pairs of markets in our sample have strengthened after the shock and, and the impact of the shock is direct. Most studies employing simple correlations arrive at similar conclusions. For instance King and Wadhwani (1990) found an increase in stock market correlations between the United States, the United Kingdom, and Japan after the 1987 crash.

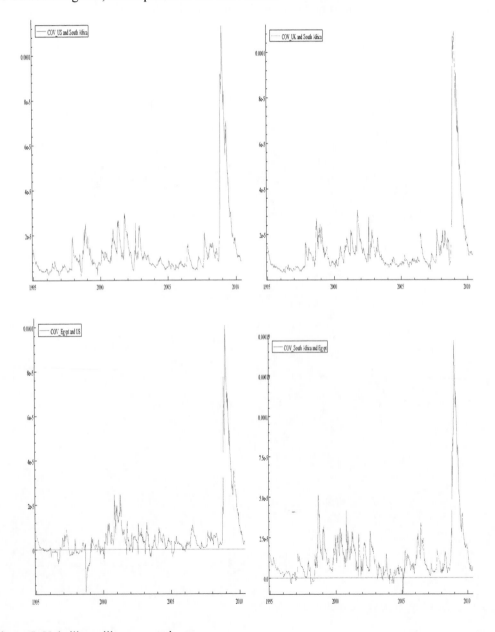

Figure 7: Volatility spillover: covariance

5. CHANNELS OF CRISIS TRANSMISSION

Private Capital Flows

One channel through which we believe the financial crisis may have direct impact on emerging economies in sub-Saharan Africa is through private capital flows. Due to lack of available data to run regressions this section is descriptive. Africa has attracted huge sums of capital in recent time, particularly after most countries liberalised their capital accounts, and relaxed restrictions on capital movements. The surge in capital flows has also been made possible by improvements in information and communications technology that allows financial transactions to change hands by the click of the mouse. Moreover, improvements in country risk perception and the generally declining number of conflicts, coupled with robust economic performance means that foreign investors consider Africa as a potential destination for investment. According to the IMF's estimates private capital flows to sub-Saharan Africa reached an estimated $50 billion in 2007. However, the evidence indicate that such flows have nearly all or partially been reversed. To see which regions and countries are most affected, we plot portfolio equity flows in US dollars for all developing regions and selected African countries in Figure 8.

Figure 8 indicates a sharp reversal in the gains following the crisis. As shown in the right hand side of the graph, portfolio equity flows declined at the onset of the recession in late 2007 and with the exception of Middle East and North Africa, the decline has been very dramatic for other developing regions of the world. The corresponding graph for the individual countries indicate that the reversal of capital inflows due to deleveraging has been one of the most significant effects of the financial crisis on Africa's emerging and frontier markets. This has been particularly evident for countries with well developed financial systems and increasingly liberalised markets. Incidentally, the more liberalised a country is, the more favoured it is a destination for global capital, but at the same time the more prone the country is to financial shocks from the global financial architecture. The right hand side of Figure 8 shows that Africa's fluid financial centres—Egypt, Nigeria and South Africa suffered most from the reversal of capital flows between 2007 and 2009. In Kenya, net portfolio equity flows declined significantly in the second quarter of 2008, with an outflow of $48 million. From $729 million in 2005, portfolio equity flows declined to $673 million in 2008 for Egypt. The Nigerian experience is even more dramatic: from $1.4 billion in 2007 equity flows were only worth $46 million by 2008. Such short term reversals and sudden stops have huge implications. For sub-Saharan the predicted loss in financial flows and export earnings on account of the financial crisis is around $49 billion between 2007 and 2009, or 6% of the entire continent's pre-crisis GDP. The impact relative to GDP is nearly double the impact of the Asian financial crisis of 1997/98. For countries that rely on external flows and base all or part of their development strategies on attracting funds from abroad, and for companies and individuals that are dependent on these flows, this fall is likely to be calamitous[11], as it put breaks on the progress towards attaining the Millennium Development Goals(MDG) of halving poverty by 2015.

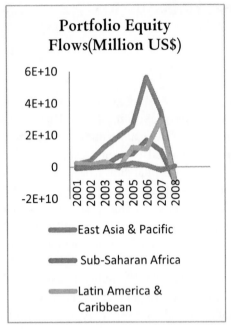
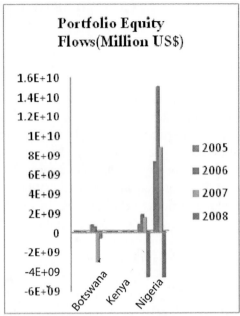

Figure 8: Portfolio Equity flows (Million US$)

Direct Investment

Compared to equity flows, FDI inflows have been resilient during and after the crisis, growing slower with the recession. Figure 9 shows net FDI flows for various developing regions and selected African countries.

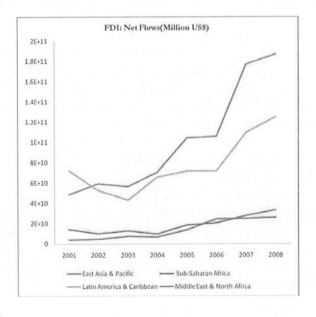

Figure 9. (Continued)

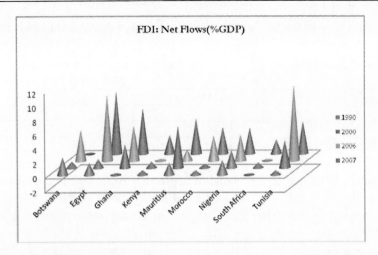

Figure 9: Net FDI Flows(Million US$)

Although the data stops at 2007, there are indications that FDI inflows to the developing world may have fallen for the first year in the decade to 2009, but continued to increase despite the crisis. This is particularly so for raw materials and extractive industry based economies.

Bank Lending

Bank lending has been another channel that has suffered most from the financial crisis. The Institute of International Finance (IIF), the international association of financial institutions, estimates that foreign bank lending to developing countries in 2008 was just 40% of the 2007 level, and by 2009 the IIF forecasts that bank lending will have dropped by more than 100% from its 2007 level. With banking sector reforms over the years, sub-Saharan Africa has attracted a significant amount of foreign banks as part of the financial deepening process. By 2007, there were 11 foreign banks in Kenya alone, representing a quarter of all banks and accounting for about 40% of commercial banks' core capital. Although there has not been any direct evidence that the share of foreign banks changed in 2008 and 2009 because of the crisis or that foreign parent banks withdrew funds in Kenya in order to offset losses in home countries, indications are that, for sub-Saharan African countries, the presence of the foreign-owned banks has had a dramatic impact on bank lending through contagion risk. Financial distress among parent foreign banks has already led to large scale withdrawal of capital. Banks' total foreign claims on Zambia declined from $2908 million in June 2008 to $2607 million in September 2008. As seen in Table 3 net flows to developing countries is negative, indicating that more money is transferred to banks overseas than is lent to developing countries.

Prior to the crisis, bond flows to sub-Saharan Africa had surged to $7.13 billion from 2006 to 2007, with individual countries accessing the international bond market to raise more funds to support development. Seychelles issued a $200 million sovereign bond in September 2006. Nigeria issued two bonds before the crisis: a $350 million private corporate bond in January 2007 and a $175 million private corporate bond in March 2007.

Table 3. Predicted losses from financial crisis to developing countries

Type of financial flow	Predicted change for developing countries, 2007-2009 (%)
Bank lending	-115
Equities	82
FDI	-34

Source: IIF, Capital Flows to Emerging Market Economies, January 2009

Ghana issued a $750 million Eurobond in September 2007; Gabon issued a $1 billion 10-year Eurobond in December 2007. However, as equity flows reversed, the cost of raising capital through bond issuance has risen largely on account of reduced risk appetite. The spread on US Treasury bonds – the least risky of all loans – and the rate charged to developing countries when they issue their own sovereign bonds, has increased from just over 2.5% in 2007 to nearly 7.5% in 2008, and is predicted to stay at around 7%. In effect, the financial crisis has made borrowing more expensive to those countries that bear least responsibility for the crisis, while reducing borrowing costs in those countries that were actually responsible.

Apart from driving the cost of borrowing up for developing countries the financial crisis has put on hold many plans for future issues. For example, Ghana cancelled planned $300 million debt issue owing to poor global market conditions. Kenya has delayed a planned debut $500 million Eurobond. Tanzania has postponed plans to issue a debut Eurobond totalling at least $500 million until market conditions improve (see Brambila and Massa, 2009). According to the IMF (2008), not a single sub-Saharan African foreign currency denominated bond (Eurobond) came to market in 2008, compared with a value of $6.5 billion in 2007.

Remittances

There are two truths about remittances. The first is that nearly all migrant income originates from the northern hemisphere and it typically flows to the south. Although there has been studies pointing to reverse remittances, i.e. flows from countries such as Mexico and Guatemala to support families suffering from the recession in the US, such events are sporadic and temporary. In 2007 the World Bank estimates that slightly under three-quarters of remittances to sub-Saharan Africa were sent from the United States and Western Europe, while the rest were sent from Gulf States, other developed countries and developing countries. The second reality is that remittance flows are intrinsically linked to migration. Thus as international migration recedes due to the recession following tighter rules on migration in developed countries, uncertainties about job prospects for existing migrants, the flow of remittances is expected to reduce.

The International Organisation of Migration (IOM) recons that there are 214 million workers worldwide. These migrants have remitted to their home countries $444 billion. Remittances to sub-Saharan Africa had been rising steadily since 1995, increasing by 11% between 2006 and 2007. Sub-Saharan Africa received US$19 billion in remittances in 2007, representing 2.5% of the regions GDP according to studies by World Bank. Worldwide $265 billion flowed to developing countries through remittances in 2007, surpassing official global development aid by 60%. The top 10 recipients of remittances worldwide have included Nigeria and Egypt. As a share of GDP, remittances exceed a quarter of the GDP of countries such as Lesotho. Over the years this source of capital flows has been critical in supporting poor families with basic necessities such as food, housing, health and education. As Figure 10 shows however, remittances began to fall with the onset of the financial crisis, with the most remarkable fall in Latin America. As panicky rich-world investors turned inward and foreign banks became increasingly reluctant to lend across borders, not only did official capital flows reverse but also remittances. The World Bank forecasts that remittance flows to developing countries could decline by 7-10% in 2009, with a possible recovery in 2010 and 2011.

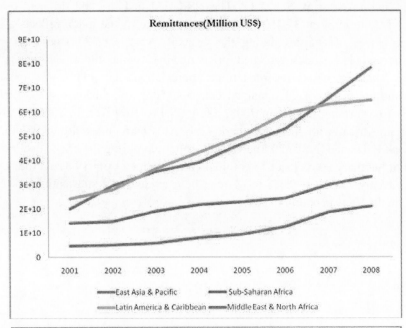

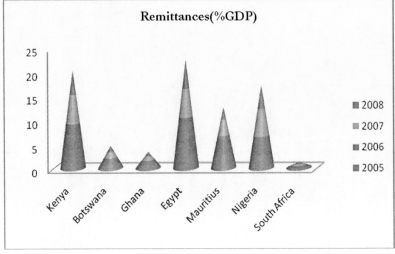

Figure 10: Workers Remittances

Impact on Stock Market

Index performance

The rising unemployment, weakened consumer demand and reduced investor confidence exerted downward pressure on the stock markets worldwide. Figure 11 shows that all markets in our sample went down with the recession and the extent of the decline was abrupt. Correspondingly Figure 12 shows the performance of African markets in local currency terms. The impact of the global economic meltdown worsened the scenario as foreign investors shunned assets considered risky while local investors sought refuge in short-term securities. The Nigerian Stock Exchange All-Share Index (ASI) dropped by 33.8% or 10,623.61 points to close at 20,827.17. The NSE ASI had in 2008 dropped by 45.8% or 26,539.44 points to close at 31,450.78. The performance of the index reflects a significant reduction in prices of equities during the year. By year end, 23 stocks recorded price appreciations and 159 stocks recorded price declines while the prices of 35 remained constant. In 2008, 78 stocks recorded price appreciations and 111 stocks recorded price declines while the prices of 24 remained constant. Globally, Ghana's stock exchange had been the best performing market in 2008, rising 58.1%. However, in 2009 it was the least performing in Africa, with the benchmark GSE All Share Index dropping -46.58%. The Nairobi Stock Exchange (NSE) 20 Share Index collapsed during the crisis, declining by 46% by the end of February 2009. Price-to-earnings ratio declined from 19.8% at the beginning of 2008 to an average value of 9.3% in March 2009: evidence of substantial loss of investor confidence in the Kenyan equity market.

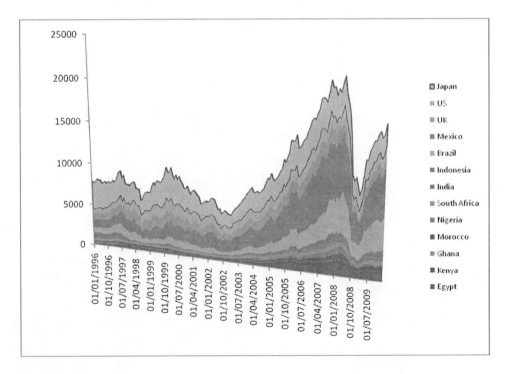

Figure 11: Share Prices ($US)

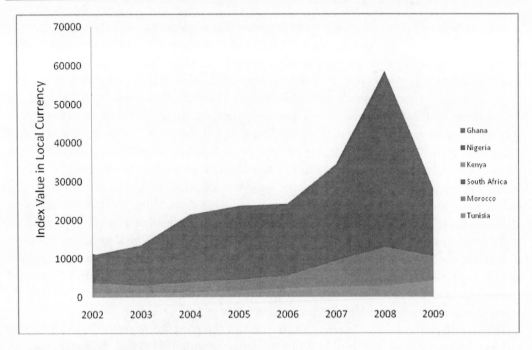

Figure 12: Share Prices (Local currency)

IPOs

In 2009, several initial public offerings (IPOs) were postponed. In Nigeria a significant portion of the funds that left the stock market for the Private Placement Market in 2007/8 remained locked-in, as many of the issuers have not yet applied to The Nigerian Stock Exchange for listing. The number of securities listed on the Exchange dropped to 266 from 299 in 2008. No new IPOs were approved in 2009 and 64 securities were delisted during the year in 2009. In Ghana there was no new listing in 2009 except Comet Properties which was provisionally listed, and some six Right Issues.

6. RESPONSE TO THE CRISIS AND REFORM

As the world economy emerges from the economic crisis and growth in Africa rebounds, a new look at the role of finance is urgently needed. This would require a substantial overhaul of the current paradigm including improving existing financial markets and institutions, to establishing new markets and instruments that would further entrench the gains made in financial development over the years. The evidence presented in this chapter clearly indicated that portfolio flows are highly volatile and subject to sudden stops. This in turn have a knock on effect in sound economic management. Very liberalised financial systems are particularly prone to capital flow reversals. Remittances have also been seen as highly procyclical. It is thus important for African countries to reduce their reliance on external capital as the major component of development finance. This in turn implies diversifying the sources of development finance. Domestic resource mobilisation is a sure way out of vulnerability. Increasing tax revenues through wider tax nets, and tackling loopholes in current tax administration hold promise for supporting growth while maintaining stability and confidence in a world financial system that is subject to frequent random shocks. But more importantly, the crisis has brought to the fore the need to improve existing financial structures through better regulation, increase the menu of options through creation of new financial products and instruments and regional integration of not only capital markets, but also the entire economy.

As shown in this chapter the more liquid and opened a market is, the more susceptible it is to capital flow reversals. Thus financial liberalisation, far from delivering the intended steady state growth effects and reducing poverty as predicted by most theoretical models, can produce significant short term welfare losses, which may then produce hysteresis type effects. A cautious approach to unfettered capital accounts opening in particular and financial liberalisation in general would be required to reduce vulnerability to financial crisis in environments of weak institutions. Available evidence indicates that blanket imposition of capital controls may not yield optimal outcomes either. Thus, in addition to raising the level of domestically generated resources, African countries would do better by minimizing the adverse impact of short term capital flows, through a mix of sound regulation of financial transactions, and Tobin taxes to put sands on the wheels of the destructive forces that hot money inflows unleash on vulnerable financial markets in Africa.

The ramifications of the financial crisis point to the need for urgent effort to integrate African capital markets regionally. While integration with the global economy may be beneficial, the evidence to date shows that entering the global economy at an uneven platform presents problems to Africa's nascent markets. A strong regional approach to capital markets development hold a long term benefit of reducing Africa's exposure to spill over effects from global markets. This would require the establishment of strong institutional agreements among African equity markets, deepening the existing networks, and removing existing impediments to capital market reform. It must however, be pointed out that capital market integration cannot occur in isolation of economic integration. Therefore, deepening trade among African countries, harmonizing policies and removing existing impediments to the free flow of goods and services is sine qua non to capital market integration. Over the years efforts at integrating Africa's stock markets have been taking place, albeit it very sluggish. The fall out of the crisis calls for a doubling of efforts to make stock market integration a reality, for a strong pan-African stock market would prove useful in the long-run. With an integrated pan-African stock market, for example, investors from the continent would be able to allocate capital to the locations in the region where it is the most productive. With more cross-border flow of funds, additional trading in individual securities will improve the liquidity of Africa's fledgling exchanges, which will in turn lower the cost of capital for firms, and lower the transaction costs investors incur. The need to access global capital markets may thus be curtailed.

Another area that deserves attention is the development of fixed income market. The vast majority of Africa's debt is currently denominated in foreign currency and highly illiquid. Very few countries have active bond markets and the paucity of a credible debt market to complement existing capital markets compounds vulnerability in the presence of financial crisis. A strong government debt market would be beneficial for African markets. At the macroeconomic level, a strong government debt market would provide a conduit for domestic funding of chronic budget deficits other than that provided by the central bank and, thereby, can reduce the need for direct and potentially damaging monetary financing of government deficits and avoid a build-up of foreign debt. Moreover, a well organised debt market can strengthen the transmission mechanism of monetary policy, including the achievement of monetary targets or inflation objectives, and can enable the use of market-based indirect monetary policy instruments. The existence of such a market can thus enable smoothing consumption and investment expenditures in response to random shocks, and if coupled with sound debt management, can also help reduce exposure to interest rate, currency, and other financial risks. A shift toward market-oriented funding of government budget deficits could reduce debt-service costs over the medium to long term through development of a deep and liquid market for government securities. At the microeconomic level, development of a domestic debt market can increase overall financial stability and improve financial intermediation through greater competition and development of related financial infrastructure, products, and services.

Beside government bonds, a sound corporate debt market helps in disintermediation, essentially allowing corporations needing funds bypass banks and go directly to the capital market. With disintermediation the requisite credit evaluation previously performed by banks must now be done by investors, who may be well equipped to fully assess the risks of their businesses. In addition a well developed corporate debt market brings on players such as pension funds and insurance companies, which tend to have a longer-term focus. Since these institutional investors employ little or no leverage, while banks are highly levered, this development should have a beneficial effect on systemic risk. However, a sound debt market requires a friendly environment to operate. For corporate bonds a crucial precondition is the absence of government interference. Investors must feel free to base their decisions on purely utilitarian characteristics such as risk and expected return. Arguably the single most important element of a well-functioning bond market is a financial reporting system for companies which are relevant, reliable, and timely. A second key ingredient of a healthy corporate bond market is a strong community of financial analysts. The role of (buy-side) financial analysts is to provide investors with independent and informed advice. In effect, the value of a sound financial reporting system is multiplied by the presence of profession of financial analysts, since their evaluation of the companies is now made easier and can therefore result in a better product. Thus, an informative accounting system also tends to raise the quality of analysts' recommendations.

Notes

1. Although most of this work supports the hypothesis that finance plays a determining factor in economic growth, there have been alternative voices urging a more cautious interpretation of the evidence, since these channels, while potentially important, may be overstressed. There have been dissenting voices that see the role of finance to be detrimental to growth and most studies suggests whole sale liberalisation of financial systems in developing countries have brought unintended consequences.

2. Bourse Régionale des Valeurs Mobilières SA, or BRVM is the regional stock exchange serving eight former French colonies in West Africa: Benin, Burkina Faso, Cote d'Ivoire, Guinea Bissau, Mali, Niger, Senegal and Togo.

3. http://www.afrol.com/articles/15679(accessed 10 April 2010)

4. With the exception of Figures 6 and 7, all other figures are based on data obtained from the online version of the World Development Indicators. All calculations and analysis are mine.

5. The fall in number of companies is largely due to delisting, particularly in South Africa and Kenya. A number of South African firms have migrated to the London Stock Exchange to access more capital over the years.

6. No tax on capital gains until end of 2010.

7. Domestic credit provided by the banking sector includes all credit to various sectors on a gross basis, with the exception of credit to the central government, which is net. The banking sector includes monetary authorities and deposit money banks, as well as other banking institutions where data are available (including institutions that do not accept transferable deposits but do incur such liabilities as time and savings deposits). Domestic credit to private sector refers to financial resources provided to the private sector, such as through loans, purchases of nonequity securities, and trade credits and other accounts receivable, that establish a claim for repayment. For some countries these claims include credit to public enterprises. Liquid liabilities are also known as broad money, or M3. They are the sum of currency and deposits in the central bank (M0), plus transferable deposits and electronic currency (M1), plus time and savings deposits, foreign currency transferable deposits, certificates of deposit, and securities repurchase agreements (M2), plus travellers checks, foreign currency time deposits, commercial paper, and shares of mutual funds or market funds held by residents.

8. The data employed are the Morgan Stanley Capital International Indices (MSCI) for each country. The data is weekly and are reported in US dollars.

9. Specifically, the test statistic is distributed as χ^2 with degrees of freedom equal to the number of restrictions. We found significant ARCH effects in each return series which suggests that past values of volatility can be used to predict current volatility.

10. The acronym BEKK is used in the literature as earlier unpublished work by Baba, Engle, Kraft, and Kroner (1990). Some researchers have used the constant correlation model, which by assuming constant correlations among the variables over time significantly reduces the number of estimated parameters. Bollerslev (1990) and Karolyi (1995) have used this model. However, Longin and Solnik (1995) argue that in equity markets the assumption of constant correlations among the variables does not hold over time. Additionally, the assumption does not permit volatility spill overs across markets. We do not favour these restrictions in the presence sense.

11. Where does it hurt? The Impact of the financial crises on developing countries, ActionAid, March 2010.

REFERENCES

Baba, Y., Engle, R. F., Kraft D., and Kroner. K. (1990). Multivariate simultaneous generalized ARCH. Unpublished manuscript, University of California-San Diego.

Beck, T., Fuchs, M., and Marilou, U. (2009). Finance in Africa: Achievements and Challenges, Policy Research Working Paper, WPS5020

Bencivenga, V. R. and B. D. Smith (1991). Financial Intermediation and Endogenous Growth. *Review of Economics Studies* 58, pp. 195-209.

Brambila,J.M and Massa, I. (2009). The global financial crises and sub-Saharan Africa, the effect of slowing private capital inflow on growth. ODI Working Paper 304.

Bollerslev, T., (1986). Generalized Autoregressive Conditional Heteroscedasticity. *Journal of Econometrics* 31, pp. 307-327.

Bollerslev, T. (1990). Modeling the coherence in short run nominal exchange rates: A multivariate generalized ARCH approach. *Review of Economics and Statistics* 72, pp. 498–505.

Caprio, G.Jr. and Demirgüç-Kunt, A. (1998). The Role of Long Term Finance: Theory and Evidence. *The World Bank Research Observer* **13**(2), pp. 171-189.

Calvo,G., Leiderman, L., and Reinhart, C. (1993). Capital Inflows and Real Exchange Rate Appreciation in Latin America: the Role of External Factors. *IMF Staff Papers* 40(1) pp. 108-51.

Cho, Y. D. (1986). Inefficiencies from financial liberalisation in the absence of well-functioning equity markets. *Journal of Money, Credit and Banking* 18(2), 191-200.

Ducker, K., 1996. Developments in African Stock Markets. International capital Markets, 16(3), pp. 18-23.

Engel, R.F., (1982). Autoregressive Conditional Heteroscedasticity with Estimates of Variance of UK Inflation. *Econometrica* 50 pp. 987-1008.

Engle, R., and Kroner, K. (1995). Multivariate simultaneous generalized ARCH. *Econometric Reviews* 11, pp.122–150.

Forbes, K.J., and Rigobon, R., (2002). No contagion, only interdependence: Measuring stock market comovements. *Journal of Finance* 57(5) pp. 2223-2261.

King, M. A., and Wadhwani, S. (1990). Transmission of volatility between stock markets. *Review of Financial Studies* 3, pp. 5–33.

International Monetary Fund (2008). Regional Economic Outlook Sub-Saharan Africa (October), Washington, DC: IMF.

Greenwood, J. and B. Jovanovic (1990). Financial Development, Growth, and the Distribution of Income. *Journal of Political Economy* 98 pp. 1076-1107.

Green, C.J., Kirkpatrick, C.H., and Murinde, V. (2005). Finance and Development: Surveys of Theory, Evidence and Policy. Edward Elga Inc, UK.

Karolyi, A. (1995). A multivariate GARCH model of international transmission of stock returns and volatility. *Journal of Business and Economic Statistics*, 13, 11–25.

Khambata, D. (2000). Impact of Foreign Investment on Volatility and Growth of Emerging Stock Market. *Multinational Business Review* 8, pp. 50-59

King, M., Sentana, A., and Wadhwani, S. (1994). Volatility and links between national stock markets. *Econometrica* 62, pp. 901–933.

King, R. G. and R. Levine (1993). Finance and Growth: Schumpeter Might Be Right. *Quarterly Journal of Economics* 108, pp. 717-738.

Kim, J., and Singal, V. (2000). Stock Market Openings: Experience of Emerging Economies. *Journal of Business* 73, pp. 25-66.

Lang, L. H.P., and Lee, Y.T. (1999). Performance of Various Transaction Frequencies under Call: the case of Taiwan. *Pacific-Basin Finance Journal* 7, pp. 23-39.

Levine, R. and S. Zervos (1998). Stock Markets, Banks, and Economic Growth. *American Economic Review* 88, pp. 537-558.

Loayza, N. and Ranciere, R. (2006). Financial Development, Financial Fragility, and Growth. *Journal of Money, Credit and Banking*, 38(4) pp. 1051-1076.

Longin, F., and Solnik, B. (1995). Is correlations in international equity returns constant: 1960–1990? *Journal of International Money and Finance* 14, pp. 3–26.

Murinde, V., and Kariisa-Kasa, J. (1997). The Financial Performance of EADB. A Retrospective Analysis. *Accounting, Business and Financial History* 7(10), pp.81-104.

Rajan, R., and Zingales, L. (1998). Financial Dependence and Growth. *American Economic Review* 88, pp. 559-586.

Singh, A., (1999). Should Africa Promote Stock Market Capitalism? *Journal of International Development* 11, pp. 343-365.

In: The Stock Market
Editor: Allison S. Wetherby

ISBN: 978-1-61122-545-7
© 2011 Nova Science Publishers, Inc.

Chapter 4

STOCK MARKET BUBBLES AND CRISES: THE CASE OF EAST ASIAN EMERGING MARKETS

Ekaterini Panopoulou[*1] *and Theologos Pantelidis*[2]
[1]Department of Statistics and Insurance Science, University of Piraeus, Greece
[2]Department of Economics, University of Crete, Greece

ABSTRACT

We investigate whether the theory of periodically collapsing speculative bubbles can explain the dynamics of East Asian emerging stock market returns. By employing three alternative measures for the deviations of actual prices from fundamental values, we estimate various two-state regime-switching models for the dynamics of excess returns of the equity markets under scrutiny. Our results indicate the existence of (usually negative) bubbles in the East Asian stock markets. While our regime-switching models seem to be able to capture the behavior of the stock markets, considerable heterogeneity among countries is evident with respect to the effect of the bubble on equity returns. Finally, our models appear to have predictive ability over the timing of a change in the state (i.e. regime) of the equity markets.

Keywords: Bubbles; Financial market crises; Regime switching
JEL Classification: G15; C3

1. INTRODUCTION

East Asian equity markets have suffered many episodes of high volatility over the past two decades. Both the investment community and the domestic economy are severely plagued by these episodes. Market turbulence originating from one country can lead to regional-wide crises through contagion transmission mechanisms. Both domestic and international investors experience huge declines in their wealth which coupled with exchange rate losses makes them

---

[*] Address for Correspondence: Department of Statistics and Insurance Science, University of Piraeus, Karaoli & Dimitriou 80, 18534 Piraeus, Greece. E-mail: apano@unipi.gr. The usual disclaimer applies.

more reluctant to invest in risky assets leading to weak capital markets with harmful consequences for economic growth.

The most prominent emerging market crisis is the East Asian crisis in 1997-1998, originating from the devaluation of the Thai baht of July 1997 and/ or the Hong Kong speculative attack of October 1997. These events led to the devaluation and float of other Asian currencies during the period and the dramatic reduction of sovereign ratings for all crisis countries. More specifically, Korea avoided a debt moratorium in December 1997 through a coordinated roll over short term debt by commercial banks. Indonesia, Korea, Malaysia and Thailand were forced to restructure their financial system, to change political leadership or to seek IMF assistance packages. For a detailed chronology of the crisis, see Bank for International Settlements (1998), IMF (1999), and Baur and Fry (2006).

In this paper, we focus on six Asian emerging stock markets, namely Indonesia, Korea, Malaysia, Philippines, Taiwan and Thailand. These countries have suffered the consequences of the crisis, however at various degrees, with Taiwan being the less affected. Our aim is to model the behavior of these markets both in turbulent and calm periods. Many studies of Asian equity markets only focus on the crisis of 1997-98 but we take a broader view and analyze a longer sample that covers over two decades. A desirable feature of our approach, outlined below, is that our analysis is free from the common problem of having very small crisis samples, often leading to low power in empirical tests. Furthermore, Ito and Hashimoto (2005) document that turbulent episodes in Asian equity markets are not confined to the 1997-98 period.

Turning to our methodology, the starting point of our analysis is the theory of periodically collapsing speculative bubbles, first proposed by Blanchard and Watson (1982), which shows that self-fulfilling expectations and speculative bubbles drive the gap between actual prices and fundamental values. In detail, during stock market booms prices start to diverge from fundamental values systematically and more importantly increasingly. This growth seems unbounded until it becomes unsustainable. At this point, a sharp reversal of market prices to fundamental values starts. Evans (1991) and van Norden and Schaller (1993) show how periodically collapsing speculative bubbles can induce regime-switching behavior in asset returns (see also Brooks and Katsaris, 2005).

In what follows, we employ the van Norden and Schaller (1993) model, also employed by van Norden (1996), Schaller and van Norden (1997, 1999, 2002) and van Norden and Vigfusson (1998), for the aforementioned emerging markets. We examine whether stock prices deviate from fundamentals in a systematic way at various periods, i.e. whether a bubble exists. We also test whether the existence of a bubble can have explanatory power for the respective returns, through our regime switching specification. As a last step, we attempt to link the outset of a crisis with the collapse of the bubble as given by the respective probability.

Our results indicate the existence of (usually negative) bubbles in the East Asian stock markets. Our regime-switching models seem to have descriptive power for the behavior of the stock markets with the effect of the bubble on equity returns varying among markets. Moreover, the examination of two historical stock market crises reveals the ability of the models to indicate a change in the state (i.e. regime) of the equity markets during the crisis. Furthermore, the results show that the six markets under scrutiny are usually in the same state and thus the benefits from international diversification in the area are limited. Finally, we estimate the probability of the equity markets under examination to experience a boom or a crash and find that the probability of a boom is greater than that of a crash. We should note that our findings are robust to the specification of the bubble measure.

The layout of this paper is as follows: Section 2 presents the alternative models employed in order to construct asset fundamental values and their deviations from prices, i.e. the measures of bubbles. Section 3 presents the econometric methodology. Section 4 presents the data and empirical results and Section 5 summarizes the main findings of the paper.

2. MEASURES OF DEVIATIONS FROM FUNDAMENTAL PRICE

In this section we review the three approaches already employed in the literature (see Schaller and van Norden, 2002) to construct the fundamental values of stock prices. These methods provide us with three measures of bubbles, i.e. deviations of stock prices from their respective fundamental values. The construction of the bubbles is the first step in our attempt to estimate regime-switching models for the equity returns.

2.1 Constant Dividend Growth Rate

The first measure of deviations from fundamental price that we use (b_t^A) is tied to the model of equilibrium asset prices. Specifically, we assume that stock market prices follow a period-to-period arbitrage condition:

$$E_t(P_{t+1}) = (1+r)(P_t + D_t)$$

where r is the required rate of return which we assume constant, while P_t and D_t are the stock market prices and dividends respectively. Further assuming that the logarithm of dividends follow a random walk with drift, the fundamental price (P_t^*) is given by a multiple of current dividends $P_t^* = \rho D_t$ where $\rho = \frac{1+r}{\exp(a+\sigma^2/2)-1}$.

Under the hypothesis that actual prices may deviate from the fundamental price, we can measure the proportional deviation from fundamental price as:

$$b_t^A = \frac{B_t}{P_t} = \frac{P_t - P_t^*}{P_t} = 1 - \rho\frac{D_t}{P_t} \tag{1}$$

where we use the mean price-dividend ratio as ρ.

2.2 Predictable Time Variation in the Dividend Growth Rate

The second method we employ allows for variation in expected dividends and is based on a simple present value model of stock prices. This method stems from Campbell and Shiller

(1987) who employ a Vector Autoregressive (VAR) model in order to estimate and test the present value model of stock prices. This method provides a way of capturing the information of dividend growth contained in the information set of market participants. If the present value of stock market prices $P_t = E_t \sum_{i=0}^{\infty} (\frac{1}{1+r})^i D_{t+i}$ were true, then a linear function of current prices and dividends (the spread as defined in Campbell and Shiller, 1987) would be the optimal linear forecast of future dividends. The spread is defined as the difference between price and a multiple of current dividends and can be estimated through a VAR representation for the change in dividends and the spread itself. More in detail, the spread (S_t) and the implied bubble measure (b_t^B) is given by the following formulas

$$S_t = P_t^* - \frac{1+r}{r} D_t = \frac{1+r}{r} \sum_{i=0}^{\infty} (\frac{1}{1+r})^i E_t(\Delta D_{t+i})$$

$$b_t^B = 1 - \frac{S_t + ((1+r)/r) * D_{t-1}}{P_t} \tag{2}$$

We set $r = \frac{1}{P_t/D_t - 1}$ to ensure that the spread has a zero mean over the whole sample.

2.3 Predictable Time Variation in the Dividend Growth Rate and in the Discount Rate

The third method we employ allows for variation in both the expected dividends and the discount rate and is also based on a simple present value model of stock prices. This method stems from Campbell and Shiller (1988a, 1988b) who employ a VAR model for the log dividend-price ratio, the discount rate and the growth rate of dividends. Specifically, the fundamental value is based on $\exp(-\delta_t^c)$ times current dividends, where δ_t^c is the predicted log dividend-price ratio calculated from the following formula (through the VAR model)

$$\delta_t^c = E_t \sum_{i=0}^{\infty} k^i (R_{t+i} - \Delta D_{t+i}) + c$$

where $k = \exp(g - h)$ with g equal to the sample mean of the dividend growth rate and h equal to the sample mean of stock returns. The implied bubble measure (b_t^C) is then given by

$$b_t^C = 1 - \exp(-\delta_t^c) \frac{D_t}{P_t} \tag{3}$$

2. ECONOMETRIC METHODOLOGY

In this section, we outline the regime switching methodology employed to link stock market returns with the respective bubbles.

Let us assume that the equity market can be in either the "Survival" (S) or the "Collapse" (C) state (i.e. we assume a two-regime model). In the former case, the bubble continues to exist (and grow), while in the latter case the bubble collapses (partly). For each one of the three bubble measures defined in the previous section (Equations 1 to 3), b_t, we estimate eight alternative regime-switching models.

Our simplest model (that is, model 1) suggests that the excess return of the equity market, R_t, can be in two different states (regimes) with the same mean but different variance. The probability of being in the first state is constant and independent of the size of the bubble. To be more specific, the first model we consider to describe the dynamics of the equity returns is given by the following three equations:

$$\text{Model 1:} \quad \left\{ \begin{array}{l} R_{s,t+1} = \beta_{s0} + \varepsilon_{s,t+1}, \text{ where } \varepsilon_{s,t+1} \sim N(0,\sigma_s^2) \\ R_{c,t+1} = \beta_{c0} + \varepsilon_{c,t+1}, \text{ where } \varepsilon_{c,t+1} \sim N(0,\sigma_c^2) \\ P(State_{t+1} = S) = q_t = \Phi(q_0) \end{array} \right\}$$

where $\beta_{s0} = \beta_{c0}$ and $R_{s,t+1}, R_{c,t+1}$ are the equity returns from period t to $t+1$ conditional on being in the survival and collapse state respectively. The estimated probability q_t will be bounded between 0 and 1 given that we adopt the same approach as in Probit models where Φ is the cumulative density function of the standard normal distribution. We expect the variance in the "collapse" state (C) to be higher compared to the variance in the "survival" state (S). Note that in the context of model 1 the bubble does not affect the behavior of the equity returns. Our next model (model 2) allows for time-varying probability q_t. In other words, model 2 is given by the following equations:

$$\text{Model 2:} \quad \left\{ \begin{array}{l} R_{s,t+1} = \beta_{s0} + \varepsilon_{s,t+1}, \text{ where } \varepsilon_{s,t+1} \sim N(0,\sigma_s^2) \\ R_{c,t+1} = \beta_{c0} + \varepsilon_{c,t+1}, \text{ where } \varepsilon_{c,t+1} \sim N(0,\sigma_c^2) \\ P(State_{t+1} = S) = q_t = \Phi(q_0 + q_1|b_t|) \end{array} \right\}$$

where $\beta_{s0} = \beta_{c0}$. We expect q_1 to be negative suggesting that the probability of survival of the bubble decreases as the bubble size increases.

Our next two models, models 3 and 4, are simple generalizations of models 1 and 2 respectively, where each regime is allowed to have a different mean (in addition to a different variance).

Model 3:
$$\left\{ \begin{array}{l} R_{s,t+1} = \beta_{s0} + \varepsilon_{s,t+1}, \text{ where } \varepsilon_{s,t+1} \sim N(0,\sigma_s^2) \\ R_{c,t+1} = \beta_{c0} + \varepsilon_{c,t+1}, \text{ where } \varepsilon_{c,t+1} \sim N(0,\sigma_c^2) \\ P(State_{t+1} = S) = q_t = \Phi(q_0) \end{array} \right\}$$

Model 4:
$$\left\{ \begin{array}{l} R_{s,t+1} = \beta_{s0} + \varepsilon_{s,t+1}, \text{ where } \varepsilon_{s,t+1} \sim N(0,\sigma_s^2) \\ R_{c,t+1} = \beta_{c0} + \varepsilon_{c,t+1}, \text{ where } \varepsilon_{c,t+1} \sim N(0,\sigma_c^2) \\ P(State_{t+1} = S) = q_t = \Phi(q_0 + q_1|b_t|) \end{array} \right\}$$

Model 3 has a constant probability q_t, contrary to model 4 where q_t depends on the size of the bubble. Models 3 and 4 are often referred in literature as the mixture of normals models.

In all four of the aforementioned models, the bubble, b_t, does not enter the conditional mean specification of the equity returns. We extend our analysis by estimating four additional models (models 5 to 8) where the bubble is included in the conditional mean equations. Specifically, models 5 and 6 are as follows:

Model 5:
$$\left\{ \begin{array}{l} R_{s,t+1} = \beta_{s0} + \beta_{s1}b_t + \varepsilon_{s,t+1}, \text{ where } \varepsilon_{s,t+1} \sim N(0,\sigma_s^2) \\ R_{c,t+1} = \beta_{c0} + \beta_{c1}b_t + \varepsilon_{c,t+1}, \text{ where } \varepsilon_{c,t+1} \sim N(0,\sigma_c^2) \\ P(State_{t+1} = S) = q_t = \Phi(q_0) \end{array} \right\}$$

Model 6:
$$\left\{ \begin{array}{l} R_{s,t+1} = \beta_{s0} + \beta_{s1}b_t + \varepsilon_{s,t+1}, \text{ where } \varepsilon_{s,t+1} \sim N(0,\sigma_s^2) \\ R_{c,t+1} = \beta_{c0} + \beta_{c1}b_t + \varepsilon_{c,t+1}, \text{ where } \varepsilon_{c,t+1} \sim N(0,\sigma_c^2) \\ P(State_{t+1} = S) = q_t = \Phi(q_0 + q_1|b_t|) \end{array} \right\}$$

where $\beta_{s0} = \beta_{c0}$ and $\beta_{s1} = \beta_{c1}$. In other words, both models 5 and 6 assume that the conditional mean equations are identical in both regimes. Model 5 has a constant probability q_t, while model 6 has a time-varying probability q_t. Models 5 and 6 are often referred in literature as the fad's models.

Finally, models 7 and 8 allow for different conditional mean specification in the two regimes. Our last two models are described by the following equations:

Model 7:
$$\left\{ \begin{array}{l} R_{s,t+1} = \beta_{s0} + \beta_{s1}b_t + \varepsilon_{s,t+1}, \text{ where } \varepsilon_{s,t+1} \sim N(0,\sigma_s^2) \\ R_{c,t+1} = \beta_{c0} + \beta_{c1}b_t + \varepsilon_{c,t+1}, \text{ where } \varepsilon_{c,t+1} \sim N(0,\sigma_c^2) \\ P(State_{t+1} = S) = q_t = \Phi(q_0) \end{array} \right\}$$

$$\text{Model 8:} \quad \left\{ \begin{array}{l} R_{s,t+1} = \beta_{s0} + \beta_{s1}b_t + \varepsilon_{s,t+1}, \text{ where } \varepsilon_{s,t+1} \sim N(0,\sigma_s^2) \\ R_{c,t+1} = \beta_{c0} + \beta_{c1}b_t + \varepsilon_{c,t+1}, \text{ where } \varepsilon_{c,t+1} \sim N(0,\sigma_c^2) \\ P(State_{t+1} = S) = q_t = \Phi(q_0 + q_1|b_t|) \end{array} \right\}$$

Model 8 is the most general model considered in our analysis, while models 1 to 7 are all nested in model 8. In other words, each one of models 1 to 7 is a restricted version of model 8.

The aforementioned models are rather standard in the literature. The general model 8 can easily be estimated by maximizing the following likelihood function

$$\prod_{t=1}^{T} [\Phi(q_0 + q_1|b_t|).\varphi\left(\frac{R_{s,t+1} - \beta_{s0} - \beta_{s1}b_t}{\sigma_s}\right)\sigma_s^{-1} +$$

$$\{1 - \Phi(q_0 + q_1|b_t|)\}.\varphi\left(\frac{R_{c,t+1} - \beta_{c0} - \beta_{c1}b_t}{\sigma_c}\right)\sigma_c^{-1}] \qquad (4)$$

where φ is the standard normal probability density function (pdf), while σ_s and σ_c are the standard deviations of $\varepsilon_{s,t+1}$ and $\varepsilon_{c,t+1}$ respectively. The probability of being in regime i at time $t+1$ is given by the formula $\Phi(1(i)(q_0 + q_1|b_t|))$, where $1(i) = 1$ in the "survival" state and -1 in the "collapse" state. The likelihood function for the remaining models considered in our study (i.e. models 1 to 7) can easily be calculated by imposing the relevant parameter restrictions of each model in equation (4).

For each model, we can calculate the ex-post probability of being in the "survival" regime, P_t^x, as follows:

$$P_t^x = \frac{q_t}{\sigma_s}\varphi\left(\frac{R_{t+1} - \beta_{s0} - \beta_{s1}b_t}{\sigma_s}\right)\left\{\frac{q_t}{\sigma_s}\varphi\left(\frac{R_{t+1} - \beta_{s0} - \beta_{s1}b_t}{\sigma_s}\right) + \frac{1-q_t}{\sigma_c}\varphi\left(\frac{R_{t+1} - \beta_{c0} - \beta_{c1}b_t}{\sigma_c}\right)\right\}^{-1} (5)$$

We can also estimate the probability of a crash (i.e. an excess return more than two standard deviations below the mean return) as follows:

$$P(R_t < x) = q_t\Phi\left(\frac{x - \beta_{s0} - \beta_{s1}b_{t-1}}{\sigma_s}\right) + (1 - q_t)\Phi\left(\frac{x - \beta_{c0} - \beta_{c1}b_{t-1}}{\sigma_c}\right) \qquad (6)$$

where $x = \overline{R_t} - 2\sigma_{R_t}$. Similarly, the probability of a boom (i.e. an excess return more than two standard deviations above the mean return) is given by:

$$P(R_t > x) = q_t \Phi\left(\frac{-x + \beta_{s0} + \beta_{s1}b_{t-1}}{\sigma_s} \right) + (1 - q_t)\Phi\left(\frac{-x + \beta_{c0} + \beta_{c1}b_{t-1}}{\sigma_c} \right) \quad (7)$$

where $x = \overline{R_t} + 2\sigma_{R_t}$.

Table 1. Dataset

Variable	Country	Database	Code
Consumer Price Index	Indonesia	IFS	53664...ZF...
	Korea	IFS	54264...ZF...
	Malaysia	IFS	54864...ZF...
	Philippines	IFS	56664...ZF...
	Taiwan	Datastream	TWCONPRCF
	Thailand	IFS	57864...ZF...
Interest Rate	Indonesia	IFS	53660B..ZF...
	Korea	IFS	54260B..ZF...
	Malaysia	IFS	54860C..ZF...
	Philippines	IFS	56660B..ZF...
	Taiwan	Datastream	TAMM30D
	Thailand	IFS	57860B..ZF...
Stock Market Price Index	Indonesia	Datastream	TOTMKID
	Korea	Datastream	TOTMKKO
	Malaysia	Datastream	TOTMKMY
	Philippines	Datastream	TOTMKPH
	Taiwan	Datastream	TOTMKTA
	Thailand	Datastream	TOTMKTH
Dividend Yield	Indonesia	Datastream	TOTMKID(DY)
	Korea	Datastream	TOTMKKO(DY)
	Malaysia	Datastream	TOTMKMY(DY)
	Philippines	Datastream	TOTMKPH(DY)
	Taiwan	Datastream	TOTMKTA(DY)
	Thailand	Datastream	TOTMKTH(DY)

3. EMPIRICAL ANALYSIS

As already mentioned our focus is on the examination of the dynamics of the stock market returns of six emerging Asian equity markets, namely Indonesia, Korea, Malaysia, Philippines, Taiwan and Thailand. Our aim is to find sufficient empirical evidence to answer the following three questions. First, is there any evidence that supports the existence of a bubble (positive or negative) in the equity markets under scrutiny? If yes, is the behavior of the equity markets affected by the existence and the size of the bubble? And finally, how large is the probability of a boom or a crash in the six stock markets and how does the size of the bubble affect this probability?

3.1 Data

We use monthly data and our dataset spans a period of almost twenty years from April 1990 to February 2010. Our sample period is determined by the availability of data. Our analysis requires data for the Consumer Price Index (CPI), the stock market price index, the interest rates and the dividend yields for each one of the six countries under scrutiny. Table 1 provides detailed information about our dataset. All indices are expressed in local currencies, suggesting that the analysis is conducted from the point of view of a local investor. We use the CPI series to transform the price and dividend series into real variables.

3.2 Model selection

We estimate the eight models described in the previous section for the six countries at hand and for the three bubble measures considered in our analysis. For each country under scrutiny, we need to select the model that fits the data better than the remaining models. We perform our model selection procedure by means of the Log-likelihood Ratio test (LR-test) which is applicable only to cases of nested models. In this respect, there are some cases in our analysis where the LR-test cannot be used to compare specific pairs of models. For example, we can use the LR-test to choose between model 8 and each one of the remaining seven models since models 1 to 7 are all restricted versions of model 8. On the other hand, we cannot apply the LR-test to compare models 2 and 3 since these two are not nested models. However, this limitation of the LR-test does not cause any problems to our model selection procedure as we will see later.

Tables 2 to 7 present the empirical results of our study. Each table corresponds to a specific country and reports the findings for all three alternative bubble measures (b_t^A, b_t^B and b_t^C). We implement the LR-test to compare 19 different pairs of models. Tables 2 to 7 report the value of the LR-test and the associated p-value along with the value of the log-likelihood functions for all the estimated models.

We first compare the general model 8 to each one of the remaining models. If the LR-test indicates that model 8 is preferable compared to all other models, we choose model 8 to perform the rest of our analysis. Otherwise, we use the LR-test to choose among the models that seem to fit the data better than model 8. For example, in the case of Indonesia and the first bubble measure (b_t^A), the LR-test indicates that models 5, 6 and 7 are better than model 8. Moreover, the LR-test also supports the superiority of model 5 over models 6 and 7. Thus, we conclude that model 5 fits the data better than any other model considered in our analysis.

Table 2. Empirical results for Indonesia

b_t^A

Value of the log-likelihood function

Model	Log-l	Model	Log-l
{1}	230.702	{5}	238.639
{2}	231.364	{6}	238.907
{3}	230.705	{7}	239.467
{4}	231.521	{8}	239.709

	Estimation
β_{S0}	0.983
	(144.29)
β_{S1}	-0.028
	(-4.862)
β_{C0}	0.983
	(144.29)
β_{C1}	-0.028
	(-4.862)
σ_s	0.064
	(7.244)
σ_c	0.147
	(4.271)
q_0	0.654
	(1.275)
q_1	

Model	LR-stat	p-value
{8}vs{1}	18.014	0.001
{8}vs{2}	16.690	0.001
{8}vs{3}	18.009	0.000
{8}vs{4}	16.377	0.000
{8}vs{5}	2.140	0.544
{8}vs{6}	1.604	0.448
{8}vs{7}	0.484	0.486
{7}vs{1}	17.530	0.001
{7}vs{3}	17.525	0.000
{7}vs{5}	1.656	0.437
{6}vs{1}	16.410	0.000
{6}vs{2}	15.086	0.000
{6}vs{5}	0.536	0.464
{5}vs{1}	15.874	0.000
{4}vs{1}	1.637	0.441
{4}vs{2}	0.313	0.576
{4}vs{3}	1.633	0.201
{3}vs{1}	0.005	0.944
{2}vs{1}	1.324	0.250
Selected Model	**{5}**	

b_t^B

Value of the log-likelihood function

Model	Log-l	Model	Log-l
{1}	230.702	{5}	238.649
{2}	231.711	{6}	238.856
{3}	230.705	{7}	239.459
{4}	231.749	{8}	239.671

	Estimation
β_{S0}	0.996
	(180.465)
β_{S1}	-0.055
	(-4.863)
β_{C0}	0.996
	(180.465)
β_{C1}	-0.055
	(-4.863)
σ_s	0.064
	(7.241)
σ_c	0.147
	(4.27)
q_0	0.654
	(1.274)
q_1	

Model	LR-stat	p-value
{8}vs{1}	17.937	0.001
{8}vs{2}	15.919	0.001
{8}vs{3}	17.932	0.000
{8}vs{4}	15.842	0.000
{8}vs{5}	2.044	0.563
{8}vs{6}	1.629	0.443
{8}vs{7}	0.423	0.516
{7}vs{1}	17.514	0.001
{7}vs{3}	17.509	0.000
{7}vs{5}	1.621	0.445
{6}vs{1}	16.308	0.000
{6}vs{2}	14.290	0.000
{6}vs{5}	0.415	0.519
{5}vs{1}	15.893	0.000
{4}vs{1}	2.094	0.351
{4}vs{2}	0.076	0.783
{4}vs{3}	2.090	0.148
{3}vs{1}	0.005	0.944
{2}vs{1}	2.018	0.155
Selected Model	**{5}**	

b_t^C

Value of the log-likelihood function

Model	Log-l	Model	Log-l
{1}	229.099	{5}	236.502
{2}	229.782	{6}	236.841
{3}	229.100	{7}	237.699
{4}	229.923	{8}	237.975

	Estimation
β_{S0}	0.985
	(150.546)
β_{S1}	-0.020
	(-4.827)
β_{C0}	0.985
	(150.546)
β_{C1}	-0.020
	(-4.827)
σ_s	0.064
	(7.1)
σ_c	0.146
	(4.414)
q_0	0.626
	(1.223)
q_1	

Model	LR-stat	p-value
{8}vs{1}	17.751	0.001
{8}vs{2}	16.385	0.001
{8}vs{3}	17.750	0.000
{8}vs{4}	16.102	0.000
{8}vs{5}	2.946	0.400
{8}vs{6}	2.267	0.322
{8}vs{7}	0.550	0.458
{7}vs{1}	17.201	0.001
{7}vs{3}	17.200	0.000
{7}vs{5}	2.396	0.302
{6}vs{1}	15.485	0.000
{6}vs{2}	14.118	0.000
{6}vs{5}	0.679	0.410
{5}vs{1}	14.806	0.000
{4}vs{1}	1.649	0.438
{4}vs{2}	0.282	0.595
{4}vs{3}	1.648	0.199
{3}vs{1}	0.002	0.967
{2}vs{1}	1.367	0.242
Selected Model	**{5}**	

Notes: {i}, i=1, 2,…,8 corresponds to model i. The t-statistics are reported in the parentheses.

Table 3. Empirical results for Korea

b_t^A

Value of the log-likelihood function

Model	Log-l	Model	Log-l
{1}	231.426	{5}	232.061
{2}	236.431	{6}	236.773
{3}	234.932	{7}	236.303
{4}	240.517	{8}	240.594

Estimation

Parameter	Estimate	(t-stat)
β_{S0}	0.992	(161.836)
β_{S1}		
β_{C0}	1.113	(13.567)
β_{C1}		
σ_s	0.073	(13.567)
σ_c	0.150	(-4.328)
q_0	2.070	(-4.074)
q_1	-2.792	(-2.635)

Model	LR-stat	p-value
{8}vs{1}	18.335	0.001
{8}vs{2}	8.325	0.040
{8}vs{3}	11.323	0.010
{8}vs{4}	0.153	0.926
{8}vs{5}	17.065	0.001
{8}vs{6}	7.641	0.022
{8}vs{7}	8.582	0.003
{7}vs{1}	9.753	0.021
{7}vs{3}	2.740	0.254
{7}vs{5}	8.483	0.014
{6}vs{1}	10.694	0.005
{6}vs{2}	0.684	0.408
{6}vs{5}	9.424	0.002
{5}vs{1}	1.270	0.260
{4}vs{1}	18.182	0.000
{4}vs{2}	8.172	0.004
{4}vs{3}	11.170	0.001
{3}vs{1}	7.012	0.008
{2}vs{1}	10.010	0.002

Selected Model {4}

b_t^B

Value of the log-likelihood function

Model	Log-l	Model	Log-l
{1}	231.426	{5}	232.030
{2}	236.790	{6}	237.076
{3}	234.932	{7}	236.300
{4}	240.507	{8}	240.898

Estimation

Parameter	Estimate	(t-stat)
β_{S0}	0.993	(157.762)
β_{S1}		
β_{C0}	1.103	(12.821)
β_{C1}		
σ_s	0.072	(12.821)
σ_c	0.152	(-4.873)
q_0	2.021	(3.95)
q_1	-9.494	(-2.738)

Model	LR-stat	p-value
{8}vs{1}	18.943	0.001
{8}vs{2}	8.216	0.042
{8}vs{3}	11.931	0.008
{8}vs{4}	0.780	0.677
{8}vs{5}	17.734	0.000
{8}vs{6}	7.642	0.022
{8}vs{7}	9.196	0.002
{7}vs{1}	9.747	0.021
{7}vs{3}	2.735	0.255
{7}vs{5}	8.538	0.014
{6}vs{1}	11.300	0.004
{6}vs{2}	0.574	0.449
{6}vs{5}	10.092	0.001
{5}vs{1}	1.209	0.272
{4}vs{1}	18.162	0.000
{4}vs{2}	7.436	0.006
{4}vs{3}	11.150	0.001
{3}vs{1}	7.012	0.008
{2}vs{1}	10.727	0.001

Selected Model {4}

b_t^C

Value of the log-likelihood function

Model	Log-l	Model	Log-l
{1}	231.525	{5}	232.278
{2}	236.751	{6}	237.129
{3}	235.009	{7}	236.439
{4}	240.505	{8}	240.620

Estimation

Parameter	Estimate	(t-stat)
β_{S0}	0.992	(162.424)
β_{S1}		
β_{C0}	1.099	(13.041)
β_{C1}		
σ_s	0.071	(13.041)
σ_c	0.153	(5.38)
q_0	2.001	(4.097)
q_1	-2.700	(-2.653)

Model	LR-stat	p-value
{8}vs{1}	18.188	0.001
{8}vs{2}	7.738	0.052
{8}vs{3}	11.220	0.011
{8}vs{4}	0.230	0.891
{8}vs{5}	16.684	0.001
{8}vs{6}	6.980	0.030
{8}vs{7}	8.360	0.004
{7}vs{1}	9.828	0.020
{7}vs{3}	2.860	0.239
{7}vs{5}	8.323	0.016
{6}vs{1}	11.208	0.004
{6}vs{2}	0.757	0.384
{6}vs{5}	9.703	0.002
{5}vs{1}	1.505	0.220
{4}vs{1}	17.958	0.000
{4}vs{2}	7.508	0.006
{4}vs{3}	10.991	0.001
{3}vs{1}	6.968	0.008
{2}vs{1}	10.451	0.001

Selected Model {4}

Notes: {i}, i=1, 2,...,8 corresponds to model i. The t-statistics are reported in the parentheses

Table 4. Empirical results for Malaysia

b_t^A

Value of the log-likelihood function

Model	Log-l	Model	Log-l		Estimation
{1}	291.063	{5}	291.992	β_{S0}	1.007
{2}	291.914	{6}	292.769		(247.775)
{3}	291.068	{7}	292.590	β_{S1}	
{4}	291.927	{8}	293.233		

Model	LR-stat	p-value		Estimation
{8}vs{1}	4.338	0.362	β_{S0}	1.007
{8}vs{2}	2.637	0.451		(247.775)
{8}vs{3}	4.330	0.228	β_{S1}	
{8}vs{4}	2.611	0.271		
{8}vs{5}	2.482	0.479	β_{C0}	1.007
{8}vs{6}	0.928	0.629		(247.775)
{8}vs{7}	1.285	0.257	β_{C1}	
{7}vs{1}	3.053	0.384		
{7}vs{3}	3.044	0.218	σ_s	0.053
{7}vs{5}	1.197	0.550		(12.346)
{6}vs{1}	3.411	0.182	σ_c	0.160
{6}vs{2}	1.709	0.191		(4.512)
{6}vs{5}	1.554	0.213	q_0	1.020
{5}vs{1}	1.857	0.173		(3.349)
{4}vs{1}	1.728	0.421	q_1	
{4}vs{2}	0.026	0.871		
{4}vs{3}	1.719	0.190		
{3}vs{1}	0.009	0.925		
{2}vs{1}	1.702	0.192		

Selected Model {1}

b_t^B

Value of the log-likelihood function

Model	Log-l	Model	Log-l		Estimation
{1}	291.063	{5}	291.980	β_{S0}	1.007
{2}	292.046	{6}	292.889		(247.775)
{3}	291.068	{7}	292.580	β_{S1}	
{4}	292.057	{8}	293.342		

Model	LR-stat	p-value		Estimation
{8}vs{1}	4.556	0.336	β_{S0}	1.007
{8}vs{2}	2.592	0.459		(247.775)
{8}vs{3}	4.548	0.208	β_{S1}	
{8}vs{4}	2.569	0.277		
{8}vs{5}	2.723	0.436	β_{C0}	1.007
{8}vs{6}	0.904	0.636		(247.775)
{8}vs{7}	1.522	0.217	β_{C1}	
{7}vs{1}	3.034	0.386		
{7}vs{3}	3.025	0.220	σ_s	0.053
{7}vs{5}	1.200	0.549		(12.346)
{6}vs{1}	3.652	0.161	σ_c	0.160
{6}vs{2}	1.687	0.194		(4.512)
{6}vs{5}	1.818	0.178	q_0	1.020
{5}vs{1}	1.834	0.176		(3.349)
{4}vs{1}	1.987	0.370	q_1	
{4}vs{2}	0.022	0.881		
{4}vs{3}	1.978	0.160		
{3}vs{1}	0.009	0.925		
{2}vs{1}	1.965	0.161		

Selected Model {1}

b_t^C

Value of the log-likelihood function

Model	Log-l	Model	Log-l		Estimation
{1}	291.063	{5}	291.953	β_{S0}	1.007
{2}	291.888	{6}	292.681		(247.775)
{3}	291.093	{7}	292.569	β_{S1}	
{4}	291.901	{8}	293.162		

Model	LR-stat	p-value		Estimation
{8}vs{1}	4.198	0.380	β_{S0}	1.007
{8}vs{2}	2.548	0.467		(247.775)
{8}vs{3}	4.138	0.247	β_{S1}	
{8}vs{4}	2.522	0.283		
{8}vs{5}	2.418	0.490	β_{C0}	1.007
{8}vs{6}	0.962	0.618		(247.775)
{8}vs{7}	1.186	0.276	β_{C1}	
{7}vs{1}	3.012	0.390		
{7}vs{3}	2.952	0.229	σ_s	0.053
{7}vs{5}	1.232	0.540		(12.346)
{6}vs{1}	3.236	0.198	σ_c	0.160
{6}vs{2}	1.586	0.208		(4.512)
{6}vs{5}	1.456	0.228	q_0	1.020
{5}vs{1}	1.780	0.182		(3.349)
{4}vs{1}	1.676	0.433	q_1	
{4}vs{2}	0.026	0.872		
{4}vs{3}	1.616	0.204		
{3}vs{1}	0.060	0.806		
{2}vs{1}	1.650	0.199		

Selected Model {1}

Notes: {i}, i=1, 2,…,8 corresponds to model i. The t-statistics are reported in the parentheses

Table 5. Empirical results for Philippines

b_t^A

Value of the log-likelihood function

Model	Log-l	Model	Log-l	Parameter	Estimation
{1}	274.504	{5}	275.021	β_{S0}	1.004 (221.563)
{2}	274.505	{6}	275.037	β_{S1}	
{3}	274.567	{7}	275.408	β_{C0}	1.004 (221.563)
{4}	274.567	{8}	275.485	β_{C1}	
				σ_s	0.060 (11.856)
				σ_c	0.161 (3.777)
				q_0	1.114 (2.975)
				q_1	

Model	LR-stat	p-value
{8}vs{1}	1.960	0.743
{8}vs{2}	1.958	0.581
{8}vs{3}	1.835	0.607
{8}vs{4}	1.835	0.400
{8}vs{5}	0.928	0.819
{8}vs{6}	0.895	0.639
{8}vs{7}	0.152	0.696
{7}vs{1}	1.808	0.613
{7}vs{3}	1.682	0.431
{7}vs{5}	0.775	0.679
{6}vs{1}	1.065	0.587
{6}vs{2}	1.063	0.302
{6}vs{5}	0.033	0.856
{5}vs{1}	1.032	0.310
{4}vs{1}	0.126	0.939
{4}vs{2}	0.124	0.725
{4}vs{3}	0.000	0.993
{3}vs{1}	0.126	0.723
{2}vs{1}	0.002	0.965
Selected Model	**{1}**	

b_t^B

Value of the log-likelihood function

Model	Log-l	Model	Log-l	Parameter	Estimation
{1}	274.504	{5}	275.027	β_{S0}	1.004 (221.563)
{2}	274.519	{6}	275.075	β_{S1}	
{3}	274.567	{7}	275.414	β_{C0}	1.004 (221.563)
{4}	274.576	{8}	275.559	β_{C1}	
				σ_s	0.060 (11.856)
				σ_c	0.161 (3.777)
				q_0	1.114 (2.975)
				q_1	

Model	LR-stat	p-value
{8}vs{1}	2.109	0.716
{8}vs{2}	2.081	0.556
{8}vs{3}	1.983	0.576
{8}vs{4}	1.966	0.374
{8}vs{5}	1.063	0.786
{8}vs{6}	0.969	0.616
{8}vs{7}	0.289	0.591
{7}vs{1}	1.820	0.611
{7}vs{3}	1.694	0.429
{7}vs{5}	0.774	0.679
{6}vs{1}	1.140	0.565
{6}vs{2}	1.112	0.292
{6}vs{5}	0.095	0.758
{5}vs{1}	1.046	0.307
{4}vs{1}	0.143	0.931
{4}vs{2}	0.115	0.734
{4}vs{3}	0.018	0.894
{3}vs{1}	0.126	0.723
{2}vs{1}	0.028	0.867
Selected Model	**{1}**	

b_t^C

Value of the log-likelihood function

Model	Log-l	Model	Log-l	Parameter	Estimation
{1}	274.504	{5}	275.400	β_{S0}	1.004 (221.563)
{2}	274.789	{6}	275.416	β_{S1}	
{3}	274.851	{7}	275.758	β_{C0}	1.004 (221.563)
{4}	274.852	{8}	275.862	β_{C1}	
				σ_s	0.060 (11.856)
				σ_c	0.161 (3.777)
				q_0	1.114 (2.975)
				q_1	

Model	LR-stat	p-value
{8}vs{1}	2.716	0.606
{8}vs{2}	2.146	0.543
{8}vs{3}	2.022	0.568
{8}vs{4}	2.020	0.364
{8}vs{5}	0.924	0.820
{8}vs{6}	0.892	0.640
{8}vs{7}	0.208	0.648
{7}vs{1}	2.508	0.474
{7}vs{3}	1.814	0.404
{7}vs{5}	0.716	0.699
{6}vs{1}	1.824	0.402
{6}vs{2}	1.254	0.263
{6}vs{5}	0.032	0.858
{5}vs{1}	1.792	0.181
{4}vs{1}	0.696	0.706
{4}vs{2}	0.126	0.723
{4}vs{3}	0.002	0.964
{3}vs{1}	0.694	0.405
{2}vs{1}	0.570	0.450
Selected Model	**{1}**	

Notes: {i}, i=1, 2,...,8 corresponds to model i. The t-statistics are reported in the parentheses

Table 6: Empirical results for Taiwan

b_t^A

Value of the log-likelihood function

Model	Log-l	Model	Log-l		Estimation
{1}	226.376	{5}	227.235	β_{S0}	0.995
{2}	228.758	{6}	229.767		(157.69)
{3}	227.414	{7}	228.363	β_{S1}	-0.008
{4}	229.483	{8}	232.529		(-1.712)
				β_{C0}	1.055
					(25.822)
				β_{C1}	-0.253
					(-1.477)
				σ_s	0.071
					(13.57)
				σ_c	0.192
					(6.187)
				q_0	0.584
					(1.344)
				q_1	1.274
					(1.191)

Model	LR-stat	p-value
{8}vs{1}	12.307	0.015
{8}vs{2}	7.542	0.056
{8}vs{3}	10.231	0.017
{8}vs{4}	6.093	0.048
{8}vs{5}	10.588	0.014
{8}vs{6}	5.525	0.063
{8}vs{7}	8.332	0.004
{7}vs{1}	3.975	0.264
{7}vs{3}	1.899	0.387
{7}vs{5}	2.256	0.324
{6}vs{1}	6.782	0.034
{6}vs{2}	2.017	0.156
{6}vs{5}	5.063	0.024
{5}vs{1}	1.719	0.190
{4}vs{1}	6.214	0.045
{4}vs{2}	1.449	0.229
{4}vs{3}	4.138	0.042
{3}vs{1}	2.076	0.150
{2}vs{1}	4.765	0.029

Selected Model {8}

b_t^B

Value of the log-likelihood function

Model	Log-l	Model	Log-l		Estimation
{1}	226.376	{5}	227.132	β_{S0}	1.000
{2}	230.601	{6}	231.498		(188.3)
{3}	227.414	{7}	228.254	β_{S1}	
{4}	231.594	{8}	233.581	β_{C0}	1.000
					(188.3)
				β_{C1}	
				σ_s	0.073
					(15.24)
				σ_c	0.230
					(4.684)
				q_0	0.429
					(1.102)
				q_1	3.738
					(2.083)

Model	LR-stat	p-value
{8}vs{1}	14.411	0.006
{8}vs{2}	5.960	0.114
{8}vs{3}	12.336	0.006
{8}vs{4}	3.975	0.137
{8}vs{5}	12.899	0.005
{8}vs{6}	4.167	0.125
{8}vs{7}	10.654	0.001
{7}vs{1}	3.757	0.289
{7}vs{3}	1.682	0.431
{7}vs{5}	2.245	0.325
{6}vs{1}	10.245	0.006
{6}vs{2}	1.794	0.180
{6}vs{5}	8.733	0.003
{5}vs{1}	1.512	0.219
{4}vs{1}	10.436	0.005
{4}vs{2}	1.985	0.159
{4}vs{3}	8.361	0.004
{3}vs{1}	2.076	0.150
{2}vs{1}	8.451	0.004

Selected Model {2}

b_t^C

Value of the log-likelihood function

Model	Log-l	Model	Log-l		Estimation
{1}	225.199	{5}	225.823	β_{S0}	0.996
{2}	227.985	{6}	228.756		(156.869)
{3}	226.210	{7}	226.881	β_{S1}	-0.004
{4}	228.687	{8}	231.538		(-1.578)
				β_{C0}	1.057
					(26.38)
				β_{C1}	-0.192
					(-1.53)
				σ_s	0.070
					(13.452)
				σ_c	0.191
					(6.346)
				q_0	0.553
					(1.29)
				q_1	0.968
					(1.207)

Model	LR-stat	p-value
{8}vs{1}	12.678	0.013
{8}vs{2}	7.106	0.069
{8}vs{3}	10.656	0.014
{8}vs{4}	5.701	0.058
{8}vs{5}	11.429	0.010
{8}vs{6}	5.564	0.062
{8}vs{7}	9.313	0.002
{7}vs{1}	3.365	0.339
{7}vs{3}	1.342	0.511
{7}vs{5}	2.116	0.347
{6}vs{1}	7.114	0.029
{6}vs{2}	1.542	0.214
{6}vs{5}	5.865	0.015
{5}vs{1}	1.249	0.264
{4}vs{1}	6.977	0.031
{4}vs{2}	1.404	0.236
{4}vs{3}	4.954	0.026
{3}vs{1}	2.023	0.155
{2}vs{1}	5.573	0.018

Selected Model {8}

Notes: {i}, i=1, 2,…,8 corresponds to model i. The t-statistics are reported in the parentheses

Table 7: Empirical results for Thailand

b_t^A

Value of the log-likelihood function

Model	Log-l	Model	Log-l
{1}	210.260	{5}	211.802
{2}	212.384	{6}	213.824
{3}	210.967	{7}	212.498
{4}	213.086	{8}	214.264

Comparison	LR-stat	p-value		Estimation
{8}vs{1}	8.010	0.091	β_{s0}	0.998 (163.051)
{8}vs{2}	3.762	0.288	β_{s1}	-0.018 (-1.764)
{8}vs{3}	6.594	0.086	β_{c0}	0.998 (163.051)
{8}vs{4}	2.357	0.308	β_{c1}	-0.018 (-1.764)
{8}vs{5}	4.925	0.177	σ_s	0.066 (10.831)
{8}vs{6}	0.880	0.644	σ_c	0.177 (8.566)
{8}vs{7}	3.534	0.060	q_0	1.108 (3.485)
{7}vs{1}	4.476	0.214	q_1	-0.761 (-1.924)
{7}vs{3}	3.060	0.216		
{7}vs{5}	1.391	0.499		
{6}vs{1}	7.130	0.028		
{6}vs{2}	2.882	0.090		
{6}vs{5}	4.045	0.044		
{5}vs{1}	3.085	0.079		
{4}vs{1}	5.653	0.059		
{4}vs{2}	1.405	0.236		
{4}vs{3}	4.237	0.040		
{3}vs{1}	1.415	0.234		
{2}vs{1}	4.248	0.039		

Selected Model: {6}

b_t^B

Value of the log-likelihood function

Model	Log-l	Model	Log-l
{1}	210.260	{5}	211.823
{2}	213.314	{6}	214.644
{3}	210.967	{7}	212.509
{4}	213.719	{8}	215.003

Comparison	LR-stat	p-value		Estimation
{8}vs{1}	9.488	0.050	β_{s0}	1.004 (178.226)
{8}vs{2}	3.379	0.337	β_{s1}	
{8}vs{3}	8.072	0.045	β_{c0}	1.004 (178.226)
{8}vs{4}	2.568	0.277	β_{c1}	
{8}vs{5}	6.360	0.095	σ_s	0.065 (10.466)
{8}vs{6}	0.718	0.698	σ_c	0.175 (9.912)
{8}vs{7}	4.990	0.026	q_0	1.125 (3.804)
{7}vs{1}	4.498	0.212	q_1	-1.779 (-2.334)
{7}vs{3}	3.083	0.214		
{7}vs{5}	1.370	0.504		
{6}vs{1}	8.770	0.012		
{6}vs{2}	2.661	0.103		
{6}vs{5}	5.642	0.018		
{5}vs{1}	3.128	0.077		
{4}vs{1}	6.920	0.031		
{4}vs{2}	0.811	0.368		
{4}vs{3}	5.504	0.019		
{3}vs{1}	1.415	0.234		
{2}vs{1}	6.109	0.013		

Selected Model: {2}

b_t^C

Value of the log-likelihood function

Model	Log-l	Model	Log-l
{1}	210.857	{5}	212.254
{2}	213.053	{6}	214.391
{3}	211.499	{7}	212.993
{4}	213.712	{8}	214.770

Comparison	LR-stat	p-value		Estimation
{8}vs{1}	7.827	0.098	β_{s0}	1.002 (179.365)
{8}vs{2}	3.433	0.329	β_{s1}	
{8}vs{3}	6.542	0.088	β_{c0}	1.002 (179.365)
{8}vs{4}	2.117	0.347	β_{c1}	
{8}vs{5}	5.033	0.169	σ_s	0.066 (10.956)
{8}vs{6}	0.759	0.684	σ_c	0.181 (9.137)
{8}vs{7}	3.555	0.059	q_0	1.047 (3.761)
{7}vs{1}	4.271	0.234	q_1	-0.435 (-1.914)
{7}vs{3}	2.987	0.225		
{7}vs{5}	1.478	0.478		
{6}vs{1}	7.068	0.029		
{6}vs{2}	2.674	0.102		
{6}vs{5}	4.274	0.039		
{5}vs{1}	2.794	0.095		
{4}vs{1}	5.709	0.058		
{4}vs{2}	1.316	0.251		
{4}vs{3}	4.425	0.035		
{3}vs{1}	1.285	0.257		
{2}vs{1}	4.393	0.036		

Selected Model: {2}

Notes: {i}, i=1, 2,…,8 corresponds to model i. The t-statistics are reported in the parentheses

3.3 Estimation results

We now turn to the presentation of the main empirical findings of this study. We first calculate the three measures of deviations from fundamentals described in the previous section, that is b_t^A, b_t^B and b_t^C. It turns out that the three alternative bubble measures are similar to each other. This is illustrated in Figure 1. However, we perform our analysis using all three alternative bubble measures for reasons of completeness. This is also a way to check the robustness of our results. An interesting characteristic of our bubble measures is that in most cases we witness negative deviations from fundamentals.

Afterwards, we estimate models 1 to 8 and implement the LR-test to choose the model that fits the data best based on the model selection procedure described in the previous subsection. Note that four of our models (that is, models 1, 3, 5 and 7) have a constant probability of partial collapse of the bubble. On the other hand, the size of the bubble affects the probability of partial collapse in the context of the other four models (models 2, 4, 6 and 8). The estimates for the selected model for each one of the countries under scrutiny are reported in Tables 2 to 7. Each table corresponds to a specific country. The tables report the results for all three bubble measures in three different panels.

Before presenting the main findings of our study, we check whether our data support the utilization of regime-switching models to describe the behavior of the series under examination. We can easily evaluate the descriptive power of our selected regime-switching model by means of the Regime Classification Measure (RCM) proposed by Ang and Bekaert (2002). The idea behind RCM is that the regime-switching model is good if it is able to classify regimes sharply. In the case of a model with two regimes, RCM is based on the ex-post probability being in the first regime, P_t^x. Specifically,

$$RCM = 400 * \frac{1}{T} \sum_{t=1}^{T} P_t^x (1 - P_t^x)$$

where T is the sample size. By construction, RCM is bounded between 0 and 100. RCM would be equal to 0 if we were certain about the regime, i.e. $P_t^x = 0$ or 1 for every t. On the other hand, RCM would equal 100 if P_t^x was equal to 0.5 for every t. To sum up, the closer RCM is to zero, the stronger the evidence in favor of the regime-switching model is. The computed values of RCM for the selected model for each country and bubble measure, reported in Table 8, range from 22.6 (Taiwan, b_t^B) to 59.8 (Indonesia, b_t^C), suggesting that the regime-switching model is a rather good model for our data.

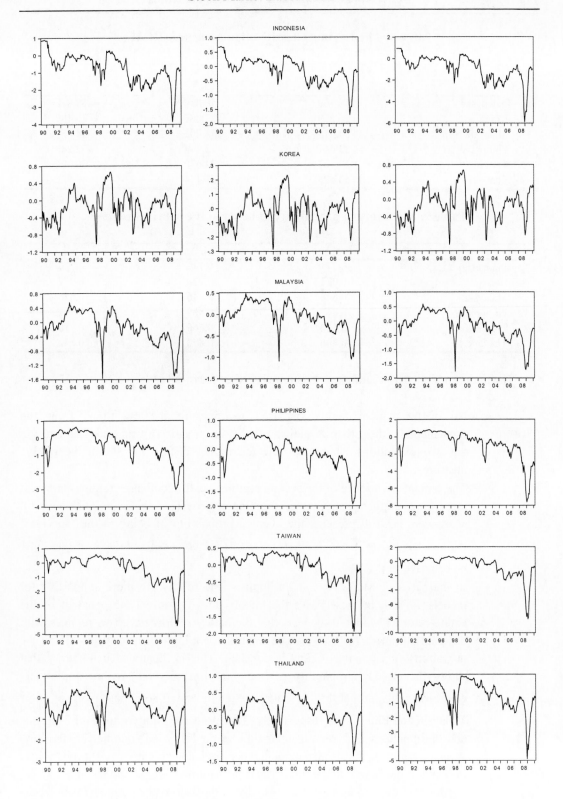

Figure 1. The bubble measures.

Table 8: The Regime Classification Measure (RCM)

	RCM		
	b_t^A	b_t^B	b_t^C
Indonesia	58.169	58.240	59.818
Korea	25.529	27.887	28.409
Malaysia	34.216	34.003	34.057
Philippines	32.467	32.244	32.289
Taiwan	29.167	22.630	30.372
Thailand	50.526	51.444	48.827

Table 9: The average probability of being in the survival regime

	b_t^A	b_t^B	b_t^C
Indonesia	0.744	0.743	0.734
Korea	0.981	0.978	0.977
Malaysia	0.846	0.846	0.846
Philippines	0.867	0.867	0.867
Taiwan	0.720	0.666	0.710
Thailand	0.866	0.870	0.852

The main findings of our study can be summarized as follows:

- No matter which method is used to measure the deviations from the fundamentals, the LR-tests indicate the same model. Taiwan and Thailand are the two exceptions where the selected model differs for alternative bubble measures.
- The estimated variance of the second regime (i.e. the "collapse" regime) is two to three times higher than that of the first regime (i.e. the "survival" regime). Moreover, Table 9 presents the average probability of being in the "survival" regime, given by $\Phi(q_0)$, that ranges from 66.6 percent (Taiwan) to 98.1 percent (Korea).
- In the cases of Malaysia and Philippines, the results are more supportive for model 1. Thus, in these cases the bubble does not affect the behavior of the equity returns. Model 1 suggests that the equity returns have two regimes with different variances (a low-variance regime and a high-variance regime) and the probability of changing regime is constant. This is illustrated in Figure 2 that shows the ex-ante probability of being in the "survival" regime for all six countries. This probability is equal to 0.846 and 0.867 (based on b_t^A) for Malaysia and Philippines respectively. Therefore, the equity returns of Malaysia and Philippines spend most of their time in the "survival" regime (i.e. the low-variance regime). This is also evident when we calculate the ex-post probabilities of being in the "survival" regime. These probabilities are plotted in Figure 3. We can see that the two processes are usually in the "survival" regime. However, the equity returns move to the "collapse" regime during some specific periods, such as the period 1997-1998 which coincides with the Asian financial crisis.

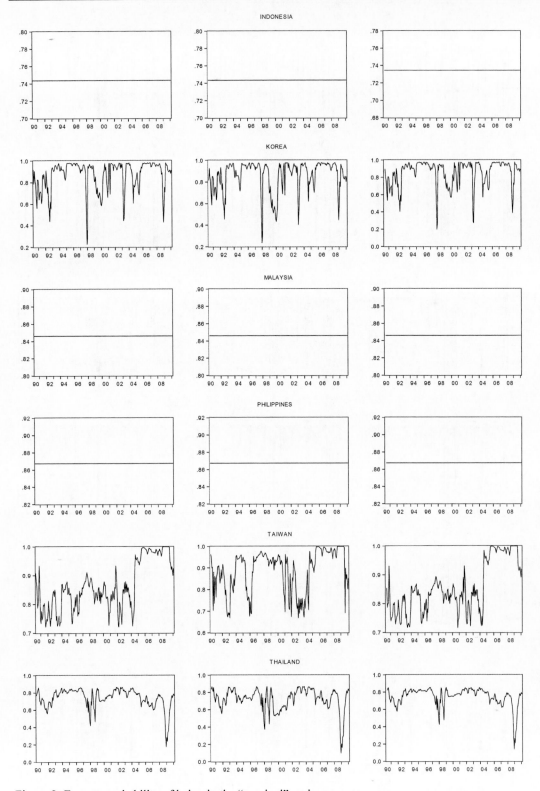

Figure 2: Ex-ante probability of being in the "survival" regime

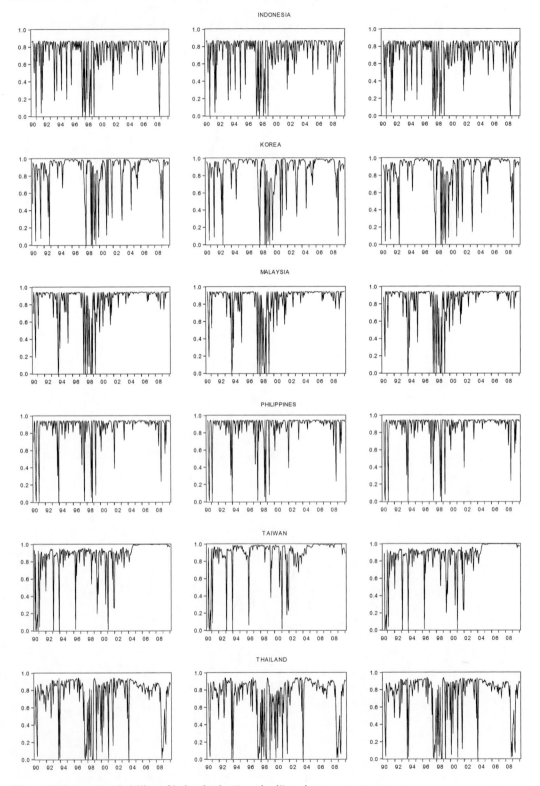

Figure 3: Ex-post probability of being in the "survival" regime

- A constant probability regime-switching model is also selected for Indonesia. However, in the case of Indonesia the bubble measure enters the conditional mean specification of each regime since model 5 is selected. The slope parameter is negative ($\beta_{s1} = \beta_{c1} = -0.028$) and (by construction) identical for both regimes. The ex-ante probability of being in the "survival" regime is 0.744 which is lower compared to the cases of Malaysia and Philippines.

- For the remaining three countries, namely Korea, Taiwan and Thailand, the selected model has a time-varying probability of changing regime. This is illustrated in Figure 2. In the cases of Korea and Thailand, we obtain a negative estimate for parameter q_1 suggesting that as the size of the bubble increases, the probability of being in the "survival" regime falls. On the other hand, the estimated value of q_1 is positive in the case of Taiwan but it is not statistically different from zero in the cases of b_t^A and b_t^C. Once again, whenever the selected model contains the slope parameters, β_{s1} and β_{c1}, the estimated values are negative.

- Interestingly, an investigation of the ex-post probabilities of being in the "survival" regime, reported in Figure 3, reveals that all six countries under scrutiny are usually in the same regime. This is a clear indication of strong interactions between the Asian equity markets that seem to follow similar paths. As a consequence, the benefits from international diversification in the context of the six equity markets under examination are limited.

- Finally, Figures 4 and 5 present the probability of a crash (given by equation (6)) and the probability of a boom (given by equation (7)) respectively. In general, the results indicate that the probability of a boom (that ranges from 0.7% to 21.7%) is substantially higher compared to the probability of a crash (which is usually less than 4% reaching a maximum of 6.9%). Both probabilities are constant in the cases of Malaysia and Philippines. For Korea, Taiwan and Thailand we observe a positive correlation between the probability of a crash and the probability of a boom. This is expected to happen when the expected value of excess returns conditional on the bubble measure is fairly constant while its variance around this expectation is not (van Norden, 1996). On the other hand, the probabilities of a crash and a boom are negatively correlated in the case of Indonesia. This is consistent with a process with a quite variable conditional mean and a stable variance (van Norden, 1996).

3.4 Examination of Two Historical Stock Market Crises

It is of great interest to examine two historical stock market crises, namely the 1997 Asian financial crisis (July 1997) and the "September 11" crisis (September 2001). We want to investigate whether our estimated models have any predictive power over the timing of a change in the state (i.e. regime) of the equity markets. The two selected historical crises have different causes. The first one, that is the 1997 Asian crisis, was probably caused by financial causes (e.g. increasing foreign debt-to-GDP ratios for most countries in the region). Therefore, if our models have any descriptive power for the dynamics of the equity markets, it is likely to find evidence of a high probability of a regime change during the period before

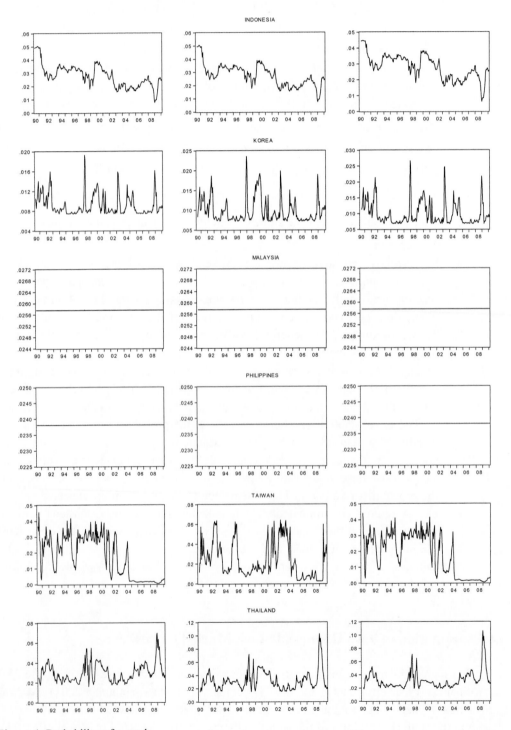

Figure 4: Probability of a crash

the crisis. On the other hand, the second one, that is the "September 11" crisis, started by the terrorist attacks in the USA. This is an event that is impossible to predict. Therefore, we would expect our models to have some predictability for the Asian financial crisis but probably not for the "September 11" crisis. We will discuss the case of our first bubble measure, b_t^A, but our results are similar for all the bubble measures considered in our study.

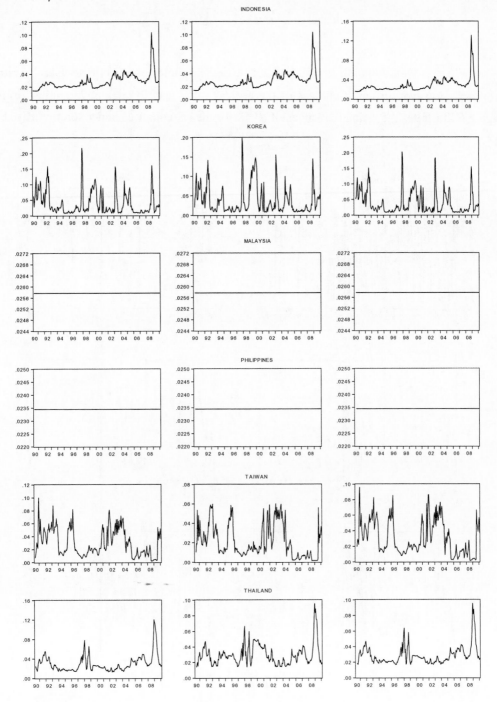

Figure 5: Probability of a boom

We examine the descriptive power of our models by means of the cumulative ex-ante probability of moving to the high-variance regime (i.e. the "collapse" state) denoted as P_t^{cum}. We estimate this cumulative probability as

$$P_t^{cum} = 1 - \prod_{n=\tau}^{t} q_n$$

where τ is the last month in which $P_t^x < 0.65$. The choice of this critical value is rather arbitrary. However, different choices of the critical value lead to qualitative similar results. Figure 6 illustrates the estimated values of P_t^{cum} for the six countries under scrutiny based on b_t^A.

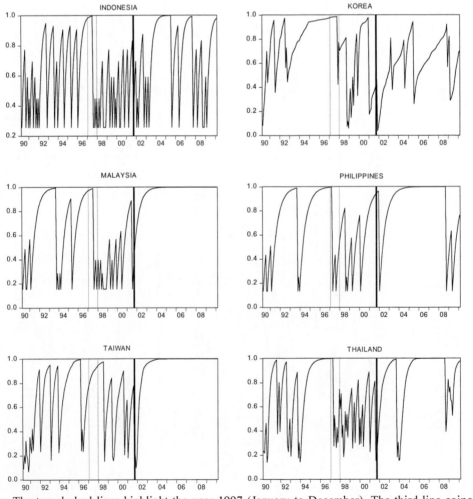

Notes: The two dashed lines highlight the year 1997 (January to December). The third line coincides with September 2001.

Figure 6: Cumulative ex-ante probability of collapse (critical value=0.65) based on b_t^A

We first investigate the 1997 Asian financial crisis that started in July 1997. Interestingly, P_t^{cum} is close to 100 percent for the months before the crisis for all six countries under examination. Specifically, the cumulative probability of being in the high-variance regime reaches 99 percent for all the countries under scrutiny with the exception of Thailand where P_t^{cum} is around 90 percent. Figure 6 shows that the 1997 Asian financial crisis clearly coincides with one of the peaks of P_t^{cum}. On the other hand, the cumulative probability of being in the "collapse" state is substantially lower for the period before the "September 11" crisis, especially for Korea, Malaysia and Thailand. In August 2001, the estimated cumulative probabilities are 0.83, 0.39, 0.28, 0.93, 0.77 and 0.15 for Indonesia, Korea, Malaysia, Philippines, Taiwan and Thailand respectively.

CONCLUSIONS

In this study, we focus on six East Asian emerging stock markets, namely Indonesia, Korea, Malaysia, Philippines, Taiwan and Thailand. We attempt to investigate whether the theory of periodically collapsing speculative bubbles can explain the dynamics of the excess returns of the aforementioned stock markets. We first implement three alternative methodologies to measure the deviation of actual prices from fundamental values (i.e. we calculate the size of the bubble). Our results indicate the existence of (usually negative) bubbles in the East Asian stock markets. Afterwards, we estimate various two-state regime-switching models in order to select the model that fits our data best. Our regime-switching models seem to have descriptive power for the behavior of the stock markets but the effect of the bubble on the equity returns differs among countries. We also examine two historical stock market crises, that is the 1997 Asian financial crisis and the "September 11" crisis (September 2001). Our results reveal the ability of the models to indicate a change in the state (i.e. regime) of the equity markets during the 1997 Asian financial crisis. On the other hand, the results are mixed for the "September 11" crisis. Moreover, we estimate the probability of a boom or a crash in the equity markets under examination and our calculations suggest that the probability of a boom is greater than that of a crash.

Finally, it is very interesting to mention that our findings show that the six markets under scrutiny are usually in the same state and thus the benefits from international diversification in the area are limited.

REFERENCES

Ang, A. and G. Bekaert, (2002). Regime switches in interest rates. *Journal of Business and Economic Statistics* 20, 163-182.

Bank for International Settlements, (1998). Chronology of the crisis. Bank for International Settlements 68th Annual Report, *Bank for International Settlements, Basle*.

Baur, D. and R.A. Fry, (2006). Endogenous contagion - A panel analysis. *CAMA Working Papers* 2006-09, Australian National University.

Blanchard, O.J. and M.W. Watson, (1982). Bubbles, rational expectations and financial markets, *NBER Working Paper Series*, No 945, 1-30.

Brooks, C. and A. Katsaris (2005). A three-regime model of speculative behavior: Modeling the evolution of the S&P500 composite index. *The Economic Journal*, 115, 767-797.

Campbell, J.Y. and R.J. Shiller, (1987). Cointegration and tests of present value models. *Journal of Political Economy* 95, 1062-1088.

Campbell, J.Y. and R.J. Shiller, (1988a). Stock prices, earnings, and expected dividends. *Journal of Finance,* 43, 661-676.

Campbell, J.Y. and R.J. Shiller, (1988b). The dividend-price ratio and expectations of future dividends and discount factors. *Review of Financial Studies,* 1, 195-228.

Evans, G.W. (1991). Pitfalls in testing for explosive bubbles in asset prices, *American Economic Review*, 81, 922-30.

International Monetary Fund, (1999). The IMF's response to the Asian crisis. *A Fact Sheet, January 1999.*

Ito, T. and Y. Hashimoto, (2005). High-frequency contagion between exchange rates and stock prices during the Asian currency crisis. In Dungey, M., Tambakis, D.M. (Eds) *Identifying International Financial Contagion: Progress and Challenges*, Oxford University Press, NY.

Schaller, H. and S. van Norden, (1997). Regime switching in stock market returns. *Applied Financial Economics*, 7, 177-191.

Schaller, H. and S. van Norden, (1999). Speculative behavior, regime-switching, and stock market crashes. In: Philip Rothman (ed) *Nonlinear Time Series Analysis of Economic and Financial Data*. Kluwer, 321-356.

Schaller, H. Ans S. van Norden, (2002). Fads or bubbles? *Empirical Economics*, 27(2), 335-362.

van Norden, S. (1996). Regime switching as a test for exchange rate bubbles. *Journal of Applied Econometrics* 11, 219-251.

van Norden, S. and H. Schaller, H (1993). The predictability of stock market regime: Evidence from the Toronto stock exchange. *Review of Economics and Statistics* 75(3), 505-510.

van Norden, S. and R. Vigfusson, (1998). Avoiding the pitfalls: Can regime-switching tests reliably detect bubbles. *Studies in Non-Linear Dynamics and Econometrics* 3(1), 1-22.

In: The Stock Market
Editor: Allison S. Wetherby

ISBN: 978-1-61122-545-7
© 2011 Nova Science Publishers, Inc.

Chapter 5

MARKET REACTIONS TO THE DISCLOSURE OF INTERNAL CONTROL WEAKNESSES UNDER THE JAPANESE SARBANES-OXLEY ACT OF 2006[*]

Hiroyasu Kawanishi[1] and Fumiko Takeda[2][*]

[1]KPMG AZSA & Co. Tokyo Sankei Building, 1-7-2,
Otemachi Chiyoda-ku, Tokyo, 100-8172 Japan
[2]Department of Technology Management for Innovation, University of Tokyo,
7-3-1 Hongo, Bunkyo-ku, Tokyo 113-8656 Japan

ABSTRACT

This article investigates how the stock market reacts to the disclosure of internal control deficiencies under the Japanese Sarbanes-Oxley Act of 2006. Given that the Japanese official agencies attempted to minimize the negative shock caused by the disclosure, we find no stock market reactions on the whole to the disclosure of internal control weaknesses. We also show that negative market reactions are intensified if firms have changed auditors in recent years, have uncertainties over their ability to continue as a going concern, have larger assets or fixed debts, or are listed on the emerging stock exchanges. In contrast, negative stock reactions are mitigated when firms have high ratios of foreign shareholders or current liabilities. Another interesting finding is that whether a firm engages a Big 4 audit firm does not seem to matter to investors evaluating firms with internal control weaknesses.

Keywords: internal control report system; event study, Sarbanes-Oxley Act, disclosure

JEL classification: M41, M48, K22

---

[*] Views expressed in this article are the authors' and do not necessarily reflect those of KPMG AZSA & Co. We would like to thank Pronexus for providing us with research papers, and participants at the 2010 Asian-Pacific Conference on International Accounting Issues for their helpful comments and suggestions. Fumiko Takeda gratefully acknowledges financial support from the Institute of Internal Auditors – Japan. All remaining errors are our own.

[*] Tel: +81-3-3548-5335; Fax: +81-3-3548-5312; E-mail: hiroyasu.kawanishi@jp.kpmg.com. Tel / Fax: +81-3-5841-1191; E-mail: takeda@tmi.t.u-tokyo.ac.jp (Corresponding author).

INTRODUCTION

Similar to the U.S. experience in which Andersen scandals led to the enactment of the so-called Sarbanes-Oxley Act of 2002 (U.S. SOX), the several high-profile corporate scandals in Japan after the fall of 2004 led to the passage of the Financial Instruments and Exchange Law (FIEL),[1] including the so-called Japanese Sarbanes-Oxley Act (J-SOX), which was intended to reinforce corporate governance and the accounting profession. Although the J-SOX was expected to induce significant benefits to investors by restoring investors' confidence and regulating internal control over financial reporting, anecdotal evidence indicates that the J-SOX has imposed nontrivial compliance costs.

Several studies have investigated the market reactions to the disclosure of internal control weaknesses under the U.S. SOX. In particular, Beneish et al. (2008) and Hammersley et al. (2008) find that SOX Section 302 internal control weakness disclosures are associated with negative stock market reactions, while Beneish et al. (2008) report that Section 404 internal control weakness disclosures are not associated with any market reactions. They also show that the market reactions vary with firms' characteristics. For instance, negative reactions are mitigated by audit quality, while they are intensified by financial and auditing risks, small size, complex operations, and so on.

This paper is in line with the existing studies on the impact of internal control reports, but investigates the Japanese case, which has not been examined in other papers, to the best of our knowledge, as many Japanese firms were required to meet the J-SOX compliance for the first time in fiscal year 2008, which ended in March 2009. The investigation of the Japanese experience provides us with a unique opportunity to examine how a different way of implementing an internal control reporting system generates different market reactions.

Prior to the implementation of the internal control reporting system, the Japanese Financial Service Agency (FSA) attempted to take into account the criticism of the U.S. SOX for imposing huge implementation costs on listed companies. The FSA incorporated a more concise and efficient implementation plan that included a top-down risk approach, an indirect reporting system, only two criteria for internal control deficiencies, and permission for the same auditor to audit both internal controls and financial reporting.[2]

In addition, prior to the mandated audit of internal control over financial reporting, the Japanese official agencies attempted to persuade investors not to react excessively to the disclosure of internal control weaknesses. For example, the FSA stressed that firms with "material weakness" would neither be penalized nor delisted from stock exchanges.[3] The FSA also insisted that "material weakness" did not mean that financial statements were qualified, and that "material weakness" should be regarded as signaling an important agenda item for managers to improve in the future.[4] In addition, for the first year of the internal control reporting system, stock exchanges did not include "material weakness" in the timely

---

[1] To be more precise, the FIEL incorporates the Amendment of the Securities and Exchange Law, which was approved and enacted at the 164th Diet session on June 7, 2006, and promulgated on June 14, 2006.

[2] These differences between the U.S. and Japan will be discussed in more detail in Section 2.

[3] See, for example, "Eleven Misunderstanding about the Internal Control Report System," published by the FSA on April 8, 2008.

[4] See, for example, "FAQs on the Internal Control Report System," published by the FSA on June 24, 2008.

disclosure items that may have significant influence on investment decisions.[5] This is different from the U.S., in which "material weakness" is one of the timely disclosure items.

Considering these differences in implementation of an internal control reporting system, we investigate how the Japanese market reacts to the disclosure of internal control weaknesses. We find that the internal control reports on "material weakness" and a disclaimer of opinion do not tend to affect the stock market on the whole. We also show that negative market reactions are intensified if firms have changed auditors in recent years, have uncertainties over their ability to continue as a going concern, have larger assets or fixed debts, or are listed on the emerging stock exchanges. In contrast, negative stock reactions are mitigated when firms have high ratios of foreign shareholders or current liabilities. Another interesting finding is that whether a firm engages a Big 4 audit firm does not seem to matter to investors evaluating firms with "material weakness" or a disclaimer of opinion.

The rest of this article is organized as follows. Section 2 provides a literature review, background, and hypothesis development. Section 3 describes research design and sample selection. A discussion of empirical results and concluding remarks are provided in Sections 4 and 5, respectively.

Literature Review, Background, and Hypothesis Development

Literature Review

A large number of studies have discussed the costs and benefits of the implementation of an internal control reporting system under the U.S. SOX. Although both the U.S. SOX and J-SOX aimed to protect investors, these acts have put a substantial burden on firms, which is arisen from satisfying the requirements of information disclosure and may damage the competitiveness of firms in international markets.

Several studies have estimated costs arising from compliance to the internal control reporting system in Japan. For instance, according to the Nikkei newspaper released on August 12, 2009, audit fees paid by 297 major Japanese companies by March 2009 had increased by 32 percent from the previous year, as the internal control reporting system requirements went into effect in fiscal year 2008. In addition, the Japan Research Institute reported on May 11, 2009, that the compliance costs of the J-SOX were Y30 million (approximately $300,000) in the prior year and Y34 million in the first year for small firms with sales amounting to less than Y10 billion, while they were Y247 million in the prior year and Y176 million in the first year for large firms with sales of more than Y50 billion. Although the Japan Research Institute states that these compliance costs are less than expected, whether the benefits exceed the costs is an interesting question.

To answer this question, several papers have examined the impact of disclosure of the internal control deficiencies by using event study methodology, finding negative reactions to the disclosure under Section 302 of the U.S. SOX. In particular, Beneish et al. (2008) perform

---

[5] The TSE later changed its stance and released the "Listing System Improvement Action Plan 2009" on September 29, 2009. This action plan required firms to disclose immediately the contents of "a decision to submit an internal control report containing the fact that the management executive finds a material weakness in the internal control system or deems the evaluation result of the internal control system cannot be disclosed." This measure was implemented for annual general shareholders' meeting pertaining to account settlement ending in March 2010.

an event study by using a sample of 330 firms making unaudited disclosures required by Section 302 and 383 firms making audited disclosures required by Section 404 of the U.S. SOX. They report that stock prices react negatively to Section 302 disclosures and that equity cost of capital of these firms increases significantly. In contrast, stock market reactions to Section 404 disclosures are insignificant. Considering the fact that Section 302 is mainly applicable to smaller firms, they conclude that "material weakness" disclosures are more informative for smaller firms, which may have suffered from information uncertainty. They also find that negative reactions are mitigated when firms employ a Big 4 audit firm.

Hammersley et al. (2008) also investigate the stock price reactions to the disclosure of internal control weaknesses under Section 302 of the U.S. SOX and to the characteristics of these weaknesses, after controlling for other material announcements in the event window. They find that the market reactions become larger as the internal control weakness becomes severer. By performing multiple regression analyses, they also report that market reactions are less negative when managers conclude that internal control is effective and when firms are audited by a Big 4 audit firm, while market reactions are more negative when internal control deficiencies are less auditable and when disclosure about weaknesses is ambiguous.

In sum, prior studies on the U.S. firms disclosing internal control weaknesses show that these firms tend to experience negative stock price reactions to the disclosure under Section 302 of the U.S. SOX, though no market reactions are found to the disclosure under Section 404. The market reactions vary with firms' characteristics. Particularly, negative reactions are mitigated by audit quality, while they are intensified by financial and auditing risks, small size, complex operations and so on.

In the case of Japan, Seino and Takeda (2009) investigate stock market reactions to news leading to the introduction of the J-SOX. They find that announcements that increase the likelihood of passage of the J-SOX raise stock prices of firms listed on the first section of the TSE. However, they report that neither the announcements of loosening the regulation set by the U.S. SOX nor the news that set the guidelines for the implementation of the J-SOX have an obvious influence on the stock market. This lack of a market reaction can be explained by the possibility that these events reduce both costs and benefits of the internal control reporting system under the J-SOX. In the next subsection we will discuss how the Japanese official agencies attempted to minimize the implementation costs of the internal control reporting system in more detail.

Japan Setting and Hypothesis Development

The internal control reporting system was introduced in Japan to pursue the same objective as that implemented in the U.S., that is, to protect investors by assuring the appropriate information disclosure. However, there are several differences in implementation of the system between the two countries, which may cause differences in market reactions to the disclosure.

First, the Japanese internal control reporting system takes into account the criticism of the U.S. SOX for imposing huge implementation costs on listed companies. To minimize the implementation costs, the Japanese official agencies incorporated a more concise and efficient implementation plan. Initially, there were four major differences between the U.S. SOX and the J-SOX implementations. The first difference was that the J-SOX incorporated a top-down risk approach, which enabled firms to focus on major risks rather than spend resources evaluating all the detailed check items under the baseline approach. The second difference was that the J-SOX employed only two criteria for deficiencies in internal control – "material weakness" and "control deficiency" - while the U.S. SOX used these two categories plus another, "significant deficiency." The third difference was that evaluation of the validity of internal controls over financial reporting is conducted by managers and then checked by independent auditors under the J-SOX. The fourth difference was that the J-SOX allowed the same auditor to audit both internal controls and financial reporting, cooperating with internal auditors, to reduce audit fees.

Second, the disclosure of internal control weaknesses was likely to be taken more lightly in Japanese stock exchanges than in the U.S. Unlike in the U.S., for the first year of the internal control reporting system, the Japanese stock exchanges did not include "material weakness" in the timely disclosure items that may have significant influence on investment decisions. This is different from the U.S., where "material weakness" is one of the timely disclosure items. The exclusion of "material weakness" from the timely disclosure items indicates that the Japanese stock exchanges did not regard "material weakness" as an important issue for investment decisions, and this stance may have assured that investors would not react to the disclosure of "material weakness."

Third, the Japanese official agencies took several measures to persuade investors not to react excessively to the internal control disclosure. For instance, the FSA published "Eleven Misunderstanding about the Internal Control Report System" on April 8, 2008, which stated that firms with "material weakness" would neither be penalized nor delisted from stock exchanges. In addition, the FSA added the "FAQs on the Internal Control Report System" on June 24, 2008, to the original version issued on October 1, 2007, which stated that "material weakness" did not mean that financial statements are qualified, but indicated the possibility that it may have serious impact on financial statements. The FSA also showed that "material weakness" should be regarded as signaling an important agenda item for managers to improve in the future.

In sum, the Japanese official agencies attempted to minimize the negative market reactions to internal reporting weakness disclosures, by taking the U.S. experience into account. These differences between the two countries may generate the difference in market reactions. Thus, we set the following null hypothesis to test by event study analysis:

Hypothesis 0. Stock prices of firms with "material weakness" or a disclaimer of opinion do not react to the disclosure of internal control weaknesses.

Research Design and Sample Selection

Event Study Analysis

To evaluate the effects of internal control disclosure on the stock prices in Japan, we employ event study methodology, per MacKinlay (1997). This methodology is based on the efficient market hypothesis, which assumes that current stock prices reflect all publicly available information and fluctuate only due to unexpected events that may change the future profitability of a firm.

In our analysis, the event day is in most cases the day when firms submitted their internal control reports. The exceptions are firms that voluntarily disclosed information beforehand.

For these firms, we set the event day as the date of early disclosure. We denote the event day as t_0, the initial date of the event window as t_1, and the final date of the event window as t_2. To ensure robustness, we select four event windows $(t_1, t_2) = (0, 1)$, $(0, 2)$, $(0, 3)$, and $(-1, 3)$. The estimation window is set at 150 transaction days before the event window.

The following market model is then estimated for each firm in the estimation window:

$$R_{it} = \alpha_i + \beta_i R_{mt} + \varepsilon_{it},$$ (1)

where ε_{it} represents the zero mean disturbance term. R_{it} is the daily stock return for firm i during period t, and R_{mt} represents the market return, which includes the Tokyo Stock Price Index (TOPIX) for firms listed on the first section of the TSE, the Tokyo Stock Exchanges Second Section Composite Index for firms listed on the second section of the TSE, the OSE Indices for firms listed on the Osaka Securities Exchange (OSE), the JASDAQ Index for firms listed on the Jasdaq Securities Exchange, the Hercules Index for firms listed on the Nippon New Market Hercules, and the S&P Japan Emerging Stock 100 Index for firms listed on Ambitious, Centrex, or Q-Board.

By using the estimated parameters $\hat{\alpha}_i$ and $\hat{\beta}_i$, we calculate an abnormal return for the stock of firm i in period t as follows:

$$AR_{it} = R_{it} - (\hat{\alpha}_i + \hat{\beta}_i R_{mt})$$ (2)

The cumulative abnormal return (CAR) is then obtained by summing up the abnormal returns over the event window, as follows:

$$CAR_i(t_1, t_2) = \sum_{t=t_1}^{t_2} AR_{it}$$ (3)

If the event does not affect stock prices, the CAR should be zero. In other words, the null hypothesis H_0 stipulating that $CAR=0$ should be rejected statistically if the event influences stock prices. To test the null hypothesis, we employ the following J-statistic:

$$J = \frac{\overline{CAR}(t_1, t_2)}{\sqrt{\overline{\sigma}^2(t_1, t_2)}} \sim N(0,1)$$ (4)

where $\overline{CAR}$ is the mean or median CAR across N firms, and its variance, $\overline{\sigma}^2(t_1, t_2)$, is the mean of the variance of the CAR, $\sigma_i^2(t_1, t_2)$, which is calculated asymptotically by the variance of abnormal returns $\sigma_{\varepsilon_i}^2$:

$$\overline{\sigma}^2(t_1, t_2) = VAR\left[\overline{CAR}(t_1, t_2)\right] = 1/N^2 \sum_{i=1}^{N} \sigma_i^2(t_1, t_2). \tag{5}$$

$$\sigma_i^2(t_1, t_2) \approx (t_2 - t_1 + 1)\sigma_{\varepsilon_i}^2 \tag{6}$$

Cross-sectional analysis

To investigate what factors contribute to individual stock price fluctuations, we conduct a cross-sectional analysis for firms with internal control weaknesses. We estimate the following multivariate regression model by using the OLS estimation:

$$CAR = \beta_1 + \beta_2 Category + \beta_3 Big4 + \beta_4 AuditorSwi tch + \beta_5 GC$$
$$+ \beta_6 Subsequent + \beta_7 Asset + \beta_8 Foreign + \beta_9 FreeFloat$$
$$+ \beta_{10} CurrentDeb t + \beta_{11} FixedDebt + \beta_{12} Emerging + \beta_{13} ListedPeri od + \varepsilon \tag{7}$$

where

Category	1 if the firm has reported a "material weakness," 0 if it has reported a disclaimer of opinion.
Big4	1 if the firm is audited by a Big 4 audit firm, 0 otherwise.
AuditorSwitch	1 if the firm changed auditors in the past two years, 0 otherwise.
GC	1 if notes to the financial statements report uncertainties that cast doubt on the firm's ability to continue as a going concern, 0 otherwise.
Subsequent	1 if notes to the financial statements report subsequent events that may have significant influence on a firm's internal control, 0 otherwise.
Foreign	foreign shareholders' ratio of total shareholders (%).
FreeFloat	weight of listed stocks available for trading in the market (%).
Asset	natural logarithm of total assets.
CurrentDebt	current liabilities divided by total assets (%).
FixedDebt	fixed liabilities divided by total assets (%).
Emerging	1 if the firm is listed on the emerging stock exchanges, 0 otherwise.
ListedPeriod	natural logarithm of a sum of months after the initial public offerings.

Category, *Big4*, and *AuditorSwitch* are three variables associated with auditing. *Category* is a dummy variable, which takes 1 if the firm has reported a "material weakness" and 0 if it has reported a disclaimer of opinion. We expect a positive sign for *Category*, because we expect that "material weakness" indicates that firms have less serious flaws in their internal control system than a disclaimer of opinion. *Big4* is a dummy variable, which takes 1 if the firm is audited by a Big4 audit firm and 0 otherwise. We expect a positive sign for *Big4*, because a Big 4 audit firm is expected to provide a higher-quality audit than that provided by other auditors. *AuditorSwitch* is also a dummy variable, which takes 1 if the firm changed auditors in the past two years and 0 otherwise. We expect a negative sign for *AuditorSwitch*, because firms that changed auditors tend to have more financial or audit risks than do other firms (Krishnan and Krishnan 1997; Shu 2000; Johnstone and Bedard 2004) and thus may be damaged severely by the disclosure of internal control weaknesses.

GC and *Subsequent* are variables representing important information given by the financial statements. *GC* is a dummy variable, which takes 1 if notes to the financial statements report uncertainties that cast doubt on the firm's ability to continue as a going concern, and 0 otherwise. *Subsequent* is a dummy variable, which takes 1 if the firm is reported to have experienced subsequent events that may have a significant influence on internal control and 0 otherwise. We expect negative signs for these variables, because when these variables are equal to 1, firms should have greater uncertainties over future profits and thus may be damaged severely by the disclosure of internal control weaknesses.

Foreign and *FreeFloat* are variables representing shareholder composition. *Foreign* is the percentage of foreign shareholders among total shareholders, and *FreeFloat* is the free float ratio, which is the weight of listed stocks available for trading in the market. We expect a positive sign for *Foreign*, because firms with high ratios of foreign shareholders are required to provide disclosure that is more demanding than that required by domestic investors and thus could have reasonably been expected to have a more effective internal control system than firms that have low foreign shareholders' ratio. The effect of the free float ratio is ambiguous. If blockholders, including main banks, provide better governance than do other short-sighted investors, CAR should be negatively associated with the free float ratio. However, if short-sighted investors are more concerned about firms' performance than blockholders are, CAR should be positively correlated with the free float ratio. Thus, whether there is a positive correlation between CAR and the free float ratio is left as an empirical question.

Asset, *CurrentDebt*, and *FixedDebt* are variables related to financial conditions. *Asset* is a natural logarithm of total assets. We predict that *Asset* is negatively associated with CAR, because investors may assume that large firms suffer from a bigger reputation loss than do small firms by disclosing internal control deficiencies. *CurrentDebt* and *FixedDebt* are current and fixed liabilities divided by total assets, respectively. The signs of these variables are empirical questions. Firms with a high liability ratio may be negatively affected by the disclosure of internal control deficiencies, which are likely to increase the bankruptcy risk. However, if main banks provide debtor firms with better governance, this would result in a positive sign for these variables. Thus, whether firms with high liability ratio experienced positive or negative stock price reactions is tested.

Emerging and *ListedPeriod* are variables associated with other firm attributes. *Emerging* is a dummy variable, which takes 1 if the firm is listed on an emerging stock exchange, including the Jasdaq Securities Exchange, the Nippon New Market Hercules, Ambitious, Centrex, or Q-Board, and 0 otherwise. These stock exchanges list mainly venture and small- and medium-sized firms in Japan. Unlike established firms listed on major stock exchanges, such as the first section of the TSE, firms listed on the emerging stock exchanges are expected to have larger information asymmetry and thus are less likely to be trusted by investors. Thus, we expect a negative sign for *Emerging*. *ListedPeriod* is a sum of months passed since the initial public offerings (IPO). Doyle et al. (2007) state that firms that have long periods after the IPO should have more opportunities to improve their internal control system and thus have little possibility to be reported to have "material weakness." This means that *ListedPeriod* is expected to have a positive sign.

Sample Selection and Data

The J-SOX was enforced on April 1, 2008, and thus firms that reported financial statements in March 2009 were required to submit internal control reports for the first time in accordance with the J-SOX. The FSA released the announcements on the submission of internal control reports on July 7, 2009, as shown in Tables 1 and 2. Among 2,670 firms that came under the new system, 56 firms were reported to have "material weakness," which consists of 2.1 percent of the total firms. In addition, 9 firms submitted a disclaimer of opinion report, because they had problems associated with "material weakness" (Machida and Pronexus 2009).

Table 1: Firms that submitted internal control reports in March 2009

	No. of firms
Firms that were obliged to submit internal control reports (1)	2,656
Of which firms that submitted internal control reports (2)	2,653
Firms that submitted internal control reports voluntarily (3)	17
All firms that submitted internal control reports (2)+(3)	2,670

Note: Voluntary submission of unlisted firms is based on the Article 24
        (4) of the Financial Instruments and Exchange Law.
Source: Financial Service Agency.

Table 2: Internal control reports in March 2009

	No. of firms	Weight (%)
Firms with effective internal control	2,605	97.6
Firms with "material weakness"	56	2.1
Firms with a disclaimer of opinion	9	0.3
Total	2,670	100.0

Source: Financial Service Agency.

The percentage of firms with "material weakness" is small, compared to the U.S. experience, in which 596 firms that account for 16.3 percent of the total 3,651 firms governed by the U.S. SOX were reported to have "material weakness." Machida (2009) attributes this difference to the fact that Japan established a long preparation period for the introduction of an internal control reporting system and that the FSA attempted to incorporate the criticisms of the U.S. SOX concerning the large costs of implementation by employing a more concise and efficient way of implementing the regulation, as explained in Section 2.

Tables 3 and 4 present the sample selection process. From the initial sample consisting of 56 firms with "material weakness," 4 firms are deleted to construct sample 1 because these firms lack stock price data for the event and estimation windows. We then delete 3 firms from sample 1 to construct sample 2 because we find confounding events around the disclosure date of internal control reports for these firms. We further delete 8 firms for sample 2 to construct sample 3, which voluntarily disclosed problems in their internal control before the disclosure date. Likewise, from 9 firms with a disclaimer of opinion, 3 firms are deleted from sample 3 to construct sample 4 because of the lack of stock price data (Table 4). We rely on *Toyo Keizai's Kabuka CD-ROM* and *Nikkei NEEDS* to obtain stock price data and other financial variables, respectively.

Table 3: Sample selection for firms with "material weakness"

		TSE 1st section	TSE 2nd section	OSE 2nd section	NSE 2nd section	Emerging
Firms with "material weakness"	56	17	4	5	1	29
less: firms without stock price data	4	1	0	1	1	1
Sample 1	52	16	4	4	0	28
less: confounding events	3	1	0	1	0	1
Sample 2	49	15	4	3	0	27
less: firms with early announcement	8	2	2	1	0	3
Sample 3	41	13	2	2	0	24

Note: 1. NSE means Nagoya Stock Exchange.
       2. Emerging includes Jasdaq Securities Exchange, the Nippon New Market Hercules, Ambitious, Centrex, and Q-Board.

Table 4: Sample selection for firms with a disclaimer of opinion

		TSE 1st section	TSE 2nd section	OSE 2nd section	Emerging
Firms with a disclaimer of opinion	9	1	1	0	7
less: firms without stock price data	3	0	0	0	3
Sample 4	6	1	1	0	4

Note: Emerging includes Jasdaq Securities Exchange, the Nippon New Market Hercules, Ambitious, Centrex, and Q-Board.

Table 5: Descriptive statistics

	Category	Big4	AuditorSwitch	GC	Subsequent	Foreign	FreeFloat	Asset	CurrentDebt	FixedDebt	Emerging	ListedPeriod
Mean	0.897	0.552	0.103	0.207	0.034	0.058	0.205	9.585	0.405	0.173	0.552	5.234
Median	1.000	1.000	0.000	0.000	0.000	0.016	0.199	9.631	0.375	0.161	1.000	5.359
Maximum	1.000	1.000	1.000	1.000	1.000	0.331	0.479	13.927	0.878	0.739	1.000	6.576
Minimum	0.000	0.000	0.000	0.000	0.000	0.000	0.010	4.682	0.064	0.000	0.000	3.178
Std. Dev.	0.307	0.502	0.307	0.409	0.184	0.081	0.116	1.932	0.214	0.140	0.502	0.968
Skewness	-2.604	-0.208	2.604	1.447	5.103	1.538	0.163	-0.008	0.542	1.422	-0.208	-0.355
Kurtosis	7.782	1.043	7.782	3.094	27.036	4.618	1.962	2.932	2.296	6.207	1.043	2.168
Observations	58	58	58	58	58	58	58	58	58	58	58	58

Table 6: Correlation Matrix

	Category	Big4	AuditorSwitch	GC	Subsequent	Foreign	FreeFloat	Asset	CurrentDebt	FixedDebt	Emerging
Big4	0.263										
AuditorSwitch	-0.071	-0.377									
GC	-0.246	-0.224	0.246								
Subsequent	-0.246	-0.210	-0.064	-0.097							
Foreign	-0.033	0.209	-0.173	0.010	0.205						
FreeFloat	0.057	0.070	-0.046	-0.193	-0.007	-0.196					
Asset	0.014	0.544	-0.377	-0.291	0.053	0.539	0.055				
CurrentDebt	-0.222	0.035	-0.072	0.138	-0.194	0.001	0.131	-0.069			
FixedDebt	0.035	0.205	-0.018	0.321	-0.184	0.089	-0.144	0.171	-0.080		
Emerging	-0.079	-0.325	0.306	0.204	0.170	-0.377	0.015	-0.565	0.033	-0.091	
ListedPeriod	-0.207	0.024	-0.124	-0.165	-0.097	0.153	0.242	0.465	-0.093	0.025	-0.453

Tables 3 and 4 also show that among 52 firms in sample 1, 28 firms (53.8 percent) are listed on emerging stock exchanges, 16 firms (30.8 percent) on the first sections of the TSE, and 8 firms (15.4 percent) on other markets. Likewise, among 49 firms in sample 2, 27 firms (55.1 percent) are listed on emerging stock exchanges, 15 firms (30.6 percent) on the first sections of the TSE, and 7 firms (14.3 percent) on other markets. Lastly, among 41 firms in sample 3, 24 firms (58.5 percent) are listed on emerging stock exchanges, 13 firms (31.7 percent) on the first sections of the TSE, and 4 firms (9.8 percent) on other markets.

Tables 5 and 6 present the descriptive statistics and correlation matrices for the variables used in our cross-sectional analysis. We note that the correlation between *Asset* and 3 variables (*Big4*, *Foreign*, and *Emerging*) is 0.544 percent, 0.539 percent, and -0.565 percent, respectively. This indicates that large firms tend to be audited by a Big 4 audit firm, have higher ratios of foreign shareholders, and be listed on the stock exchanges other than emerging stock exchanges. The negative correlation between *Asset* and *Emerging* is reasonable, because large and established stock exchanges such as the TSE allow only large firms to be listed.

Empirical Results

Event Study Analysis

Tables 7 to 10 present the results of event study analysis for 52 firms with "material weakness" (sample 1), for 49 firms without confounding events (sample 2), for 41 firms without early announcements (sample 3), and for 6 firms with a disclaimer of opinion (sample 4), respectively. For all tables, both mean CARs and median CARs are insignificant for all windows, indicating that the internal control reports on "material weakness" and a disclaimer of opinion did not tend to affect the stock market on the whole.

The lack of market reactions to the disclosure of internal control weaknesses may be due to the following factors. First, as suggested by Beneith et al. (2008), these firms may operate in rich information environments and thus the internal control disclosures may not be incremental news to the market. Second, the measures taken by the Japanese official agencies to persuade investors not to react excessively to the internal control disclosure may result in no market reactions. Third, noise induced by the clustering of annual report filings coincident with the internal control disclosure may reduce the power to detect abnormal returns. Fourth, the market reactions to the internal control disclosure may be mitigated by firms attributes such as high-quality auditing, shareholder composition, financial conditions, and so on.

Table 7: CAR for 52 firms with "material weakness" (sample 1)

	Mean		Median	
(t_1, t_2)	CAR	J-statistic	CAR	J-statistic
(0, 1)	0.61%	0.526	-0.48%	-0.413
(0, 2)	1.11%	0.775	-0.33%	-0.234
(0, 3)	1.72%	1.041	0.14%	0.082
(-1, 3)	2.47%	1.337	0.70%	0.381

Table 8: CAR for 49 firms with "material weakness" (sample 2)

(t_1, t_2)	Mean		Median	
	CAR	J-statistic	CAR	J-statistic
(0, 1)	-1.90%	-0.429	-1.40%	-0.307
(0, 2)	-0.10%	-0.017	-0.30%	-0.056
(0, 3)	-2.90%	-0.452	-1.80%	-0.287
(-1, 3)	0.60%	0.078	-0.50%	-0.066

Table 9: CAR for 41 firms with "material weakness" (sample 3)

(t_1, t_2)	Mean		Median	
	CAR	J-statistic	CAR	J-statistic
(0, 1)	-0.66%	-0.599	-0.57%	-0.519
(0, 2)	-0.13%	-0.095	-0.68%	-0.508
(0, 3)	0.49%	0.316	0.00%	-0.003
(-1, 3)	1.45%	0.837	0.33%	0.190

Table 10: CAR for 6 firms with a disclaimer of opinion (sample 4)

(t_1, t_2)	Mean		Median	
	CAR	J-statistic	CAR	J-statistic
(0, 1)	-0.62%	-0.502	-0.57%	-0.460
(0, 2)	0.19%	0.126	-0.31%	-0.203
(0, 3)	0.57%	0.327	0.14%	0.083
(-1, 3)	1.70%	0.875	0.92%	0.473

We first examine the possibility of the first factor. As shown in Tables 3 and 4, more than half of the firms with internal control weaknesses are listed on emerging stock exchanges, in which investors are likely to face more information asymmetry than that provided for firms listed on established stock exchanges such as the first section of the TSE. In addition, Japanese firms did not have a period of voluntary disclosure of internal control deficiencies prior to mandated disclosure. This is different from the U.S., where a number of U.S. firms voluntarily disclosed under Section 302 of the U.S. SOX prior to mandated disclosure under Section 404. Thus, we conclude that the possibility of the first factor is unlikely to hold in our sample.

We next consider the possibility of the second factor. As explained in Section 2, unlike the U.S, the Japanese stock exchanges did not include "material weakness" in the timely disclosure items during the sample period. In addition, the Japanese official agencies attempted to persuade investors not to react excessively to the internal control deficiencies by notifying that firms with "material weakness" would neither be penalized nor delisted from stock exchanges. Thanks to the FSA's efforts, the disclosure of the existence of "material weakness" may not have influenced investors' risk assessment. These facts suggest that the measures taken by the Japanese official agencies may lead to no market reaction.

With regard to the third factor, major items of financial statements were disclosed under the voluntary rule of stock exchanges, usually within 45 days after the settlement day, which is the end of March for our sample. This means that most of the financial data are known to the public prior to the internal control reports, whose disclosure is concentrated in the end of June with a few exceptions. Thus, it is less likely that confounding new information other than internal control reports reduces the power of our tests to detect abnormal returns as indicated.

Considering the first three factors, only the second factor, i.e., the Japanese official agencies' efforts, may have contributed to the lack of a market reaction to the disclosure. In the next subsection we will examine whether firm attributes may reduce stock price reactions as indicated by the fourth factor.

Table 11: Cross-sectional analysis

	(0,+1)		(0,+2)		(0,+3)		(-1,+3)	
	Coefficient	t-statistic	Coefficient	t-statistic	Coefficient	t-statistic	Coefficient	t-statistic
Intercept	0.200	1.654	0.217	1.892 *	0.219	1.721 *	0.154	1.248
Category	0.033	0.797	0.007	0.184	0.022	0.508	0.028	0.657
Big4	-0.002	-0.055	-0.026	-0.933	-0.039	-1.278	-0.025	-0.819
AuditorSwitch	-0.033	-0.851	-0.068	-1.842 *	-0.071	-1.747 *	-0.015	-0.384
GC	0.002	0.071	-0.030	-0.990	-0.093	-2.773 ***	-0.055	-1.702 *
Subsequent	-0.020	-0.276	-0.066	-0.973	-0.111	-1.477	-0.046	-0.634
Foreign	0.348	2.029 **	0.225	1.382	0.169	0.935	0.211	1.202
Free Float	-0.021	-0.204	0.032	0.335	-0.002	-0.019	-0.061	-0.591
Asset	-0.025	-2.619 **	-0.018	-1.911 *	-0.011	-1.087	-0.017	-1.760 *
CurrentDebt	0.042	0.750	0.079	1.493	0.125	2.126 **	0.099	1.731 *
FixedDebt	-0.107	-1.248	-0.096	-1.176	-0.157	-1.736 *	-0.117	-1.327
Emerging	-0.054	-1.921 *	-0.031	-1.186	-0.010	-0.337	0.001	0.032
ListedPeriod	0.007	0.456	-0.006	-0.444	-0.018	-1.142	0.004	0.227
F-statistic	1.594		1.794 *		3.070 ***		1.716 *	
Adj. R^2	11.1%		14.3%		30.3%		13.1%	
Obs.	58		58		58		58	

Note: ***, **, and * indicate statistical significance at the 1%, 5%, and 10% level, respectively.

Cross-sectional analysis

We next estimate equation (7) by OLS regression to examine the relationship between CARs and firm attributes for 4 event windows. The results are presented in Table 11.

First, we investigate the effect of three variables associated with auditing, that is, *Category*, *Big4*, and *AuditorSwitch*. Neither *Category* nor *Big4* is significantly associated with CARs. This means that the difference between "material weakness" and a disclaimer of opinion does not generate any difference in CARs. Also, whether firms are audited by a Big 4 audit firm does not matter for investors. The effect of *AuditorSwitch* on CARs is significantly negative at the 10 percent level for two event windows. This result is consistent with our prediction, indicating that firms that have changed auditors in recent years tend to experience more negative stock price responses by disclosing "material weakness" or a disclaimer of opinion.

Second, we examine the relationship between CARs and variables representing important information given by the financial statements, that is, *GC* and *Subsequent*. Although coefficients of *Subsequent* are insignificant for all windows, coefficients of *GC* are significantly negative at the 1 percent and 10 percent level for 4-day and 5-day windows, respectively. The result of *GC* is consistent with our prediction, indicating that firms that had uncertainties over their ability to continue as a going concern tended to experience more negative stock responses.

Third, with regard to the effect of variables representing shareholder composition, that is, *Foreign* and *FreeFloat*, one coefficient of *Foreign* is significantly positive at the 5 percent level for the 2-day event window, while coefficients of *FreeFloat* are insignificant for all windows. The result of *Foreign* is consistent with our prediction, in the sense that the negative effect of firms with a high foreign shareholders ratio are mitigated, perhaps because foreign shareholders are more demanding regarding disclosure and better performance.

Fourth, we investigate the influence of variables related to financial conditions, that is, *Asset*, *CurrentDebt*, and *FixedDebt*. Coefficients of *Asset* are significantly negative at the 5 percent, 10 percent and 10 percent level for 2-day, 3-day, and 5-day windows, respectively. This result is consistent with our prediction, meaning that large firms tend to experience more negative stock price responses, because they may suffer more from reputation loss generated by the disclosure of internal control deficiencies than would small firms. The coefficients of *CurrentDebt* are significantly positive at the 5 percent and 10 percent level for 4-day and 5-day windows, respectively. In contrast, one coefficient of *FixedDebt* is significantly negative at the 10 percent level for the 4-day event window.

The result of *CurrentDebt* contrasts with those of Gupta and Nayar (2007), which find a negative correlation between CARs and current liabilities because internal control deficiencies might have increased the likelihood of bankruptcy of firms with more short-term debts.[6] The difference in results may be caused by the difference in the governance structure between Japan and the U.S. In other words, a positive effect of short-term debt means that Japanese main banks are expected to provide debtor firms with better governance. Our results are consistent with those of Numata and Takeda (2010) and Seino and Takeda (2009), which find positive correlations between CARs and leverage in events of audit failure and events leading to the passage of the J-SOX, respectively.

Lastly, among variables associated with other firm characteristics, that is, *Emerging* and *ListedPeriod*, the coefficient of *Emerging* is significantly negative at the 10 percent level for the 2-day event window, while coefficients of *Listed Period* are insignificant for all windows. This result is consistent with our prediction, in the sense that firms listed on the emerging stock exchanges may face larger information asymmetry between managers and investors, which results in negative stock responses.

In sum, our multivariate analysis shows that firms that changed auditors in recent years, that have uncertainties over their ability to continue as a going concern, that have larger assets or fixed debts, or that are listed on the emerging stock exchanges, tended to experience more negative stock price responses by disclosing "material weakness" or a disclaimer of opinion. In contrast, negative stock reactions were mitigated when firms have a high ratio of foreign shareholders or a high ratio of current liabilities. Another interesting finding is that whether a firm engages a Big 4 audit firms does not seem to matter to investors to evaluate firms with "material weakness" or a disclaimer of opinion.

---

[6] Gupta and Nayar (2007) focus on 90 firms that voluntarily disclosed internal control deficiencies during the period between November 2003 and July 2004, which corresponds to the period prior to the mandated internal control audits. They find that stock prices of firms with internal control deficiencies react negatively to the disclosure. This reaction is less negative when firms engaged a Big 4 audit firm, while the reaction is more negative for firms with large current liabilities to total assets.

CONCLUDING REMARKS

We investigate how the stock market reacts to the disclosure of internal control weaknesses under the Japanese Sarbanes-Oxley Act of 2006. We find that the internal control reports on "material weakness" and a disclaimer of opinion do not tend to affect the stock market on the whole, perhaps because the Japanese official agencies attempted to minimize the implementation costs of the new system. We also show that negative market reactions are intensified if firms have changed auditors in recent years, have uncertainties over their ability to continue as a going concern, have larger assets or fixed debts, or are listed on the emerging stock exchanges. In contrast, negative stock reactions are mitigated when firms have a high ratio of foreign shareholders or a high ratio of current liabilities. Another interesting finding is that whether a firm engaged a Big 4 audit firms does not seem to matter to investors evaluating firms with "material weakness" or a disclaimer of opinion.

REFERENCES

Beneish, M., Billings, D. M. B. & Leslie D. Hodder, L. D. (2008). Internal Control Weaknesses and Information Uncertainty. The Accounting Review, 83(3), 665-703.

Doyle, J., Ge, W., & McVay, S. (2007). Determinants of weaknesses in internal control over financial reporting. Journal of Accounting and Economics, 44,193–223.

Gupta, P. P., & Nayar, N. (2007). Information content of control deficiency disclosures under the Sarbanes -Oxley Act: An empirical investigation. International Journal of Disclosure and Governance, 4 (1), 3–23.

Hammersley, J. S., Myers, L. A., & Shakespeare, C. (2008). Market reaction to the disclosure of internal control weakness and to the characteristics of those weaknesses under section 302 of the Sarbanes Oxley Act of 2002. Review of Accounting Studies, 13,141-165.

Johnstone, K. M., & Bedard, C. (2004). Audit firm portfolio management decisions. Journal of Accounting Research, 42, 659-690.

Krishnan, J., & Krishnan, J. (1997). Litigation Risk and Auditor Resignations. The Accounting Review, 72 (4), 539-560.

Krishnamurthy, S., & Zhou, N. (2006). Auditor Reputation, Auditor Independence and the Stock Market Impact of Andersen's Indictment on its Client Firms. Contemporary Accounting Research, 23, 465-490.

Machida, Y. (2009). Knowledge on Internal Control (Naibu Tosei no Chishiki in Japanese). Nikkei Newspaper Inc.: Tokyo, Japan.

Machida, Y., and Pronexus. (2009). Analysis on Internal Control Reports (Naibu Tosei Houkoku no Jittai Chosa Kekka no Bunseki in Japanese). Weekly Report On Financial Accounting (Shukan Keiei Zaimu), No. 2927, 22-29.

MacKinlay, A. C. (1997). Event studies in economics and finance. Journal of Economic Literature, 35, 13-39.

Numata, S., & Takeda, F. (2010). Audit Reputation and Stock Market Reaction in Japan: The Case of Kanebo and Chuo Aoyama. International Journal of Accounting, 45(2), 175-199.

Seino, K., & Takeda, F. (2009). Stock Market Reactions to the Japanese Sarbanes-Oxley Act of 2006. Corporate Ownership & Control, 7(2), 126-136.

Shu, S. Z. (2000). Auditor resignations: clientele effects and legal liability. Journal of Accounting and Economics, 29, 173-205.

In: The Stock Market
Editor: Allison S. Wetherby

ISBN 978-1-61122-545-7
© 2011 Nova Science Publishers, Inc.

Chapter 6

ADAPTIVE WAVE MODELS FOR OPTION PRICING EVOLUTION

Vladimir G. Ivancevic
Defence Science & Technology Organisation, Australia

Abstract

Adaptive wave model for financial option pricing is proposed, as a high-complexity alternative to the standard Black–Scholes model. The new option-pricing model, representing a controlled Brownian motion, includes two wave-type approaches: nonlinear and quantum, both based on (adaptive form of) the Schrödinger equation. The nonlinear approach comes in two flavors: (i) for the case of constant volatility, it is defined by a single adaptive nonlinear Schrödinger (NLS) equation, while for the case of stochastic volatility, it is defined by an adaptive Manakov system of two coupled NLS equations. The linear quantum approach is defined in terms of de Broglie's plane waves and free-particle Schrödinger equation. In this approach, financial variables have quantum-mechanical interpretation and satisfy the Heisenberg-type uncertainty relations. Both models are capable of successful fitting of the Black–Scholes data, as well as defining Greeks. Based on the two models, as well as the rogue solutions of the NLS equation, I propose a new financial research program.

Keywords: Black–Scholes option pricing, adaptive nonlinear Schrödinger equation, adaptive Manakov system, rogue NLS-waves, quantum-mechanical option pricing, market-heat potential, new financial research program

1. Introduction

Recall that the celebrated Black–Scholes partial differential equation (PDE) describes the time–evolution of the market value of a *stock option* [1, 2]. Formally, for a function $u = u(t, s)$ defined on the domain $0 \leq s < \infty$, $0 \leq t \leq T$ and describing the market value of a stock option with the stock (asset) price s, the *Black–Scholes PDE* can be written (using the physicist notation: $\partial_z u = \partial u / \partial z$) as a diffusion–type equation:

$$\partial_t u = -\frac{1}{2}(\sigma s)^2 \, \partial_{ss} u - rs \, \partial_s u + ru, \tag{1}$$

where $\sigma > 0$ is the standard deviation, or *volatility* of s, r is the short–term prevailing continuously–compounded risk–free interest rate, and $T > 0$ is the time to maturity of the stock option. In this formulation it is assumed that the *underlying* (typically the stock) follows a *geometric Brownian motion* with 'drift' μ and volatility σ, given by the stochastic differential equation (SDE) [3]

$$ds(t) = \mu s(t)dt + \sigma s(t)dW(t), \tag{2}$$

where W is the standard Wiener process. The Black-Scholes PDE (1) is usually derived from SDEs describing the geometric Brownian motion (2), with the stock-price solution given by:

$$s(t) = s(0)\,e^{(\mu - \frac{1}{2}\sigma^2)t + \sigma W(t)}.$$

In mathematical finance, derivation is usually performed using Itô lemma [4] (assuming that the underlying asset obeys the Itô SDE), while in physics it is performed using Stratonovich interpretation [5, 6] (assuming that the underlying asset obeys the Stratonovich SDE [8]).

The Black-Sholes PDE (1) can be applied to a number of one-dimensional models of interpretations of prices given to u, e.g., puts or calls, and to s, e.g., stocks or futures, dividends, etc. The most important examples are European call and put options, defined by:

$$u_{\text{Call}}(s, t) = s\,\mathcal{N}(d_1)\,e^{-T\delta} - k\,\mathcal{N}(d_2)\,e^{-rT}, \tag{3}$$

$$u_{\text{Put}}(s, t) = k\,\mathcal{N}(-d_2)\,e^{-rT} - s\,\mathcal{N}(-d_1)\,e^{-T\delta}, \tag{4}$$

$$\mathcal{N}(\lambda) = \frac{1}{2}\left(1 + \text{erf}\left(\frac{\lambda}{\sqrt{2}}\right)\right),$$

$$d_1 = \frac{\ln\left(\frac{s}{k}\right) + T\left(r - \delta + \frac{\sigma^2}{2}\right)}{\sigma\sqrt{T}}, \qquad d_2 = \frac{\ln\left(\frac{s}{k}\right) + T\left(r - \delta - \frac{\sigma^2}{2}\right)}{\sigma\sqrt{T}},$$

where $\text{erf}(\lambda)$ is the (real-valued) error function, k denotes the strike price and δ represents the dividend yield. In addition, for each of the call and put options, there are five Greeks (see, e.g. [9, 10]), or sensitivities, which are partial derivatives of the option-price with respect to stock price (Delta), interest rate (Rho), volatility (Vega), elapsed time since entering into the option (Theta), and the second partial derivative of the option-price with respect to the stock price (Gamma).

Using the standard *Kolmogorov probability* approach, instead of the market value of an option given by the Black–Scholes equation (1), we could consider the corresponding probability density function (PDF) given by the backward Fokker–Planck equation (see [6, 7]). Alternatively, we can obtain the same PDF (for the market value of a stock option), using the *quantum–probability* formalism [11, 12], as a solution to a time–dependent linear or nonlinear *Schrödinger equation* for the evolution of the complex–valued wave ψ–function for which the absolute square, $|\psi|^2$, is the PDF. The adaptive nonlinear Schrödinger (NLS) equation was recently used in [10] as an approach to option price modelling, as briefly reviewed in this section. The new model, philosophically founded on adaptive markets hypothesis [13, 14] and Elliott wave market theory [15, 16], as well as my own recent work on quantum congition [17, 18], describes adaptively controlled Brownian market behavior. This nonlinear approach to option price modelling is reviewed in the next section. Its important limiting case with low interest-rate reduces to the linear Schrödinger equation. This linear approach to option price modelling is elaborated in the subsequent section.

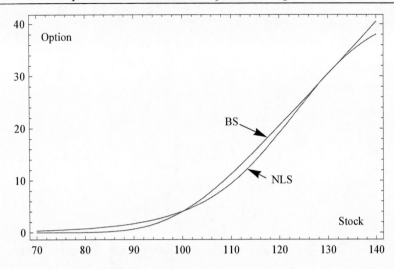

Figure 1. Fitting the Black–Scholes call option with $\beta(w)$-adaptive PDF of the shock-wave NLS-solution (10).

2. Nonlinear Adaptive Wave Model for General Option Pricing

2.1. Adaptive NLS Model

The adaptive, wave–form, nonlinear and stochastic option–pricing model with stock price s, volatility σ and interest rate r is formally defined as a complex-valued, focusing (1+1)–NLS equation, defining the time-dependent *option–price wave function* $\psi = \psi(s, t)$, whose absolute square $|\psi(s, t)|^2$ represents the probability density function (PDF) for the option price in terms of the stock price and time. In natural quantum units, this NLS equation reads:

$$i\partial_t\psi = -\frac{1}{2}\sigma\partial_{ss}\psi - \beta|\psi|^2\psi, \qquad (i = \sqrt{-1}), \tag{5}$$

where $\beta = \beta(r, w)$ denotes the adaptive market-heat potential (see [19]), so the term $V(\psi) = -\beta|\psi|^2$ represents the ψ–dependent potential field. In the simplest nonadaptive scenario β is equal to the interest rate r, while in the adaptive case it depends on the set of adjustable synaptic weights $\{w_j^i\}$ as:

$$\beta(r, w) = r\sum_{i=1}^{n} w_1^i \operatorname{erf}\left(\frac{w_2^i s}{w_3^i}\right). \tag{6}$$

Physically, the NLS equation (5) describes a nonlinear wave (e.g. in Bose-Einstein condensates) defined by the complex-valued wave function $\psi(s, t)$ of real space and time parameters. In the present context, the space-like variable s denotes the stock (asset) price.

The NLS equation (5) has been exactly solved using the power series expansion method [20, 21] of Jacobi elliptic functions [22]. Consider the ψ–function describing a single plane wave, with the wave number k and circular frequency ω:

$$\psi(s, t) = \phi(\xi)\,e^{i(ks-\omega t)}, \qquad \text{with } \xi = s - \sigma k t \text{ and } \phi(\xi) \in \mathbb{R}. \tag{7}$$

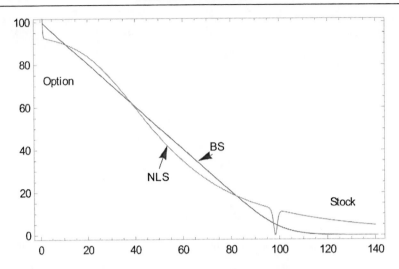

Figure 2. Fitting the Black–Scholes put option with $\beta(w)$–adaptive PDF of the shock-wave NLS $\psi_2(s,t)$ solution (10). Notice the kink near $s = 100$.

Its substitution into the NLS equation (5) gives the nonlinear oscillator ODE:

$$\phi''(\xi) + \left[\omega - \frac{1}{2}\sigma k^2\right]\phi(\xi) + \beta\phi^3(\xi) = 0. \tag{8}$$

We can seek a solution $\phi(\xi)$ for (8) as a linear function [21]

$$\phi(\xi) = a_0 + a_1\mathrm{sn}(\xi),$$

where $\mathrm{sn}(s) = \mathrm{sn}(s, m)$ are Jacobi elliptic sine functions with *elliptic modulus* $m \in [0, 1]$, such that $\mathrm{sn}(s, 0) = \sin(s)$ and $\mathrm{sn}(s, 1) = \tanh(s)$. The solution of (8) was calculated in [10] to be

$$\phi(\xi) = \pm m\sqrt{\frac{-\sigma}{\beta}}\,\mathrm{sn}(\xi), \qquad \text{for } m \in [0, 1]; \text{ and}$$

$$\phi(\xi) = \pm\sqrt{\frac{-\sigma}{\beta}}\,\tanh(\xi), \qquad \text{for } m = 1.$$

This gives the exact periodic solution of (5) as [10]

$$\psi_1(s,t) = \pm m\sqrt{\frac{-\sigma}{\beta(w)}}\,\mathrm{sn}(s - \sigma kt)\,\mathrm{e}^{\mathrm{i}[ks - \frac{1}{2}\sigma t(1+m^2+k^2)]}, \qquad \text{for } m \in [0, 1); \tag{9}$$

$$\psi_2(s,t) = \pm\sqrt{\frac{-\sigma}{\beta(w)}}\,\tanh(s - \sigma kt)\,\mathrm{e}^{\mathrm{i}[ks - \frac{1}{2}\sigma t(2+k^2)]}, \qquad \text{for } m = 1, \tag{10}$$

where (9) defines the general solution, while (10) defines the *envelope shock-wave*[1] (or,

---

[1]A shock wave is a type of fast-propagating nonlinear disturbance that carries energy and can propagate through a medium (or, field). It is characterized by an abrupt, nearly discontinuous change in the characteristics of the medium. The energy of a shock wave dissipates relatively quickly with distance and its entropy increases. On the other hand, a soliton is a self-reinforcing nonlinear solitary wave packet that maintains its shape while it travels at constant speed. It is caused by a cancelation of nonlinear and dispersive effects in the medium (or, field).

'dark soliton') solution of the NLS equation (5).

Alternatively, if we seek a solution $\phi(\xi)$ as a linear function of Jacobi elliptic cosine functions, such that $\mathrm{cn}(s,0) = \cos(s)$ and $\mathrm{cn}(s,1) = \mathrm{sech}(s)$,[2]

$$\phi(\xi) = a_0 + a_1 \mathrm{cn}(\xi),$$

then we get [10]

$$\psi_3(s,t) \quad = \quad \pm m \sqrt{\frac{\sigma}{\beta(w)}} \, \mathrm{cn}(s - \sigma kt) \, \mathrm{e}^{\mathrm{i}[ks - \frac{1}{2}\sigma t(1 - 2m^2 + k^2)]}, \qquad \text{for } m \in [0,1); \quad (11)$$

$$\psi_4(s,t) \quad = \quad \pm \sqrt{\frac{\sigma}{\beta(w)}} \, \mathrm{sech}(s - \sigma kt) \, \mathrm{e}^{\mathrm{i}[ks - \frac{1}{2}\sigma t(k^2 - 1)]}, \qquad \text{for } m = 1, \quad (12)$$

where (11) defines the general solution, while (12) defines the *envelope solitary-wave* (or, 'bright soliton') solution of the NLS equation (5).

In all four solution expressions (9), (10), (11) and (12), the adaptive potential $\beta(w)$ is yet to be calculated using either unsupervised Hebbian learning, or supervised Levenberg–Marquardt algorithm (see, e.g. [23, 24]). In this way, the NLS equation (5) becomes the *quantum neural network* (see [18]). Any kind of numerical analysis can be easily performed using above closed-form solutions $\psi_i(s,t)$ $(i = 1, ..., 4)$ as initial conditions.

The adaptive NLS–PDFs of the shock-wave type (10) has been used in [10] to fit the Black–Scholes call and put options (see Figures 1 and 2). Specifically, the adaptive heat potential (6) was combined with the spatial part of (10)

$$\phi(s) = \left| \sqrt{\frac{\sigma}{\beta}} \tanh(s - kt\sigma) \right|^2, \tag{13}$$

while parameter estimates where obtained using 100 iterations of the Levenberg–Marquardt algorithm.

As can be seen from Figure (2) there is a kink near $s = 100$. This kink, which is a natural characteristic of the spatial shock-wave (13), can be smoothed out (Figure 3) by taking the sum of the spatial parts of the shock-wave solution (10) and the soliton solution (12) as:

$$\phi(s) = \left| \sqrt{\frac{\sigma}{\beta}} [d_1 \tanh(s - kt\sigma) + d_2 \mathrm{sech}(s - kt\sigma)] \right|^2. \tag{14}$$

The adaptive NLS–based Greeks (Delta, Rho, Vega, Theta and Gamma) have been defined in [10], as partial derivatives of the shock-wave solution (10).

---

[2]A closely related solution of an anharmonic oscillator ODE:

$$\phi''(s) + \phi(s) + \phi^3(s) = 0$$

is given by

$$\phi(s) = \sqrt{\frac{2m}{1 - 2m}} \, \mathrm{cn}\left(\sqrt{1 + \frac{2m}{1 - 2m}} \, s, \, m \right).$$

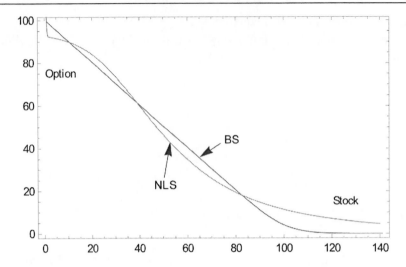

Figure 3. Smoothing out the kink in the put option fit, by combining the shock-wave solution with the soliton solution, as defined by (14).

2.2. Adaptive Manakov System

Next, for the purpose of including a *controlled stochastic volatility*[3] into the adaptive–NLS model (5), the full bidirectional quantum neural computation model [18] for option-price forecasting has been formulated in [10] as a self-organized system of two coupled self-focusing NLS equations: one defining the *option–price wave function* $\psi = \psi(s, t)$ and the other defining the *volatility wave function* $\sigma = \sigma(s, t)$:

$$\text{Volatility NLS}: \quad i\partial_t \sigma = -\frac{1}{2}\partial_{ss}\sigma - \beta(r, w)\left(|\sigma|^2 + |\psi|^2\right)\sigma, \tag{15}$$

$$\text{Option price NLS}: \quad i\partial_t \psi = -\frac{1}{2}\partial_{ss}\psi - \beta(r, w)\left(|\sigma|^2 + |\psi|^2\right)\psi. \tag{16}$$

In this coupled model, the σ–NLS (15) governs the (s, t)–evolution of stochastic volatility, which plays the role of a nonlinear coefficient in (16); the ψ–NLS (16) defines the (s, t)–evolution of option price, which plays the role of a nonlinear coefficient in (15). The purpose of this coupling is to generate a *leverage effect*, i.e. stock volatility is (negatively) correlated to stock returns[4] (see, e.g. [27]). This bidirectional associative memory effectively performs quantum neural computation [18], by giving a spatio-temporal and quantum generalization of Kosko's BAM family of neural networks [28, 29]. In addition, the shock-wave and solitary-wave nature of the coupled NLS equations may describe brain-like effects frequently occurring in financial markets: volatility/price propagation, reflection and collision of shock and solitary waves (see [30]).

The coupled NLS-system (15)–(16), without an embedded w–learning (i.e., for constant $\beta = r$ – the interest rate), actually defines the well-known *Manakov system*,[5] proven

---

[3]Controlled stochastic volatility here represents volatility evolving in a stochastic manner but within the controlled boundaries.

[4]The hypothesis that financial leverage can explain the leverage effect was first discussed by F. Black [26].

[5]Manakov system has been used to describe the interaction between wave packets in dispersive conservative

by S. Manakov in 1973 [31] to be completely integrable, by the existence of infinite number of involutive integrals of motion. It admits 'bright' and 'dark' soliton solutions. The simplest solution of (15)–(16), the so-called *Manakov bright 2–soliton*, has the form resembling that of the sech-solution (12) (see [34, 35, 36, 37, 38, 39, 40]), and is formally defined by:

$$\psi_{\text{sol}}(s,t) = 2b\,\mathbf{c}\,\text{sech}(2b(s+4at))\,e^{-2i(2a^2t+as-2b^2t)}, \tag{17}$$

where $\psi_{\text{sol}}(s,t) = \begin{pmatrix} \sigma(s,t) \\ \psi(s,t) \end{pmatrix}$, $\mathbf{c} = (c_1, c_2)^T$ is a unit vector such that $|c_1|^2 + |c_2|^2 = 1$. Real-valued parameters a and b are some simple functions of (σ, β, k), which can be determined by the Levenberg–Marquardt algorithm. I have argued in [10] that in some short-time financial situations, the adaptation effect on β can be neglected, so our option-pricing model (15)–(16) can be reduced to the Manakov 2–soliton model (17), as depicted and explained in Figure 4.

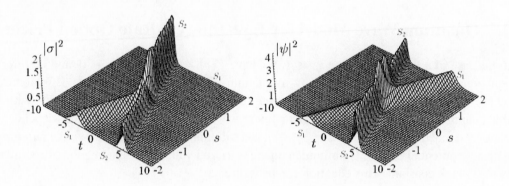

Figure 4. Hypothetical market scenario including sample PDFs for volatility $|\sigma|^2$ and $|\psi|^2$ of the Manakov 2–soliton (17). On the left, we observe the (s,t)–evolution of stochastic volatility: we have a collision of two volatility component-solitons, $S_1(s,t)$ and $S_2(s,t)$, which join together into the resulting soliton $S_2(s,t)$, annihilating the $S_1(s,t)$ component in the process. On the right, we observe the (s,t)–evolution of option price: we have a collision of two option component-solitons, $S_1(s,t)$ and $S_2(s,t)$, which pass through each other without much change, except at the collision point. Due to symmetry of the Manakov system, volatility and option price can exchange their roles.

3. Financial Rogue Waves

In addition, two new wave-solutions of the NLS equation (5) have been recently provided in [41], in the form of rogue waves,[6] using the deformed Darboux transformation method developed in [44]:

---

media, and also the interaction between orthogonally polarized components in nonlinear optical fibres (see, e.g. [32, 33] and references therein).

[6]Rogue waves are also known as *freak waves*, *monster waves*, *killer waves*, *giant waves* and *extreme waves*. They are found in various media, including optical fibers [42]. The basic rogue wave solution was first presented by Peregrine [43] to describe the phenomenon known as *Peregrine soliton* (or Peregrine breather).

1. The *one-rogon* solution:

$$\psi_{1\mathrm{rogon}}(s,t) = \alpha\sqrt{\frac{\sigma}{2\beta}}\left[1 - \frac{4(1+\sigma\alpha^2 t)}{1 + 2\alpha^2(s-\sigma k t)^2 + \sigma^2\alpha^4 t^2}\right]e^{i[ks+\sigma/2(\alpha^2-k^2)t]}, \quad \sigma\beta > 0,$$

(18)

where α and k denote the scaling and gauge.

2. The *two-rogon* solution:

$$\psi_{2\mathrm{rogon}}(s,t) = \alpha\sqrt{\frac{\sigma}{2\beta}}\left[1 + \frac{P_2(s,t) + iQ_2(s,t)}{R_2(s,t)}\right]e^{i[ks+\sigma/2(\alpha^2-k^2)t]}, \quad \sigma\beta > 0,$$

(19)

where P_2, Q_2, R_2 are certain polynomial functions of s and t.

Both rogon solutions can be easily made adaptive by introducing a set of 'synaptic weights' for nonlinear data fitting, in the same way as before.

4. Quantum Wave Model for Low Interest-Rate Option Pricing

In the case of a low interest-rate $r \ll 1$, we have $\beta(r) \ll 1$, so $V(\psi) \to 0$, and therefore equation (5) can be approximated by a quantum-like *option wave packet*. It is defined by a continuous superposition of *de Broglie's plane waves*, 'physically' associated with a free quantum particle of unit mass. This linear wave packet, given by the time-dependent complex-valued wave function $\psi = \psi(s,t)$, is a solution of the *linear Schrödinger equation* with zero potential energy, Hamiltonian operator $\hat{H}$ and volatility σ playing the role similar to the Planck constant. This equation can be written as:

$$i\sigma\partial_t\psi = \hat{H}\psi, \qquad \text{where} \qquad \hat{H} = -\frac{\sigma^2}{2}\partial_{ss}.$$

(20)

Thus, we consider the ψ-function describing a single de Broglie's plane wave, with the wave number k, linear momentum $p = \sigma k$, wavelength $\lambda_k = 2\pi/k$, angular frequency $\omega_k = \sigma k^2/2$, and oscillation period $T_k = 2\pi/\omega_k = 4\pi/\sigma k^2$. It is defined by (compare with [45, 46, 12])

$$\psi_k(s,t) = Ae^{i(ks-\omega_k t)} = Ae^{i(ks-\frac{\sigma k^2}{2}t)} = A\cos(ks - \frac{\sigma k^2}{2}t) + Ai\sin(ks - \frac{\sigma k^2}{2}t), \quad (21)$$

where A is the amplitude of the wave, the angle $(ks - \omega_k t) = (ks - \frac{\sigma k^2}{2}t)$ represents the phase of the wave ψ_k with the *phase velocity:* $v_k = \omega_k/k = \sigma k/2$.

The space-time wave function $\psi(s,t)$ that satisfies the linear Schrödinger equation (20) can be decomposed (using Fourier's separation of variables) into the spatial part $\phi(s)$ and the temporal part $e^{-i\omega t}$ as:

$$\psi(s,t) = \phi(s)\,e^{-i\omega t} = \phi(s)\,e^{-\frac{i}{\sigma}Et}.$$

The spatial part, representing *stationary* (or, *amplitude*) *wave function*, $\phi(s) = Ae^{iks}$, satisfies the *linear harmonic oscillator,* which can be formulated in several equivalent forms:

$$\phi'' + k^2\phi = 0, \qquad \phi'' + \left(\frac{p}{\sigma}\right)^2\phi = 0, \qquad \phi'' + \left(\frac{\omega_k}{v_k}\right)^2\phi = 0, \qquad \phi'' + \frac{2E_k}{\sigma^2}\phi = 0. \quad (22)$$

Planck's *energy quantum* of the option wave ψ_k is given by: $E_k = \sigma\omega_k = \frac{1}{2}(\sigma k)^2$.

From the plane-wave expressions (21) we have: $\psi_k(s,t) = Ae^{\frac{i}{\sigma}(ps - E_k t)} -$ for the wave going to the 'right' and $\psi_k(s,t) = Ae^{-\frac{i}{\sigma}(ps + E_k t)} -$ for the wave going to the 'left'.

The general solution to (20) is formulated as a linear combination of de Broglie's option waves (21), comprising the option wave-packet:

$$\psi(s,t) = \sum_{i=0}^{n} c_i \psi_{k_i}(s,t), \qquad (\text{with } n \in \mathbb{N}). \tag{23}$$

Its absolute square, $|\psi(s,t)|^2$, represents the probability density function at a time t.

The *group velocity* of an option wave-packet is given by: $v_g = d\omega_k/dk$. It is related to the phase velocity v_k of a plane wave as: $v_g = v_k - \lambda_k dv_k/d\lambda_k$. Closely related is the *center* of the option wave-packet (the point of maximum amplitude), given by: $s = td\omega_k/dk$.

The following quantum-motivated assertions can be stated:

1. Volatility σ has dimension of *financial action*, or *energy* $\times$ *time*.

2. The total energy E of an option wave-packet is (in the case of similar plane waves) given by Planck's superposition of the energies E_k of n individual waves: $E = n\sigma\omega_k = \frac{n}{2}(\sigma k)^2$, where $L = n\sigma$ denotes the *angular momentum* of the option wave-packet, representing the shift between its growth and decay, and *vice versa*.

3. The average energy $\langle E \rangle$ of an option wave-packet is given by Boltzmann's partition function:

$$\langle E \rangle = \frac{\sum_{n=0}^{\infty} nE_k e^{-\frac{nE_k}{bT}}}{\sum_{n=0}^{\infty} e^{-\frac{nE_k}{bT}}} = \frac{E_k}{e^{\frac{E_k}{bT}} - 1},$$

where b is the Boltzmann-like kinetic constant and T is the market temperature.

4. The energy form of the Schrödinger equation (20) reads: $E\psi = i\sigma\partial_t\psi$.

5. The eigenvalue equation for the Hamiltonian operator $\hat{H}$ is the *stationary Schrödinger equation:*

$$\hat{H}\phi(s) = E\phi(s), \qquad \text{or} \qquad E\phi(s) = -\frac{\sigma^2}{2}\partial_{ss}\phi(s),$$

which is just another form of the harmonic oscillator (22). It has oscillatory solutions of the form:

$$\phi_E(s) = c_1 e^{\frac{i}{\sigma}\sqrt{2E_k}\,s} + c_2 e^{-\frac{i}{\sigma}\sqrt{2E_k}\,s},$$

called *energy eigen-states* with energies E_k and denoted by: $\hat{H}\phi_E(s) = E_k\phi_E(s)$.

The Black–Scholes put and call options have been fitted with the quantum PDFs (see Figures 5 and 6) given by the absolute square of (23) with $n = 7$ and $n = 3$, respectively. Using supervised Levenberg–Marquardt algorithm and *Mathematica* 7, the following

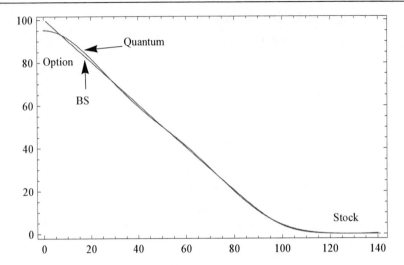

Figure 5. Fitting the Black–Scholes put option with the quantum PDF given by the absolute square of (23) with $n = 7$.

coefficients were obtained for the Black–Scholes put option:

$\sigma^* = -0.0031891$, $t^* = -0.0031891$, $k_1 = 2.62771$, $k_2 = 2.62777$, $k_3 = 2.65402$, $k_4 = 2.61118$, $k_5 = 2.64104$, $k_6 = 2.54737$, $k_7 = 2.62778$, $c_1 = 1.26632$, $c_2 = 1.26517$,
$c_3 = 2.74379$, $c_4 = 1.35495$, $c_5 = 1.59586$, $c_6 = 0.263832$, $c_7 = 1.26779$,
with $\sigma_{BS} = -94.0705\sigma^*$, $t_{BS} = -31.3568t^*$.

Using the same algorithm, the following coefficients were obtained for the Black–Scholes call option:

$\sigma^* = -11.9245$, $t^* = -11.9245$, $k_1 = 0.851858$, $k_2 = 0.832409$,
$k_3 = 0.872061$, $c_1 = 2.9004$, $c_2 = 2.72592$, $c_3 = 2.93291$,
with $\sigma_{BS} - 0.0251583\sigma^*$, $t = -0.00838609t^*$.

Now, given some initial option wave function, $\psi(s, 0) = \psi_0(s)$, a solution to the initial-value problem for the linear Schrödinger equation (20) is, in terms of the pair of Fourier transforms $(\mathcal{F}, \mathcal{F}^{-1})$, given by (see [46])

$$\psi(s, t) = \mathcal{F}^{-1}\left[e^{-i\omega t}\mathcal{F}(\psi_0)\right] = \mathcal{F}^{-1}\left[e^{-i\frac{\sigma k^2}{2}t}\mathcal{F}(\psi_0)\right]. \tag{24}$$

For example (see [46]), suppose we have an initial option wave-function at time $t = 0$ given by the complex-valued Gaussian function:

$$\psi(s, 0) = e^{-as^2/2}e^{i\sigma ks},$$

where a is the width of the Gaussian, while p is the average momentum of the wave. Its

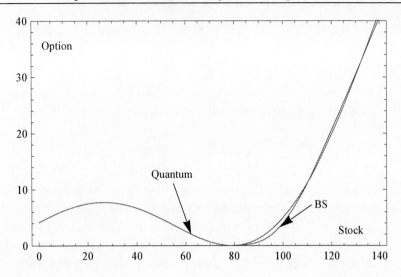

Figure 6. Fitting the Black–Scholes call option with the quantum PDF given by the absolute square of (23) with $n = 3$. Note that fit is good in the realistic stock region: $s \in [75, 140]$.

Fourier transform, $\hat{\psi}_0(k) = \mathcal{F}[\psi(s, 0)]$, is given by

$$\hat{\psi}_0(k) = \frac{e^{-\frac{(k-p)^2}{2a}}}{\sqrt{a}}.$$

The solution at time t of the initial value problem is given by

$$\psi(s, t) = \frac{1}{\sqrt{2\pi a}} \int_{-\infty}^{+\infty} e^{i(ks - \frac{\sigma k^2}{2}t)} \, e^{-\frac{a(k-p)^2}{2a}} \, dk,$$

which, after some algebra becomes

$$\psi(s, t) = \frac{\exp\left(-\frac{as^2 - 2isp + ip^2 t}{2(1 + iat)}\right)}{\sqrt{1 + iat}}, \qquad \text{(with } p = \sigma k\text{)}.$$

As a simpler example,[7] if we have an initial option wave-function given by the real-valued Gaussian function,

$$\psi(s, 0) = \frac{e^{-s^2/2}}{\sqrt[4]{\pi}},$$

---

[7]An example of a more general Gaussian wave-packet solution of (20) is given by:

$$\psi(s, t) = \sqrt{\frac{\sqrt{a/\pi}}{1 + iat}} \, \exp\left(\frac{-\frac{1}{2}a(s - s_0)^2 - \frac{i}{2}p_0^2 t + ip_0(s - s_0)}{1 + iat} \right),$$

where s_0, p_0 are initial stock-price and average momentum, while a is the width of the Gaussian. At time $t = 0$ the 'particle' is at rest around $s = 0$, its average momentum $p_0 = 0$. The wave function spreads with time while its maximum decreases and stays put at the origin. At time $-t$ the wave packet is the complex-conjugate of the wave-packet at time t.

the solution of (20) is given by the complex-valued $\psi-$function,

$$\psi(s,t) = \frac{\exp(-\frac{s^2}{2(1+\mathrm{i}t)})}{\sqrt[4]{\pi}\sqrt{1+\mathrm{i}t}}.$$

From (24) it follows that a stationary option wave-packet is given by:

$$\phi(s) = \frac{1}{\sqrt{2\pi}} \int_{-\infty}^{+\infty} e^{\frac{\mathrm{i}}{\sigma}ks}\,\hat{\psi}(k)\,dk, \qquad \text{where} \qquad \hat{\psi}(k) = \mathcal{F}[\phi(s)].$$

As $|\phi(s)|^2$ is the stationary stock PDF, we can calculate the *expectation values* of the stock and the wave number of the whole option wave-packet, consisting of n measured plane waves, as:

$$\langle s \rangle = \int_{-\infty}^{+\infty} s|\phi(s)|^2 ds \qquad \text{and} \qquad \langle k \rangle = \int_{-\infty}^{+\infty} k|\hat{\psi}(k)|^2 dk. \tag{25}$$

The recordings of n individual option plane waves (21) will be scattered around the mean values (25). The width of the distribution of the recorded $s-$ and $k-$values are uncertainties Δs and Δk, respectively. They satisfy the Heisenberg-type uncertainty relation:

$$\Delta s\,\Delta k \geq \frac{n}{2},$$

which imply the similar relation for the total option energy and time:

$$\Delta E\,\Delta t \geq \frac{n}{2}.$$

Finally, Greeks for both put and call options are defined as the following partial derivatives of the option $\psi-$function PDF:

Delta $= \partial_s |\psi(s,t)|^2 =$
$2\mathrm{i}\sum_{j=1}^{n} c_j k_j\, e^{k_j\left(\mathrm{i}s - \frac{1}{2}\mathrm{i}\sigma k_j t\right)} \mathrm{Abs}\left[\sum_{j=1}^{n} c_j\, e^{k_j\left(\mathrm{i}s - \frac{1}{2}\mathrm{i}\sigma k_j t\right)}\right] \mathrm{Abs}'\left[\sum_{j=1}^{n} c_j\, e^{k_j\left(\mathrm{i}s - \frac{1}{2}\mathrm{i}\sigma k_j t\right)}\right]$

Vega $= \partial_\sigma |\psi(s,t)|^2 =$
$-\mathrm{i}t\sum_{j=1}^{n} c_j k_j{}^2\, e^{k_j\left(\mathrm{i}s - \frac{1}{2}\mathrm{i}\sigma k_j t\right)} \mathrm{Abs}\left[\sum_{j=1}^{n} c_j\, e^{k_j\left(\mathrm{i}s - \frac{1}{2}\mathrm{i}\sigma k_j t\right)}\right] \mathrm{Abs}'\left[\sum_{j=1}^{n} c_j\, e^{k_j\left(\mathrm{i}s - \frac{1}{2}\mathrm{i}\sigma k_j t\right)}\right]$

Theta $= \partial_t |\psi(s,t)|^2 =$
$-\mathrm{i}\sigma\sum_{j=1}^{n} c_j k_j{}^2\, e^{k_j\left(\mathrm{i}s - \frac{1}{2}\mathrm{i}\sigma k_j t\right)} \mathrm{Abs}\left[\sum_{j=1}^{n} c_j\, e^{k_j\left(\mathrm{i}s - \frac{1}{2}\mathrm{i}\sigma k_j t\right)}\right] \mathrm{Abs}'\left[\sum_{j=1}^{n} c_j\, e^{k_j\left(\mathrm{i}s - \frac{1}{2}\mathrm{i}\sigma k_j t\right)}\right]$

Gamma $= \partial_{ss} |\psi(s,t)|^2 =$
$-2\sum_{j=1}^{n} c_j k_j{}^2\, e^{k_j\left(\mathrm{i}s - \frac{1}{2}\mathrm{i}\sigma k_j t\right)} \mathrm{Abs}\left[\sum_{j=1}^{n} c_j\, e^{k_j\left(\mathrm{i}s - \frac{1}{2}\mathrm{i}\sigma k_j t\right)}\right] \mathrm{Abs}'\left[\sum_{j=1}^{n} c_j\, e^{k_j\left(\mathrm{i}s - \frac{1}{2}\mathrm{i}\sigma k_j t\right)}\right] -$
$\left(\sum_{j=1}^{n} c_j k_j\, e^{k_j\left(\mathrm{i}s - \frac{1}{2}\mathrm{i}\sigma k_j t\right)}\right)^2 \mathrm{Abs}'\left[\sum_{j=1}^{n} c_j\, e^{k_j\left(\mathrm{i}s - \frac{1}{2}\mathrm{i}\sigma k_j t\right)}\right]^2 -$
$\left(\sum_{j=1}^{n} c_j k_j\, e^{k_j\left(\mathrm{i}s - \frac{1}{2}\mathrm{i}\sigma k_j t\right)}\right)^2 \mathrm{Abs}\left[\sum_{j=1}^{n} c_j\, e^{k_j\left(\mathrm{i}s - \frac{1}{2}\mathrm{i}\sigma k_j t\right)}\right] \mathrm{Abs}''\left[\sum_{j=1}^{n} c_j\, e^{k_j\left(\mathrm{i}s - \frac{1}{2}\mathrm{i}\sigma k_j t\right)}\right],$

where Abs denotes the absolute value, while Abs' and Abs'' denote its first and second derivatives.

5. A New Stock-Market Research Program

Based on the above wave stock-market analysis, I propose a new financial research program as follows.

Firstly, define the *general adaptive wave model for option pricing evolution* as a (linear) combination of the previously defined particular solutions to the adaptive NLS-equation (5). The five wave-components of this general model are:

1. the linear wave packet $\psi_{\text{packet}}(s, t)$, given by (23);

2. the shock-wave $\psi_{\text{shock}}(s, t)$, given by (10);

3. the soliton $\psi_{\text{soliton}}(s, t)$, given by (12);

4. the one-rogon $\psi_{\text{1rogon}}(s, t)$, given by (18); and

5. the two rogon $\psi_{\text{2rogon}}(s, t)$ (19).

Formally, the general adaptive wave model is defined by:

$$
\begin{aligned}
\psi_{\text{general}}(s, t) \;=\; & A_1 \sum_{i=0}^{n} c_i \mathrm{e}^{\mathrm{i}(ks - \omega_k t)} \\
\pm\; & A_2 \sqrt{\frac{-\sigma}{\beta}} \tanh(s - \sigma k t)\, \mathrm{e}^{\mathrm{i}[ks - \frac{1}{2}\sigma t(2 + k^2)]} \\
\pm\; & A_3 \sqrt{\frac{\sigma}{\beta}} \operatorname{sech}(s - \sigma k t)\, \mathrm{e}^{\mathrm{i}[ks - \frac{1}{2}\sigma t(k^2 - 1)]} \\
+\; & A_4 \alpha \sqrt{\frac{\sigma}{2\beta}} \left[1 - \frac{4(1 + \sigma\alpha^2 t)}{1 + 2\alpha^2(s - \sigma k t)^2 + \sigma^2\alpha^4 t^2} \right] \mathrm{e}^{\mathrm{i}[ks + \sigma/2(\alpha^2 - k^2)t]} \\
+\; & A_5 \alpha \sqrt{\frac{\sigma}{2\beta}} \left[1 + \frac{P_2(s, t) + \mathrm{i}Q_2(s, t)}{R_2(s, t)} \right] \mathrm{e}^{\mathrm{i}[ks + \sigma/2(\alpha^2 - k^2)t]},
\end{aligned}
\tag{26}
$$

where A_i, $(i = 1, ..., 5)$ denote adaptive amplitudes of the five waves, while the other parameters are defined in the previous section.

Secondly, we need to find the most representative financial index or contemporary markets data that clearly show in their evolution both the *efficient markets hypothesis* [13] and *adaptive markets hypothesis* [14]. Once we find such a representative data, we need to fit it using our general wave model (26) and the powerful Levenberg-Marquardt fitting algorithm. I remark here that, based on my empirical experience, the general wave model (26) is capable of fitting any financial data, provided we use appropriate number of fitting coefficients (see [10] for technical details).

Once we have successfully fitted the most representative market data we will have a model that can be used for *prediction* of many possible outcomes of the current *global financial storm*.

6. Conclusion

I have proposed an adaptive–wave alternative to the standard Black-Scholes option pricing model. The new model, philosophically founded on adaptive markets hypothesis [13, 14] and Elliott wave market theory [15, 16], describes adaptively controlled Brownian market behavior. Two approaches have been proposed: (i) a nonlinear one based on the adaptive NLS (solved by means of Jacobi elliptic functions) and the adaptive Manakov system (of two coupled NLS equations); (ii) a linear quantum-mechanical one based on the free-particle Schrödinger equation and de Broglie's plane waves. For the purpose of fitting the Black-Scholes data, the Levenberg-Marquardt algorithm was used.

The presented adaptive and quantum wave models are spatio-temporal dynamical systems of much higher complexity [25] then the Black-Scholes model. This makes the new wave models harder to analyze, but at the same time, their immense variety is potentially much closer to the real financial market complexity, especially at the time of financial crisis.

Based on the two models, as well as the rogue solutions of the NLS equation, I have proposed a new financial research program. Its aim is to develop a general adaptive wave model for option pricing evolution, consisting of a linear wave packet, a shock-wave, a soliton, a one-rogon and a two rogon. This general wave model will be capable of fitting any stock-market data, provided we use an appropriate number of fitting coefficients.

References

[1] F. Black, M. Scholes, The Pricing of Options and Corporate Liabilities, *J. Pol. Econ.* **81**, 637-659, (1973)

[2] R.C. Merton, *Bell J. Econ. and Management Sci.* **4**, 141-183, (1973)

[3] M.F.M. Osborne, *Operations Research* **7**, 145-173, (1959)

[4] K. Itô, *Mem. Am. Math. Soc.* **4**, 1-51, (1951)

[5] J. Perello, J. M. Porra, M. Montero, J. Masoliver, *Physica A* **278**, **1-2**, 260-274, (2000)

[6] C.W. Gardiner, *Handbook of Stochastic Methods*, Springer, Berlin, (1983)

[7] J. Voit, *The Statistical Mechanics of Financial Markets*. Springer, (2005)

[8] R.L. Stratonovich, *SIAM J. Control* **4**, 362-371, (1966)

[9] M. Kelly, Black-Scholes Option Model & European Option Greeks. *The Wolfram Demonstrations Project,* http://demonstrations.wolfram.com/EuropeanOptionGreeks, (2009)

[10] V. Ivancevic, Cogn. Comput. Springer-online first, (January 2010)

[11] V. Ivancevic, T. Ivancevic, Complex Dynamics: Advanced System Dynamics in Complex Variables. Springer, Dordrecht, (2007)

[12] V. Ivancevic, T. Ivancevic, *Quantum Leap: From Dirac and Feynman, Across the Universe, to Human Body and Mind*. World Scientific, Singapore, (2008)

[13] A.W. Lo, *J. Portf. Manag.* **30**, 15-29, (2004)

[14] A.W. Lo, *J. Inves. Consult.* **7**, 21-44, (2005)

[15] A.J. Frost, R.R. Prechter, Jr., *Elliott Wave Principle: Key to Market Behavior.* Wiley, New York, (1978); (10th Edition) Elliott Wave International, (2009)

[16] P. Steven, *Applying Elliott Wave Theory Profitably*. Wiley, New York, (2003)

[17] V. Ivancevic, E. Aidman, *Physica A* **382**, 616–630, (2007)

[18] V. Ivancevic, T. Ivancevic, *Quantum Neural Computation,* Springer, (2009)

[19] H. Kleinert, H. Kleinert, *Path Integrals in Quantum Mechanics, Statistics, Polymer Physics, and Financial Markets* (3rd ed), World Scientific, Singapore, (2002)

[20] S. Liu, Z. Fu, S. Liu, Q. Zhao, *Phys. Let. A* **289**, 69–74, (2001)

[21] G-T. Liu, T-Y. Fan, *Phys. Let. A* **345**, 161–166, (2005)

[22] M. Abramowitz, I.A. Stegun, (Eds): *Jacobian Elliptic Functions and Theta Functions.* Chapter 16 in Handbook of Mathematical Functions with Formulas, Graphs, and Mathematical Tables (9th ed). Dover, New York, 567-581, (1972)

[23] V. Ivancevic, T. Ivancevic, *Neuro-Fuzzy Associative Machinery for Comprehensive Brain and Cognition Modelling*. Springer, Berlin, (2007)

[24] V. Ivancevic, T. Ivancevic, *Computational Mind: A Complex Dynamics Perspective.* Springer, Berlin, (2007)

[25] V. Ivancevic, T. Ivancevic, *Complex Nonlinearity: Chaos, Phase Transitions, Topology Change and Path Integrals,* Springer, (2008)

[26] F. Black, *1976 Meet. Ame. Stat. Assoc. Bus. Econ. Stat.* 177—181, (1976)

[27] H.E. Roman, M. Porto, C. Dose, *EPL* **84**, 28001, (5pp), (2008)

[28] B. Kosko, *IEEE Trans. Sys. Man Cyb.* **18**, 49–60, (1988)

[29] B. Kosko, *Neural Networks, Fuzzy Systems, A Dynamical Systems Approach to Machine Intelligence.* Prentice–Hall, New York, (1992)

[30] S.-H. Hanm, I.G. Koh, *Phys. Rev. E* **60**, 7608–7611, (1999)

[31] S.V. Manakov, (in Russian) *Zh. Eksp. Teor. Fiz.* **65** 505–516, (1973); (transleted into English) *Sov. Phys. JETP* **38**, 248–253, (1974)

[32] M. Haelterman, A.P. Sheppard, *Phys. Rev. E* **49**, 3376–3381, (1994)

[33] J. Yang, *Physica D* **108**, 92–112, (1997)

[34] D.J. Benney, A.C. Newell, *J. Math. Phys.* **46**, 133-139, (1967)

[35] V.E. Zakharov, S.V. Manakov, S.P. Novikov, L.P. Pitaevskii, *Soliton theory: inverse scattering method.* Nauka, Moscow, (1980)

[36] A. Hasegawa, Y. Kodama, *Solitons in Optical Communications.* Clarendon, Oxford, (1995)

[37] R. Radhakrishnan, M. Lakshmanan, J. Hietarinta, *Phys. Rev. E.* **56**, 2213, (1997)

[38] G. Agrawal, *Nonlinear fiber optics* (3rd ed.). Academic Press, San Diego, (2001).

[39] J. Yang, *Phys. Rev. E* **64**, 026607, (2001)

[40] J. Elgin, V. Enolski, A. Its, *Physica D* **225** (22), 127-152, (2007)

[41] Z. Yan, Financial rogue waves (in press) arXiv.q-fin.PR:0911.4259; *Optical Rogue Waves* (Rogons), Wolfram Demonstration Project, (2009)

[42] D.R. Solli, C. Ropers, P. Koonath, B. Jalali, Optical Rogue Waves, *Nature*, **450**, 10541057, (2007)

[43] D.H. Peregrine, Water Waves, Nonlinear Schrödinger Equations and Their Solutions, *J. Austral. Math. Soc. Ser.* **B25**, 1643, (1983)

[44] N. Akhmediev, A. Ankiewicz, M. Taki, Waves That Appear from Nowhere and Disappear without a Trace, *Phys. Lett.* **A373**(6), 675678, (2009); N. Akhmediev, A. Ankiewicz, J. M. Soto-Crespo, Rogue Waves and Rational Solutions of the Nonlinear Schrdinger Equation, Phys. Rev. **E80**(2), 026601, (2009)

[45] D.J. Griffiths, *Introduction to Quantum Mechanics* (2nd ed.), Pearson Educ. Int., (2005)

[46] B. Thaller, *Visual Quantum Mechanics,* Springer, New York, (2000)

In: The Stock Market
Editor: Allison S. Wetherby
ISBN 978-1-61122-545-7
© 2011 Nova Science Publishers, Inc.

Chapter 7

RECONSIDERING STOCK RETURNS AND EQUITY MUTUAL FUND FLOWS IN THE U.S. STOCK MARKET: A MACRO APPROACH

Heung-Joo Cha[1] *and Jaebeom Kim*[2,*]
[1]Department of Business Administration, University of Redlands, CA, USA
[2]Department of Economics, Oklahoma State Unversity, USA

Abstract

We study dynamic and causal relations between stock returns and aggregate equity mutual fund flows in the U.S. stock market. More specifically, Granger (1969) and Sims (1972) causality tests and an ECM indicate that there is unidirectional causality from stock returns to mutual fund flows. Furthermore, if there is a deviation from long-run equilibrium, the stock returns force the deviation to go toward the long-run equilibrium. Thus, it is likely that stock returns lead mutual fund flows and appear to be the most important element explaining fund flows in the U.S. financial market.

Keywords: Equity mutual fund flows; stock returns; causality.

JEL Classification: G11

1. Introduction

The main purpose of this paper is to study dynamics and the possibility of a causality between stock returns and aggregate equity mutual fund flows in the U.S. stock market. There is an intense debate over whether mutual fund flows have any relevance at all to the market's direction. The degree to which prior stock market returns influence investor demand for mutual fund shares and to what extent this demand drives returns have important implications for the stability of the U.S. stock market. Substantial efforts have been made

---

*E-mail address: jb.kim@okstate.edu. Tel.: 405.744.7359. Fax: 405.744.5180. Corresponding Author. We thank seminar participants at Multinational Finance Association Conference in the UK and the SEA conference for their helpful comments and discussions. We also thank Ms. Bev Dunham for her ready assistant. All remaining errors are our own.

to detect the relationships explained by stock prices and mutual fund flows. However, empirical evidence on the issue has not been clear.

In analyzing the relations between stock returns and mutual fund flows, studies have mainly employed two different approaches, a micro approach and a macro approach.[1] The former focuses attention on how mutual funds flows are analyzed on individual bases. The empirical literature at the individual level including Grinblatt et al. (1995) and Sirri and Tufano (1998) shows that the flow of funds is a function of past performance, so that investors tend to move cash into the funds that had the highest returns in the preceding years. The macro approach, on the other hand, studies large scale movements of money into and out of the market without regard to which fund it goes into or comes from. Hence, the research at the macro level has centered on the relationship between stock market returns and aggregate mutual fund flows.

Warther (1995) pioneers study at the macro level and finds some evidence for the price pressure hypothesis and for a positive relation between flows and subsequent returns but a negative relation between returns and subsequent flows. His results support the popular belief that fund inflows and returns are positively related. The aggregate fund literature including Edelen and Warner (2001), Goetzmann and Massa (2003), Boyer and Zheng (2004) and Braverman, Kandel, and Wohl (2005) indicates that in general there exits a high positive correlation between aggregate mutual fund flows and stock market returns. Further, the positive correlation between aggregate mutual fund flows and stock returns are supported by theoretical approaches such as the price pressure theory, the information revelation hypothesis, and investor's sentiment.[2]

However, it is not clear whether the stock market is driven by aggregate mutual fund flows due to following reasons. First, the high positive correlation between stock returns and aggregate equity mutual fund flows does not necessarily imply that the former causes the latter and vice versa because there might be other possible reasons for the causal relationship[3] Furthermore, prior research that has established the positive relation on stock returns and mutual fund flows employs overly simple regression approaches such as least squares methodologies with logged differenced or normalized time series data, which ignores the unit root or permanent component of the data and therefore avoids the complications related to unit roots and spurious regressions. Since business cycle activity comprises both temporary and permanent components, which are often related with each other, the removal of the permanent component loses valuable long term information concerning the evolvement of short-term movements.

This study provides a different perspective on the interactions in stock market by pro-

---

[1] Some recent papers argue that investor sentiments are important factors in overall market movements. See Goetzmann, Massa, and Rouwenhorst (2000), Goetzmann and Massa (2003), Indro (2004), and Frazzini and Lamont (2005) for details.

[2] Price pressure theory implies that when inflows in mutual funds increase, this stimulates a demand to hold stocks, and causes stock prices to go up. Information revelation hypothesis shows that based on the assumption that the market is to react to available information instead of responding to the fund flows, well-informed investors's purchases may signal to other less-informed investors to buy mutual fund, thus cause stock prices to rise. Further, investor sentiment is also considered as one of important factor affecting mutual fund market.

[3] See Potter and Schneeweis (1998), Remolona, Kleiman, and Gruenstein (1997), and Fortune (1998) for details.

viding dynamic and causal relationships between stock returns and aggregate mutual fund flows. To examine the dynamic and causal relations, we employ Park's (1992) Canonical Cointegration Regression (CCR), an Error Correction Model (ECM), and two causality tests proposed by Granger (1969) and Sims (1972). Our empirical evidence indicates that there is unidirectional causality between stock returns and mutual fund flows, implying that prior changes in stock returns cause changes in equity fund flows. The most significant factor explaining equity mutual fund flows in our study appears to be stock market performance in the U.S. financial market.

2.   Econometric Methodologies

To test a long run relationship and to estimate a cointegrating vector between the stock prices and equity mutual fund flows, we employ Park's (1992) CCR. Consider a cointegrated system where y_t and X_t are difference stationary. To obtain an asymptotically efficient OLS estimator, Park suggests a transformed model:

$$y_t^* = y_t + \Pi_y' w_t \tag{1}$$

$$X_t^* = X_t + \Pi_x' w_t. \tag{2}$$

The idea of CCR is to choose Π_y and Π_x, so that the OLS estimator is asymptotically efficient when y_t^* is regressed on X_t^*. The $H(p, q)$ tests basically apply Park's $G(p, q)$ tests to CCR residuals for the null of stationarity to OLS regressions. [4] The $H(p, q)$ statistic converges in distribution to a χ_{p-q}^2 random variable under the null hypothesis of cointegration. In particular, the $H(0, 1)$ statistic tests the deterministic cointegrating restriction and the $H(1, q)$ statistic tests stochastic cointegration restriction. [5]

For short-run dynamics between the fund flows and the returns based on the Granger representation theorem (Engle and Granger (1987)), we consider an ECM under the assumption that $Z_t = Y_t - X_t'\gamma$ is stationary:

$$\Delta Y_t = \mu_{0i} + \lambda_{0i}\widehat{Z}_{t-1} + \sum_{j=1}^{k} \gamma_{1j}\Delta X_{t-j} + \sum_{j=1}^{k} \gamma_{2j}\Delta Y_{t-j} + u_{1t} \tag{3}$$

$$\Delta X_t = \mu_{1i} + \lambda_{1i}\widehat{Z}_{t-1} + \sum_{j=1}^{k} \phi_{1j}\Delta X_{t-j} + \sum_{j=1}^{k} \phi_{2j}\Delta Y_{t-j} + u_{2t} \tag{4}$$

Equations (3) and (4) imply that stock returns and net cash flows are cointegrated with the cointegrating vector $(1, -\gamma)$. This two equation system assumes that the long run relationship between the two variables should be unique, but the short run relationship may vary according to government policies, regulations, transaction costs, and the like. The point estimates of λ have important economic contents. First, the stationarity requires λ_{0i}

---

[4]See Park (1990) for more explanation.

[5]One reason for using CCR is that Monte Carlo simulations in Park and Ogaki (1991) have shown that the CCR estimators have better small sample properties in terms of mean squared error than Johansen's (1988) Maximum Likelihood (ML) estimators when the sample size is small.

$\leq 0$and $\lambda_{1i} \geq 0$. Second, the weak exogeneity of X_t with respect to the long run parameters requires $\lambda_{1i} = 0$, so the deviation from the long run equilibrium, $\widehat{Z}_t$, does not affect X_t. Third, the point estimates of λ_{0i} measure the speed of adjustment to the long run equilibrium. The larger the absolute value of λ_{0i}, the faster is the convergence of the deviation toward the long-run equilibrium.

For the hypothesis of causal relationships between stock returns and aggregate mutual fund flows we adopt the notion of Granger causality (1969). Granger formally defines his linear causality in the means of two jointly covariance stationary series L and F conditional on the information set. According to Granger, L causes F if, and only if, the variance of the error in forecasting F using the information in L, together with all the other relevant information, is less than the variance of the error in forecasting F without the knowledge of L. Thus, L causes F if

$$\sigma^2(F_t|F_{t-j}, L_{t-j}) < \sigma^2(F_t|F_{t-j}) \tag{5}$$

where σ^2 is the variance of the error in forecasting F. Various researchers have used one of the two asymptotically equivalent test procedures attributed to Granger (1969) and Sims (1972) for testing the null hypothesis of unidirectional causality against the alternative of feedback. These procedures test for the additional contribution made by the hypothesized causal variable in explaining the variability in the effect variable using least square methodologies. The Granger (1969) causality test is basically a test of the predictability of time-series models and means that if X_t Granger-causes Y_t, then X_t is a useful predictor of Y_t, given the other variables in the regression of the forms in equations (3) and (4). The null hypothesis implies that the regressors have no predictive content for Y_t beyond that contained in the other regressors, and the test of this null hypothesis is called the Granger causality test. On the other hand, Sims'(1972) procedure is to run a regression of the form:

$$Y_t = \delta_0 + \sum_{i=-m}^{m} \theta_i X_{t-i} + \eta_t \tag{6}$$

Sims proved that in the distributed lag regression, $\theta_i = 0$ for all $i < 0$ if, and only if, Y fails to Granger cause X.

3. Empirical Results

This study employs data from the Investment Company Institute (ICI) on aggregate monthly stock mutual fund flows from 1984:1 to 2006:12.[6] The data is divided into 21 categories by the investment objective of the funds. Within each group, cash flows are further broken down into total sales, redemptions, exchange sales, and exchange redemptions. Total sales and redemptions represent outside flows, while exchange sales and exchange redemptions represent flows among funds within a fund family. Our interest is in tracking the net flows of mutual fund money into different sectors of the market. Thus, we compute net flows (net sales) as total sales minus redemptions, plus exchange sales minus exchange redemptions.

---

[6]Because mutual funds played a much smaller role in the pre-1984 markets, our attention concentrates on the period beginning January 1984.

**Table 1. Unit Root and Cointegration Tests for Stock Price
and Stock Mutual Fund Flow**

	ADF test $t_{\hat{\rho}=1}$			KPSS test η_μ	
ln(SPI)	-1.704			4.549**	
SCF	-1.787			0.823**	

Y_t	X_t	CCR $\hat{\beta}^{(a)}$	$H(0,1)^{(b)}$	$H(1,2)^{(b)}$	$H(1,3)^{(b)}$	$H(1,4)^{(b)}$
ln(SPI)	SCF	0.0001	80.300	3.148	3.651	4.087
		(0.0000)	(0.0000)	(0.076)	(0.161)	(0.252)
SCF	ln(SPI)	7184.011	2.493	0.017	0.702	4.766
		(995.632)	(0.114)	(0.896)	(0.704)	(0.190)

Note: ** and * represent denote significance at the 5% and 10% levels, respectively. The Critical values for t-statistic with 100 observations are -2.89 and -2.58 for 5% and 10% significance levels, respectively. For KPSS tests, the critical values are 0.463, and 0.347 for 5%, and 10 % levels of significance, respectively. For column (a): numbers in parenthesis are standard errors. For columns (b): numbers in parenthesis are p-values. The H(0,1) statistic tests the deterministic cointegrating restriction and the H(1,q) statistic tests stochastic cointegration. SPI: S&P 500 Index. SCF: Stock mutual fund net cash flow.

The ICI defines larger fund categories as follows: Equity Funds, Bond and Income Funds, and Money Market Funds. Monthly stock price (return) data comes from the Stocks, Bonds, Bills and Inflation Series of Ibbotson and Associates. We use the realized S&P 500 total return index that includes both cash income (dividends or coupons) and capital value changes.

Table 1 shows the results of two unit root tests, ADF and KPSS tests, [7] and of cointegration test. The ADF test fails to reject the null hypothesis of unit roots and the KPSS test rejects the null of stationarity for the series of the S&P 500 return index and mutual fund flows. According to the results, it is likely that the stock prices and fund flows are integrated of order one, I(1). As seen from the results based on the CCR, the deterministic and stochastic cointegrating restrictions are not rejected at the 5% significance level when fund flows are used as dependent variables, implying that there is a positive long run relationship between stock returns and mutual fund flows and the two variables move together in the long run. [8]

Next, we employ the ECM and its results are presented in Table 2. The last two columns contain the F-statistics that test for long-term and short-term relations between stock returns and fund flows. We have statistically significant coefficients for $\hat{\lambda}_0$, which indicates a long-term relation between stock returns and mutual fund flows. This result is interesting because it also implies that if there is a deviation from long-run equilibrium, the stock

---

[7]For details, see appendix.
[8]This is the test for the null of cointegration.

Table 2. ECM Results

$$\Delta Y_t = \mu_{0i} + \lambda_{0i}\widehat{Z}_{t-1} + \sum_{j=1}^{n} \gamma_{1j}\Delta X_{t-j} + \sum_{j=1}^{n} \gamma_{2j}\Delta Y_{t-j} + u_{1t}$$
$$\Delta X_t = \mu_{1i} + \lambda_{1i}\widehat{Z}_{t-1} + \sum_{j=1}^{k} \phi_{1j}\Delta X_{t-j} + \sum_{j=1}^{k} \phi_{2j}\Delta Y_{t-j} + u_{2t}$$

	$\widehat{\lambda}^{(a)}$	Long term effect[b]	Short term effect[b]
ln(SPI)	-0.009	4.143	3.584
	(0.004)	(0.042)	(0.611)
SCF	706.123	14.707	10.810
	(939.839)	(0.000)	(0.055)

Note: For column (a): numbers in parenthesis are standard errors. For columns (b): numbers in parenthesis are p-values. SPI is S&P 500 Index and SCF is stock mutual fund net cash flow.

returns force the deviation to go toward the long-run equilibrium. The fund flows are weakly exogenous because $\lambda_{1i} = 0$ in the second equation of the system, so the fund flows are not likely to respond to eliminate this deviation. This result indicates that the mutual fund flows do not affect stock returns. Furthermore, the hypothesis of neither the long-term nor short-term relation between the two variables is rejected at the 5% level.

Based on the Granger and Sims causality tests presented in Table 3, we reject the null hypothesis, which implies stock returns lead fund flows. [9] The positive causality from stock returns to fund flows indicates that changes in the past and current returns cause changes in the current and next returns, resulting in changes in the current and next equity fund flows in the same direction. When stock returns are used as dependent variables for the Granger causality test, the stock market may not be affected by monthly cash flows in the prior month because of the insignificant point estimates of $\widehat{\alpha}_1$ at the 5% level. On the other hand, as mutual fund flows are used as dependent variables, the point estimates of $\widehat{\alpha}_1$ are positive and statistically significant at the 5% level, implying that the net cash flows into the stock markets are affected by the returns in the previous month. This evidence is different from Warther (1995) in that he finds that flows are negatively related to past returns. Moreover, as mutual fund flows are used as the dependent variables, we have a significant positive coefficient for the first lag, which is consistent with a feedback trader hypothesis. This evidence also contrasts with Warther (1995) who finds no evidence for the hypothesis. The Granger and Sims causality tests provides strong evidence that stock returns causes aggregate equity fund flows. These findings are interesting because as stock market performance increases, investors are likely to react to the level of the stock market and are encouraged to invest more in the market.

---

[9] We test the causality hypothesis that stock returns (equity fund flows) do not lead fund flows (stock returns).

Table 3. Granger and Sims Causality Tests

Granger Causality Test

$$\Delta Y_t = \alpha_0 + \sum_{i=1}^{k} \alpha_i \Delta X_{t-i} + \sum_{j=1}^{k} \beta_j \Delta Y_{t-j} + \xi_t$$

ΔY_t	ΔX_t	α_1	α_2	β_1	β_2	F-Statistic	p-value	$X_t \overset{G.C}{\rightarrow} Y_t$
ln(SPI)	SCF	0.318E-8	0.518E-9	0.943**	0.049	0.526	0.591	NO
SCF	ln(SPI)	3.739E+4**	3.423E+4**	0.344**	0.169**	9.694	0.000	YES

Sims Causality Test

$$\Delta Y_t = \delta_0 + \sum_{i=-m}^{m} \theta_i \Delta X_{t-i} + \eta_t$$

ΔY_t	ΔX_t	θ_1	θ_2	θ_0	θ_{-1}	θ_{-2}	F-Statistic	p-value	$Y_t \overset{G.C}{\rightarrow} X_t$
ln(SPI)	SCF	0.921E-5**	0.155E-4**	0.872E-5**	0.766E-5**	0.126E-4**	3.972	0.018	YES
SCF	ln(SPI)	1.798E+4**	-6.507E+4	7.959E+4**	5662.841	5095.436	0.554	0.574	NO

Note: SPI is S&P 500 Index and SCF is stock mutual fund net cash flow. * and ** denote significance at the 10% and 5% levels, respectively. "Yes (No)" indicates presence (absence) of causality with a p-value of equal or less than 0.05.

4. Conclusion

This paper investigated the possibility of a causality in which stock prices may affect mutual fund flows and vice versa in the U.S. financial market. The empirical findings from the ECM and the Granger and Sims causality tests indicate that the mutual fund flows are weakly exogenous and there exists unidirectional causality from stock returns to mutual fund flows, implying that stock returns Granger cause the fund flows. Even though there is no standard way to interpret the empirical results, our findings from weak exogeneity of the mutual fund flows as well as the positive causality from stock returns to mutual fund flows can be explained by the investor sentiment. Several empirical studies have shown the significance and the profound impact of investor sentiment on U.S. equity market.

Our empirical evidence implies that at the aggregate level, there is evidence that investors move into the stock markets in response to recent returns at monthly frequency. Investors are likely to react to fund performance and to look at the recent performance of the stock market when deciding whether to put their money into the stock market. This type of behavior seems to be rational for those who try to maximize their individual returns; in addition, this investment strategy disciplines fund managers and aligns their interests with those of investors as well. Our empirical findings are not likely to support the popular notion of mutual fund flows as a driving force behind rallies in security markets. The most important element explaining equity mutual fund flows seems to be stock market performance in the U.S. financial market.

5. Appendix

5.1. Unit Root Tests

To examine the dynamic relationship between stock prices and aggregate mutual fund flows, we employ two types of unit root tests. They are the ADF test and the KPSS test. The standard test for unit root nonstationarity is the ADF (1979) test. The ADF test is based on the following regression:

$$\Delta X_t = \theta + (\rho - 1)X_{t-1} + \sum_{i=1}^{p} \beta_i \Delta X_{t-i} + u_t \qquad (A1)$$

and the null hypothesis is $(\rho - 1) = 0$, i.e. X_t possesses a unit root. One issue in computing the ADF test is the choice of the maximum lag in equation (A1). An insufficiently small number of lags will result in a test of incorrect size, but too large choice of lags results in a test of lower power. The method used here to decide the maximum lag is the one suggested by Hall's general-to-specific method recommended by Campbell and Perron (1991).[10]

The KPSS test is the test of the null hypothesis of mean stationarity in order to determine whether variables are stationary or integrated. The KPSS test is based on the statistic:

$$\eta(u) = \frac{T^{-2} \sum_{t=1}^{T} S_t^2}{\sigma_i^2} \text{ where } S_t = \sum_{t=1}^{T} v_i, t = 1, ..., T \qquad (A2)$$

---

[10] Starting with a reasonably large value of p (24) and decrease it until the coefficient on the last included lag is significant.

with v_i being a residual, σ^2 a consistent long-run variance estimate of X_t , and T representing the sample size. Kwiatkowski et al. (1992) show that the statistic $\eta(u)$ has a non-standard distribution and critical values have been provided therein. If the calculated value of $\eta(u)$ is large, the null of stationarity for the KPSS test is rejected.

References

Boyer, B., & Zheng, L. (2004). Who moves the market? A study of stock prices and sector cash flows. *Working paper.*

Braverman, O., Kandel, S., & Wohl, A. (2005). The (bad?) timing of mutual fund investors. *Centre for Economic Policy Research Discussion Paper* **5243**.

Campbell, J., & Perron, P. (1991). Pitfalls and opportunities: What macroeconomists should know about unit roots. *NBER Macroeconomics Annual,* 1991, 141-201.

Dickey, D. A., & Fuller, W. A. (1979). Distribution of the estimators for autoregressive time series with a unit root. *Journal of the American Statistical Association,* **74**, 427-431.

Edelen, R., & Warner, J. B. (2001). Aggregate price effects of institutional trading: A study of mutual fund flow and market returns. *Journal of Financial Economics,* **59**, 195-220.

Engle, R. F. & Granger, W. J. (1987). Cointegration and error correction: Representation, estimation and testing. *Econometrica*, **55**, 251-276.

Fant, L. F. (1999). Investment behavior of mutual fund shareholders: The evidence from aggregate fund flows. *Journal of Financial Markets*, **2**, 391-402.

Fortune, P. (1998). Mutual funds, part II: Fund flows and security returns. *New England Economic Review*, January/February, 3-22.

Frazzini, A., & Lamont, O. (2005). Dumb money: Mutual fund flows and the cross-section of stock returns. *NBER Working Paper* **11526**.

Goetzmann, W. N. & Massa, M. (2003). Index funds and stock market growth. *Journal of Business,* **76**, 1-28.

Goetzmann, W. N., Massa, M. & Rouwenhorst, G. (2009).   Behavioral factors in mutual fund flows. *Yale ICF Working paper* No.00-14.

Granger, C. W. (1969).   Investigating causal relations by econometric models and cross-spectral methods. *Econometrica*, **37**, 424-438.

Grinblatt, M., Titman, S., & Wermers, R. (1995). Momentum investment strategies, portfolio performance and herding: A study of mutual fund behavior. *American Economic Review,* **85**, 1088-1105.

Indro, D. (2004). Does mutual fund flow reflect investor sentiment? *Journal of Behavioral Finance,* **5** (2), 105-115.

Ippolito, R. A. (1992). Consumer reaction to measures of poor quality: Evidence from the mutual find industry. *Journal of Law and Economics*, **35**, 45-70.

Kwiatkowski, D., Phillips, P. C. B., Schmidt, P., & Shin, Y. C. (1992). Testing the null hypothesis of stationarity against the alternative of a unit-root - How sure are we that economic time-series have a unit-root. *Journal of Econometrics,* **54** (1-3), 159-178.

Ogaki, M., & Park, J. Y. (1998). A Cointegration approach to estimating preference parameters. *Journal of Econometrics*, **82**, 107-134.

Park, J. Y. (1990). Testing for unit roots and cointegration by variable addition. *Advances in Econometrics Series*, 107-133.

Park, J. Y. (1992). *Canonical cointegrating regressions. Econometrica* , **60**, 119-143.

Park, J. Y., & Ogaki, M. (1991). Seemingly unrelated canonical cointegrating regressions. *RCER Working Papers* **280**, Center for Economic Research.

Potter, M., & Schneeweis, T. (1998). *The relationship between aggregate mutual fund flows and security returns.* Working paper.

Remolona, E., Kleiman, P., & Gruenstein, D. (1997). Market returns and mutual fund flows. *FRBNY Economic Policy Review,* July, 33-52.

Sims, C. A. (1972). Money, income, and causality. *American Economic Review,* **62**, 540-552.

Sirri, E. R., & Tufano, P. (1998). Costly search and mutual fund flows. *Journal of Finance,* **53**, 1589-1622.

Warther, V. A. (1995). Aggregate mutual fund flows and security returns. *Journal of Financial Economics,* **39**, 209-235.

In: The Stock Market
Editor: Allison S. Wetherby

ISBN: 978-1-61122-545-7
© 2011 Nova Science Publishers, Inc.

Chapter 8

REEXAMINING COVARIANCE RISK DYNAMICS IN GLOBAL STOCK MARKETS USING QUANTILE REGRESSION ANALYSIS[*]

Ming-Yuan Leon Li

Department of Accountancy and Graduate Institute of Finance and Banking,
National Cheng Kung University, Taiwan

ABSTRACT

This investigation is one of the first to adopt quantile regression to examine covariance risk dynamics in international stock markets. Feasibility of the proposed model is demonstrated in G7 stock markets. Additionally, two conventional random-coefficient frameworks, including time-varying betas derived from GARCH models and state-varying betas implied by Markov-switching models, are employed and subjected to comparative analysis. The empirical findings of this work are consistent with the following notions. First, several types of beta distortions are demonstrated: the "beta smile" ("beta skew") curve for the Italian, U.S. and U.K. (Canadian, French and German) markets. That is, covariance risk among global stock markets in extremely bull and/or bear market states is significantly higher than that in stable period. Additionally, the Japanese market provides a special case, and its beta estimate at extremely bust state is significantly lower, not higher than that at the middle region. Second, this study hypothesizes two sorts of asset reallocation processes: "stock-to-stock" and "stock-to-bond", and employs them to explain these different types of beta distortions among various markets. Third, the quantile-varying betas are identified as possessing two key advantages. Specifically, the comparison of the system with quantile-varying betas against that with time-varying betas implied by GARCH models provides meaningful implications for correlation-volatility relationship among international stock markets. Furthermore, the quantile-varying beta design in this study releases a simple dual beta setting implied by Markov-switching models of Ramchand and Susmel (1998) and can identify dynamics of asymmetry in betas.

---

[*] A version of this chapter was also published in *Emerging Markets: Identification, New Developments and Investments,* edited by John V. Reynolds, published by Nova Science Publishers, Inc. It was submitted for appropriate modifications in an effort to encourage wider dissemination of research.

JEL classification: G12, G15, C53

Keywords: Quantile regression; beta; ICAPM; GARCH; Markov-switching I. Introduction

This study is one of the first to apply the quantile regression model to examine covariance risk dynamics in global stock markets. Specifically, this investigation sets up an international capital asset pricing model (hereafter, ICAPM) based on consideration of the perspective of international portfolios, and takes both individual country stock index returns and global stock returns as individual asset returns and market portfolio returns, respectively[1]. The ICAPM provides investors with a theoretical price for the stock assets of each country and the beta coefficient of each country stock market derived from the ICAPM represents the corresponding covariance risk in relation to the global market[2]. Furthermore, two conventional random-coefficient frameworks are employed; including time-varying betas derived from GARCH models and state-varying betas implied by Markov-switching models, and a comparative analysis is presented[3].

The research direction of covariance risk dynamics in international stock markets has generated considerable interest, as demonstrated by Mark (1998), Harvey (1991), Ferson and Harvey (1993), Bekaert and Harvey (1995), Dumas and Solnik (1995), De Santis and Gerard (1997). All these studies invariably established a framework in which time-varying betas are estimated using the time-varying conditional variances and covriances derived from multivariate ARCH/GARCH specifications as inputs[4]. Furthermore, Bhardwaj and Brooks (1993), Braun et al. (1995), Pettengill et al. (1995), Fletcher (2000) and Gregory and Johan (2002) introduced asymmetry dynamics into beta estimations. Additionally, Ramchand and Susmel (1998) and Bekaert and Harvey (1995) proposed an ICAPM system that models beta as state dependent. Specifically, Ramchand and Susmel (1998) adopted the Markov-switching ARCH (SWARCH) model to identify high and low volatility states and allowed beta parameters to vary according to phase of market state[5]. Moreover, Bekaert and Harvey (1995) devised a model linking two-state beta to degree of emerging market integration with world stock markets.

This investigation departs from previous related studies in the way beta is modeled and proposes a new approach to questions regarding the dynamics of beta coefficients. Specifically, this work is one of the first to examine nonlinearity in the systematic risk-return performance of international stock markets using quantile regression. Constant-coefficient regression models have been extensively applied in statistics. Various random-coefficient models have also emerged as viable competitors particularly fields of application. One variant of the latter class of models, though perhaps not immediately recognizable as such, is the

---

[1] Markowitz (1952) used the mean-variance model and capital market line (CML) to establish an internationally efficient portfolio, and demonstrated the advantages of international investing. Furthermore, Sharp (1964), Lintner (1965a, 1965b) and Mossin (1966) followed Markowitz (1952) to establish a capital asset pricing model (CAPM). In the market equilibrium, the expected returns of individual securities are a linear function of market portfolio returns and beta.

[2] The ICAPM model only considers the influence of systematic risk on individual country asset returns and assumes investors can achieve an effectively diversified portfolio that completely eliminates individual asset specific risk. All that remains that cannot be eliminated by diversification is thus market risk, and a risk premium can only be obtained via market risk.

[3] The Engle's (1982) ARCH (auto-regressive conditional heteroskedasticity) or Bollerslev's (1986) are the most commonly used methods to characterize the volatility of stock returns.

[4] Refer to Bollerslev et al. (1992), Mark (1988) and Ng (1991) for related discussions.

[5] See Hamilton (1989), Cai (1994) and Hamilton and Susmel (1994) for relevant discussions of SWARCH models.

quantile regression model. This investigation established a quantile model in which the beta coefficients can be expressed as a monotone function of a single, scalar random variable. The model can capture systematic influences of conditioning variables on the location, scale, and shape of the conditional distribution of the response and thus constitutes a significant extension of the beta coefficient model in which the effects of conditioning are limited to a location shift.

The key feature of quantile regression models is examining the entire distribution of stock returns rather than a single measure of their central tendency. Consequently, quantile systems can assess the relative magnitude of beta coefficients at different points of stock return distribution. Restated, the quantile framework permits identification of differences in the impacts of market returns on individual stock returns for different return quantiles.

One key question asked by this study is whether the beta coefficient is consistent with different levels of return quantiles. To answer this question, the parameterization in the model presented here allows domestic stock returns to depend on a world factor such that the nature of dependence is based on stock return quantile variability. In brief, the beta in the proposed model is modeled as depending on return qantile. Particularly, this investigation permits the proportionality factor or beta to depend on return quantile states, and generates a different beta for every return quantil state. In this sense the parameterization of this study captures a non-linear relationship between domestic and global stock returns, in which the determining factor is the return quantile of local returns.

The remainder of this paper is organized as follows: Section 2 reviews the underlying models used. Section 3 then presents the empirical results and finally Section 4 presents conclusions.

2. MODEL SPECIFICATION

2.1 ICAPM wth Single Beta

The ICAPM is based on the realization that the appropriate risk premium for a country asset is determined by its contribution to the risk of investors' international portfolios. Furthermore, nonsystematic risk can be reduced to an arbitrarily low level through diversification, and thus investors do not require a risk premium to compensate for bearing nonsystematic risk and instead require compensation only for bearing systematic risk, which cannot be diversified. Additionally, the contribution of individual country asset to the risk of a large diversified international portfolio depends entirely on the systematic risk of the country asset as measured by its beta. Comparing the ratio of risk premium to systematic risk for the international portfolio, which has a beta of 1.0, with the corresponding ratio for the stock assets of the i-th country, it can be concluded that:

$$E(R_i) - R_f(R_w - R_f) = \beta_i 1 \tag{1}$$

where R_i denotes the stock index returns of the i-th country, $E(R_i)$ is R_i's mean return, R_f is the risk-free asset return and R_w is the global stock market return[6]. Rearranging the relationships in the ICAPM's expected return-beta relationship:

$$E(R_i) - R_f = \beta_i \times (R_w - R_f) \qquad (2)$$

In words, the rate of return on the i-th country's stock assets exceeds the risk-free rate by a risk premium equal to the systematic risk measure of the assets, namely β_i, times the risk premimum of the global market portfolio. Furthermore, the ICAPM explains the relationship between individual country's expected returns and world market returns when investors create an effectively diversified portfolio. In the traditional one-single β model above, the β_i coefficient represents the regression coefficient in the following linear regression setting:

$$R_{i,t}^{\bullet} = \alpha_i + \beta_i \times R_{w,t}^{\bullet} + e_{i,t} \qquad (3)$$

where $R_{i,t}^{\bullet}$ and $R_{w,t}^{\bullet}$ denote the excess returns of the i-th country's stock index and the global stock index at time t, respectively. Apparently, the β_i parameter measures co-movement size between the i-th individual market and the world market. A key limitation in Equ. 3: the beta, β_i is a constant for the whole sample. Furthermore, by using ordinary least squares (OLS), the estimators for α_i and β_i are obtained from:

$$\min \sum 1 \times (e_{i,t})^2 = \min \sum 1 \times (R_{i,t}^{\bullet} - \alpha_i - \beta_i \times R_{w,t}^{\bullet})^2 \quad tt \qquad (4)$$

The sum of the absolute error can also be minimized to yield the estimates of least absolute deviations (hereafter LAD):

$$\min \sum 1 \times | e_{i,t} | = \min \sum 1 \times | R_{i,t}^{\bullet} - \alpha_i - \beta_i \times R_{w,t}^{\bullet} | \qquad (5)$$
tt

Notably, the unity term in Eqs. 4 and 5 represents each of the error term square, $e_{i,t}^2$ and the absolute error term, $|e_{i,t}|$ is averaged by equal weight and thus $(\alpha_i + \beta_i \times R_{w,t}^{\bullet})$ represents the conditional mean and the conditional median functions in the optimization technique of OLS and LAD, respectively. Restated, a key limitation of the OLS and LAD estimates is that they provide only a single measure of beta, and consider the central tendency of stock return distribution while failing to picture tail behaviors.

2.2 ICAPM with Quantile-Varying Betas

This investigation states that traditional optimization techniques, including OLS and LAD, suffer from ignoring distinctive behaviors in the tail regions of return distributions, and relationships between individual and world stock market returns change in the tail regions. To

---

[6] Market return denotes the return of a representative benchmark portfolio.

characterize stock return tail behaviors, this study employs quantile regression to establish an ICAPM using dynamic beta coefficients. This study uses the quantile regression technique established by Koenker and Basset (1978) to examine the dynamics of the relationship between individual and world returns. Particularly, this work demonstrates that, for various countries, the unconditional version of the ICAPM with a constant proportionality factor is misspecified.

Same with Eq. 3, $R_{i,t}^{*}$ and $R_{w,t}^{*}$, t=1, 2, 3,...T denote the excess returns of the i-th country's stock index and the world stock index, respectively. Assuming that the θ-th conditional quantile of $R_{i,t}^{*}$ is liner in $R_{w,t}^{*}$, the conditional quantile regression model is presented as follows:

$$R_{i,t}^{*} = \alpha_{i,\theta} + \beta_{i,\theta} \times R_{w,t}^{*} + u_{i,\theta,t} \tag{6}$$

$$Quant_{\theta}(R_{i,t}^{*}$$

$$R_{w,t}^{*}) \equiv \inf \left\{ R_{i} : F_{t}(R_{i} R_{w}) \theta \right\} = \alpha_{i,\theta} + \beta_{i,\theta} \times R_{w,t} \tag{7}$$

$$R_{w,t}^{*}) = 0 \tag{8}$$

$$Quant_{\theta}(u_{i,\theta,t}^{*}$$

where $Quant_{\theta}(R_{i,t}^{*} R_{w,t}^{*})$ denotes the θ-th conditional quantile of $R_{i,t}^{*}$ on the regressor vector $R_{w,t}^{*}$; $\alpha_{i,\theta}$and $\beta_{i,\theta}$ are two parameters to be estimated for different values of θ in (0,1); $u_{i,\theta,t}$ is the error term assumed to be continuously differentiable c.d.f. (cumulative density function) of F $(\cdot R^{*})$ and a density function f $(\cdot R_{w}^{*})$. The $u_{i,\theta w}$ $u_{i,\theta}$ value $F_{t}(.|R_{w}^{*})$ denotes the conditional distribution of R_{i} conditional on R_{w}^{*}. Varying the value of θ from 0 to 1 reveals the entire distribution of R_{i} conditional on R_{w}^{*}.

The estimators for $\alpha_{i,\theta}$ and $\beta_{i,\theta}$ are obtained from:

$$\min \sum_{t:u_{i,\theta,t}>0} \theta \times |u_{i,\theta,t}| + \sum_{t:u_{i,\theta,t}<0} (1-\theta) \times |u_{i,\theta,t}|$$

$$= \min \sum_{t:R_{i,t}^{*}-\alpha_{i},\theta-\beta_{i},\theta \times R_{W}^{*},t>0} \theta \times |R_{i,t}^{*} - \alpha_{i,\theta} - \beta_{i,\theta} \times R_{w,t}^{*}| \tag{9}$$

$$+ \sum_{t:R_{i,t}^{*}-\alpha_{i},\theta-\beta_{i},\theta \times R_{w,t}<0} (1-\theta) \times |R_{i,t}^{*} - \alpha_{i,\theta} - \beta_{i,\theta} \times R_{w,t}^{*}|$$

Notably, the estimators do not have an explicit form, but the resulting minimization problem can be solved by liner programming techniques[7]. Restated, one feature of quantile regression is the ability to trace the entire distribution of dependent variable conditional on the independent variable. Comparing Eq. 9 with Eqs. 4 and 5 reveals a key feature of quantile

---

[7] See Koenker (2000) and Koenker and Hallock (2001) for the related discussions.

regression technique: the estimators for $\alpha_{i,\theta}$ and $\beta_{i,\theta}$ vary with θ. By varying the value of θ from 0 to 1, one then can evaluate co-movement patterns between the individual and world stock markets at various levels of return quantiles and trace the entire distribution of R_i^* conditional on R_w^*.

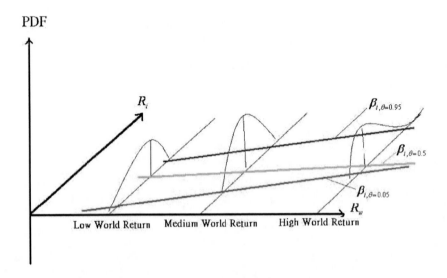

Figure 1. The perspective of quantile-varying betas (a) Canada (b) France

Fig. 1 illustrates the perspective of quantile-varying beta under the heterogeneous distribution of R_i^* conditional on R_w^*. Specially, three possible heterogeneous conditional distributions are defined at Fig. 1. Furthermore, the present results show that the median value of EWW returns is 0.004% and approximately approaches to zero and thus this study defines high (low) world market return as highly positive (negative) return and medium world market return as zero return. Additionally, this study hypothesizes that global stock markets invariably rise and fall together particularly during periods of volatility. Consequently, this investigation denotes that the conditional distribution of R_i^* on R_w^* would be highly right (left) skewed under high (low) world market returns. In other words, owing to remarkable co-movement process among global stock markets during volatile periods, this study generalizes that individual stock market has much higher possibility to exhibit positive (negative) return performances when global stock markets rise (decline) highly.

Restated, the conventional OLS and LAD models average error terms with equal loading (See Equs. 4 and 5) and thus capture the central tendency of stock return distribution. Additionally, the LAD beta estimate is a special case of quantile-varying betas with the restriction θ =0.5, namely $\beta_{i,\theta=0.5}$ and represents the line through the mid points of the conditional distributions. Apparently, the line with $\beta_{i,\theta=0.5}$ provide only a single measure of beta, considering the central tendency of the conditional distribution of individual stock market returns while failing to picture the tail behaviors.

This study thus adopts quantile regression models to capture the beta dynamics at the tail regions. The key advantage of quantile regression models lies in tracing the entire distribution of the dependent variable conditional on the independent variable via various loadings on positive and negative error terms. Specifically, to picture the beta estimate at quantile 0.95, namely $\beta_{i,\theta=0.95}$, the quantile regression model weighs positive (negative) error terms using the loading of 0.95 (0.05) and thus graphs the line in which the points of 0.95 percentile of R_i^* conditional on R_w^* go through (See Fig. 1). Notably, the results of this investigation indicate that that the line with $\beta_{i,\theta}$ given $\theta=0.5$ is considerably different with the line with $\beta_{i,\theta}$ given $\theta=0.95$ or $\theta=0.05$.

Intuitively, to analyze the beta dynamics across various return quantiles, criteria such as the magnitude of stock returns can be applied to segment the sample into various subsets before implementing traditional optimization techniques such as OLS and LAD to fit the subsets. For example, return observations can be separated using the criterion of positive/negative returns and thus beta dynamics for boom and bust markets can be investigated separately based on the OLS and LAD methods. However, this analytical framework is based on an unconditional distribution of return samples. Furthermore, this study denotes that this form of "sample truncation" may yield invalid results. Heckman (1979) demonstrated that such methods frequently display sample selection bias.

Last but not the least; the design matrix bootstrap method is employed to estimate standard errors for the coefficients in quantile regression[8]. In a Monte Carlo study, Buchinsky (1995) first recommended bootstrap methods for relatively small samples because the methods are robust to changes in bootstrap sample size relative to the data sample size[9]. Additionally, the percentile method proposed by Koenker and Hallock (2001) could be used to construct confidence intervals for each parameter in β_θ, where the intervals are computed from the empirical distribution of the sample of the bootstrapped estimates[10]. Notably, in comparison with standard asymptotic confidence intervals, the bootstrap percentile intervals do not generally by symmetric around the underlying parameter estimate[11]. These bootstrap procedures can be extended to deal with joint distribution of various quantile regression estimators, which allows equality of slope parameters to be tested across various quantiles[12].

2.3 ICAPM with Time-varying Betas

The research direction of dynamic beta coefficient has generated considerable interest. As is well known, the establishment of a beta coefficient depends heavily on two key variables: covariance between individual, market returns and their variances. Prior studies invariably established frameworks with dynamic beta coefficient are estimated using as input the time-varying variances and covariances derived from ARCH or GARCH Models.

Let $R_{i,t}^*$ and $R_{w,t}^*$, t=1, 2, 3,...T, to be the excess returns of the i-th country's stock index and the world stock index, respectively. The bivariate GARCH model used in this study is specified as follows:

---

[8] As is well known, two approaches are generally used to estimate the covariance matrix of the regression parameter vector. The first derives the asymptotic standard error of the estimator while the second uses bootstrap methods to compute these standard errors and construct confidence intervals.

[9] The matrix bootstrap method is valid under many forms of heterogeneity. Specifically, the bootstrap matrix performs very well even when the errors are homoskedastic.

[10] See Buchinsky (1998) for a detailed discussion of the percentile method.

[11] It is useful when the true sampling distribution is not symmetric.

[12] See Koenker and Hallock (2001) for a related discussion.

$$R_{i,t}^{\cdot} = \varphi_{i,0} + \sum_{l=1}^{l=p} \varphi_{i,l} R_{i,t-l}^{\cdot} + e_{i,t} \tag{10}$$

$$R_{w,t}^{\cdot} = \varphi_{w,0} + \sum_{l=1}^{l=p} \varphi_{w,l} R_{w,t-l}^{\cdot} + e_{w,t} \tag{11}$$

$$e_t | \psi_{t-1} = \begin{bmatrix} e_{i,t} \\ e_{w,t} \end{bmatrix} | \psi_{t-1} \sim BN(0, H_t) \tag{12}$$

$$H_t = \begin{bmatrix} h_t^i & h_t^{i,w} \\ h_t^{i,w} & h_t^w \end{bmatrix} \tag{13}$$

where $e_{i,t}$ and $e_{w,t}$ are residuals at time t, ψ_{t-1} refers to the information available at time t-1, BN denotes the bivariate normal distribution, and H_t is a time-varying 2x2 positive definite conditional variance-covariance matrix, which is specified in the following equations:

$$h_t^i = \eta_{i,0} + \sum_{m=1}^{rs} \eta_{i,t-m} (e_{i,t-m})^2 + \sum_{n=1}^{rs} \lambda_{i,t-n} h_{t-n}^i \tag{14}$$

$$h_t^w = \eta_{w,0} + \sum_{m=1}^{rs} \eta_{w,t-m} (e_{w,t-m})^2 + \sum_{n=1}^{rs} \lambda_{w,t-n} h_{t-n}^w \tag{15}$$

$$h_t^{i,w} = \rho \times (h_t^i \cdot h_t^w)^{1/2} \tag{16}$$

where h_t^i and h_t^w are conditional variances of individual and world market returns, respectively; $h_t^{i,w}$ and ρ are conditional covariance and correlation coefficient between individual and world market returns. Furthermore, the time-varying beta coefficient by GARCH model is then[13]:

$$\beta_{i,t}^{i,w} = \frac{h_t^{i,w}}{h_t^w} \tag{17}$$

In the bivariate GARCH model, this study sets the order of auto-regression for the individual and world market returns as unity, namely p=1 and a GARCH (1, 1) setting with r=1 and s=1 is designed to capture the variance dynamics of stock returns[14].

Notably, the bivariate GARCH model suffers two limitations. First, one key assumption of ARCH/GARCH family models is that, the variance on one day is a function of the variance on the previous day. However, while estimating stock return series, numerous studies have pointed out that ARCH/GARCH models could not well control structure changes. Specifically, Diebold (1986) and Lamoreux and Lastrapes (1990) argued that the usual high persistence found in ARCH/GARCH models is due to the presence of structural breaks. Nelson (1991) and Engle and Mustafa (1992) showed that ARCH/GARCH models didn't able to account for events like the Crash of 1987. Secondly, although the GARCH model

---

[13] See Mark (1988) and Ng (1991) for the related discussions. Moreover, Braun et al. (1995) further considered asymmetric effect of negative news on beta; however, they found no evidence for this particular time-variation of beta.

[14] As is well known, the GARCH (1, 1) model with r=1 and s=1 is the most common setting for picturing stock return variance dynamics.

employs a time-varying framework to capture the variance/covariance dynamics of individual and world market returns and then establish a time-varying beta; however the time-varying beta derived from GARCH model fails to provide economic and financial implications of why the beta or covariance risk changes over time.

2.4 ICAPM with State-Varying Betas

Owing to ARCH/GARCH models failing to capture structural changes during estimation periods, Ramchand and Susmel (1998) established a system with sate-varying betas by using Markov-switching techniques. Specifically, they adopted a switching ARCH (SWARCH) model to identify two market volatility states: high and low volatility states and allowed beta parameters to vary according to the phase of market state. They showed that beta in ICAPM is linked to the volatility regime of the underlying stock returns.

Let $R_{i,t}$ and $R_{w,t}^{\cdot}$, t=1, 2, 3,...T, to be the excess returns of the i-th country's stock index and the world stock index, respectively. The system with state-varying betas used in this study is specified as follows:

$$R_{i,t}^{\cdot} = \alpha_i + \beta_{i,s_t} \cdot R_{w,t}^{\cdot} + e_{i,t} \tag{18}$$

$$e_{i,t} = \sqrt{g_{s_t}} \; g_{s_t} u_{i,t} \tag{19}$$

$$u_{i,t} = \sqrt{h_t^i} \; h_t^i v_t \tag{20}$$

$$h_t^i = \pi_{i,0} + \pi_{i,1} u_{i,t-1}^2 + \pi_{i,2} u_{i,t-2}^2 + ... + \pi_{i,m} u_{i,t-m}^2, \tag{21}$$

where v_t is a Guassian distribution with unit standard error, s_t is an unobservable state variable with possible values: 1, 2,..., k. For the setting with two volatility states, namely $s_t=1$ or 2, the transition probabilities for state variables are presented as follows:

$$p(s_t=1| s_{t-1} = 1) = p_{11}, \; p(s_t=2| s_{t-1} = 1) = p_{12} \tag{22}$$
$$p(s_t=2| s_{t-1} = 2) = p_{22}, \; p(s_t=1| s_{t-1} = 2) = p_{21}$$

where p11+p12=p21+p22=1 and 1 > pij > 0, for i (j)=1 or 2. Notably, $u_{i,t}$ is a standard ARCH (m) setting. Moreover, when st=1 (st=2), ei,t equals ui,t multiplied by $\sqrt{g_1}$ g_1).

Without losing the generalization principle, this study sets up g1 =1. This $(\sqrt{g_2}$ means that the volatility of state II is g2 times state I. If the g2 estimate is significantly greater than unity, then we could conclude state I (II) as the low (high) volatility state.

For capturing beta dynamics among global stock markets, this study follows with Ramchand and Susmel (1998) to establish the setting in which beta parameter varies according to the phase of the volatility regime. Specifically, two volatility regimes are defined in the above setting: (1) regime I or the low volatility regime (namely st=1), the beta parameter of the i-th individual stock market is $\beta_{i,1}$, while (2) regime II or the high volatility regime (namely $s_t=2$), the beta parameter is $\beta_{i,2}$.

In the estimation processes of the system with state-varying betas, this paper sets the number of orders in ARCH to be two, namely, $m=2$. Furthermore, we use OPTIMUM, a package program from GAUSS, and the built-in BFGS algebra to get the negative minimum likelihood function.

3. EMPIRICAL RESULTS

3.1 Data

This investigation uses weekly (Wednesday to Wednesday) US dollar stock returns for G7 equity markets compiled by Morgan Stanley Capital International Perspective. The country indices comprise at least 80% of the stock market capitalization of each country. To concert returns to excess returns, the weekly Eurodollar deposit rate is subtracted from the raw returns. The data cover the period January 1993 through the last week of August 2004, and include 608 observations. All the stock prices are stated in dollar terms.

Undeniably, several alternative measures exist for the proxy variable of world factors. One such measure is the world index conducted by Morgan Stanley Capital International (MSCI). However, the MSCI world index is weighted by market capitalization and may suffer from excessive loading of a specific country market with high capitalization. Additionally, this study states that an efficient international diversification should be a portfolio that not only contains large numbers of assets, but also balances the weights of various assets.

Table 1. Summary statistics of return rates of various stock market indices

	Canada	France	Germany	Italy	Japan	U. K	U. S	EWW
Mean	0.1111	0.0893	0.0796	0.1235	-0.0401	0.0437	0.0929	0.0202
Std. Dev.	0.1012	0.1175	0.1259	0.1351	0.1234	0.0908	0.0919	0.0865
Variance	2.4958	2.8976	3.1055	3.3310	3.0422	2.2379	2.2663	2.1329
Kurtosis	6.2291	8.3962	9.6439	11.0953	9.2548	5.0080	5.1363	4.5493
Skewness	1.5940	2.6930	2.7362	0.8716	1.1417	2.5196	2.1059	1.2396
Min.	-0.2603	-0.0305	-0.2462	-0.0263	0.4568	0.1470	0.0016	-0.1782
Max	-11.2081	-13.3977	-12.4331	-12.2774	-8.8411	-9.4155	-8.8294	-1.7192

Notes:

This study uses weekly (Wednesday to Wednesday) US dollar stock returns of G7 equity markets compiled by Morgan Stanley Capital International Perspective. The country indices account for at least 80% of each country's stock market capitalization.

To concert returns to excess returns, the weekly Eurodollar deposit rate is subtracted from the raw returns.

The data cover the period January 1993 through the last week of August 2004 for 608 observations. All the stock prices are in terms of dollar.

This study averages all the G7 stock market indices with equal weights to arrive at an equally weighted world (hereafter, EWW) stock index as a replacement for the international portfolio

The mean and skewness coefficient are closed to zero, however, the kurtosis coefficient is grater than 3 for all cases.

Following the above line of thought and avoiding the high correlation between the MSCI world index and the largest market represented within the index, namely the U.S. market, this investigation averages all the G7 stock market indices while assigning equal weightings to each to produce an equally weighted world (hereafter, EWW) stock index to substitute for the international portfolio[15].

Table 1 lists several basic statistics for the sample markets. Initially, the return mean and skewness coefficient is near 0 for all cases. However, the kurtosis coefficient markedly exceeds three for cases. Generally, the term used to describe probability distributions with a kurtosis exceeding that of the normal distribution is leptokurtosis. Furthermore leptokurtosis can also be considered a measure of the fatness of the distribution tails. This finding is consistent with the notion that most markets display more extreme movements than those associated with a normal distribution. Furthermore, this study states that key feature of the quantile model is providing enhanced description of the extreme tail region. Table 2 shows the correlation coefficient estimates across various stock markets.

Table 2. Correlation matrix of stock index returns
Canada, France, Germany, Italy, Japan, U. K, U. S, EWW

	Canada	France	Germany	Italy	Japan	U. K	U. S	EWW
Canada	1.0000							
France	0.5526	1.0000						
Germany	0.5676	0.8109	1.0000					
Italy	0.4196	0.6597	0.6233	1.0000				
Japan	0.3153	0.3229	0.3298	0.2461	1.0000			
U. K.	0.5078	0.7472	0.6834	0.5691	0.2701	1.0000		
U. S.	0.7040	0.6000	0.6387	0.4307	0.2886	0.6182	1.0000	
EWW	0.6586	0.7975	0.8022	0.6216	0.7441	0.7230	0.7011	1.0000

Notes:

The weekly data cover the period January 1993 through the last week of August 2004 for 608 observations. All the stock prices are in terms of dollar.

The correlation estimates between Japan stock market and other stock markets are considerably lower compared to other cases.

3.2 One-Single Beta versus Quantile-Varying Betas

Table 3 lists the beta estimates of the ICAMP with single beta using OLS and LAD methods. The beta coefficient estimates clearly are significantly positive at 1% for all cases. Furthermore, the LAD beta estimates are below the OLS beta estimates[15]; however, the inequality between the OLS and LAD beta estimates is insignificant[16]. For simplicity, this work adopts the LAD beta estimates as measures of one-single beta in the following discussions.

---

[15] Ramchand and Susmel (1998) also recommended adopting EWW instead of the MSCI world index.

[16] One explanation is that the OLS estimates are more influenced by outliers than the LAD estimates. Furthermore, those rare extreme observations are consistent with the tail region data, and this study demonstrated the tail regions correspond to higher beta estimates and thus the OLS beta estimates exceed LAD. Specifically, the 90% confidence levels of the OLS and LAD beta estimates overlap with each other for all cases.

Table 3. Beta estimates of ICAM with one-single beta using OLS and LAD for various stock markets

	OLS	LAD
Canada	0.7706 (0.0357)*	0.7245 (0.0352)*
France	1.0834 (0.0332)*	1.0455 (0.0310)*
Germany	1.1680 (0.0353)*	1.1401(0.0327)*
Italy	0.9707 (0.0496)*	0.9176 (0.047)*
Japan	1.0613 (0.0387)*	1.1499 (0.0320)*
U.K	0.7586 (0.0294)*	0.7064 (0.0299)*
U.S	0.7450 (0.0307)*	0.6965 (0.0286)*

Notes:

The weekly data cover the period January 1993 through the last week of August 2004 for 608 observations. All the stock prices are in terms of dollar.

Please refer to Equs. 3 and 4 (Equs. 3 and 5) for the detail of model specification and estimation process of the ICAPM with one-single beta measure using OLS (LAD) model.

The * denote the significance in 1%. The value in the parenthesis denotes the estimated standard error of the estimate.

Apparently, all the beta coefficient estimates are significantly positive in 1%. Furthermore, the LAD beta estimates are lower than the OLS beta estimates for all cases; however, the inequality between the LAD and OLS beta estimates is insignificant. For reason of simplicity, this study adopts the LAD beta estimates as measures of one-single beta in following discussions.

Restated, the LAD and OLS estimates focus only on the averaging behavior of the beta coefficients, and do not consider that the beta can differ for the extreme return regions. Furthermore, this investigation demonstrates that all the stock markets display more extreme price movements than the normal distribution (please refer to Table 1). As is well known, the OLS and LAD technique does not effectively describe those extreme observations. This study is concerned with whether the beta coefficients are consistent in the tail regions of the returns distribution. Furthermore, this study also examines whether the beta estimates in the tail regions are larger/smaller than those in the central region.

Table 4 lists conditional quantile-varying beta estimates and Fig. 2 presents graphs of beta estimates in different return quantiles. The empirical findings are listed below. First, the quantile-varying beta estimates with 0.5 quantile (namely, $\theta=0.5$) are equivalent to the LAD beta estimates. Comparing Eqns. 9 and 5 reveals that the LAD estimate is a special case of quantile-varying betas with $\theta=0.5$. Second, although the sign and significance of beta estimates are consistent across various quantiles; however, the magnitude of the estimated beta coefficients varies significantly with changes in the conditional distribution. Furthermore, this study defines two types of beta distortions among international stock markets. That is, examining Figs. 2 (d), (f) and (g) for the case of Italy, U.K. and U.S., respectively, reveals that beta estimates deep outside the central region (namely, $\theta=0.95$ and 0.05) are significantly higher than beta estimate at the central quantile (namely, $\theta=0.5$). This investigation thus proposes a distortion of beta coefficients: "beta smile".

The "beta smile" phenomenon is explained below. First, this study states that situations involving extreme return quantiles (namely, $\theta=0.95$ and 0.05) directly correspond to unstable periods. Additionally, the nature of "beta smile" is consistent with the literature describing the high correlations among international stock markets during the volatile periods[17]. Briefly, international stock markets invariably rise and fall together during periods of high volatility.

Additionally, examining Fig. 2 (a), (b) and (c) for Canadian, French, and German stock markets, respectively, demonstrates another type of beta distortion: "beta skew". Specifically, in the case of Canada (France and Germany), the shape of the quantile-varying beta estimates substantially increases for the left-tail (right-tail) region but the right-tail (left-tail). Consequently, the Canadian stock market tends to simultaneously decrease with global stock markets during its extreme bear markets; in contrast, the French and German stock markets display significant correlation with global stock markets during their strong bull markets.

Finally, this work denotes the Japanese stock market as a special case. Specifically, the beta estimate of the Japanese stock market is considerably lower, not higher, in the left-tailed region (namely, $\theta=0.05$). This empirical finding is consistent with the extremely poor performance of the Japanese stock market during the 1990s. Additionally, in a world with increasingly integrated financial markets, the Japanese stock market performed extremely poorly compared to all other countries and sunk individually through the 1990s.

Table 4. Beta estimates of ICAPM with quantile-varying beta for various stock markets

	$\theta=0.05$	$\theta=0.1$	$\theta=0.25$	$\theta=0.5$ (LAD)	$\theta=0.75$	$\theta=0.9$	$\theta=0.95$
Canada	0.8520*	0.7672*	0.7811*	0.7245*	0.7163*	0.7494*	0.7555*
	(0.1032)	(0.0585)	(0.0508)	(0.0352)	(0.0515)	(0.0745)	(0.0939)
France	1.0351*	1.0065*	1.0558*	1.0455*	1.0876*	1.1027*	1.2081*
	(0.1667)	(0.0915)	(0.0392)	(0.031)	(0.041)	(0.0696)	(0.176)
Germany	1.1418*	1.1775*	1.1226*	1.1401*	1.1237*	1.3202*	1.3332*
	(0.2547)	(0.1238)	(0.0681)	(0.0327)	(0.0481)	(0.0649)	(0.1401)
Italy	1.1188*	1.0572*	0.9472*	0.9176*	0.9667*	1.0112*	1.1043*
	(0.1135)	(0.0986)	(0.0821)	(0.047)	(0.0839)	(0.0712)	(0.1205)
Japan	0.8517*	0.9212*	1.1501*	1.1499*	1.1335*	1.1518*	1.2060*
	(0.195)	(0.0869)	(0.061)	(0.032)	(0.0727)	(0.1074)	(0.2823)
U.K.	0.7872*	0.7762*	0.7541*	0.7064*	0.7358*	0.7807*	0.8435*
	(0.1176)	(0.0587)	(0.0417)	(0.0299)	(0.0401)	(0.0572)	(0.1526)
U.S.	0.7622*	0.7620*	0.7468*	0.6965*	0.6790*	0.7562*	0.8245*
	(0.1327)	(0.0545)	(0.0434)	(0.0286)	(0.0471)	(0.0787)	(0.1254)

Notes:

The weekly data cover the period January 1993 through the last week of August 2004 for 608 observations. All the stock prices are in terms of dollar.

Please refer to Equs. 6-9 for the detail of model specification and estimation process of the ICAPM with quantile-varying betas. The * denotes the significance at 1%.

The value in the parenthesis denotes the estimated standard error of the estimate.

The quantile-varying beta estimates with 0.5 quantile (namely, $\theta=0.5$) are equivalent to the LAD beta estimates.

Although the sign and significance of beta estimates are consistent across various quantiles; however, there is large variation in the magnitude of the estimated beta coefficients as the conditional distribution is changed.

---

[17] See Login and Solnik (1995), Ramchand and Susmel (1997, 1998).

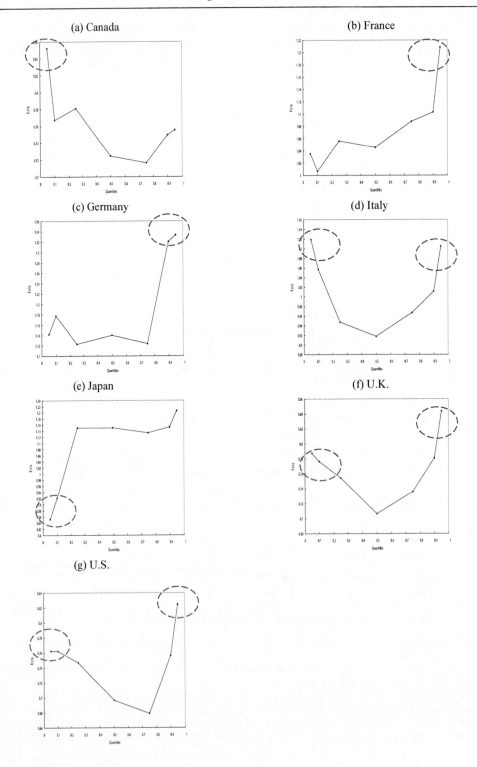

Figure 2. The quantile-varying beta estimates under various return quantiles

Table 5. Beta difference percentage of quantile-varying beta versus one-single (LAD) beta

	θ=0.05	θ=0.1	θ=0.25	θ=0.5 (LAD)	0.75	θ=0.9	θ=0.95
Canada	**17.60%**	5.89%	7.81%*	0.00%	-1.13%	3.44%	4.28%
France	-0.99%	-3.73%	0.99%	0.00%	4.03%	5.47%	**15.55%**
Germany	0.15%	3.28%	-1.53%	0.00%	-1.44%	15.80%	**16.94%**
Italy	**21.93%**	15.21%	3.23%	0.00%	5.35%	10.20%	**20.35%**
Japan	**-25.93%**	-19.89%	0.02%	0.00%	-1.43%	0.17%	4.88%
U.K	**11.44%**	9.88%	6.75%	0.00%	4.16%	10.52%	**19.41%**
U.S	**9.43%**	9.40%	7.22%	0.00%	-2.51%	8.57%	**18.38%**

Notes:
For benchmark purpose, this paper considers the LAD beta estimate and uses it to calculate beta difference percentage across various return quantiles: Beta difference % of the θ-th beta against LAD beta =-100*(the θ-th beta estimate - LAD beta estimate)/ (LAD beta estimate)

Remarkably, most of the deviation percentage estimates are over 10% at tail regions. Specifically, using LAD beta estimate as a benchmark, the three selected stock markets: Italy, U.S. and

U.K. with "beta smile" characteristics experience 20.35%, 19.41% and 18.38% (21.93%, 11.44% and 9.43%) inequality at the right (left tail) region, namely θ=0.95 (θ=0.05).

3. Furthermore, the three stock markets with "beta skew" phenomena: Canada, France and Germany show 17.60% deviation at θ=0.05, 15.55% deviation at θ=0.95 and 16.94% at θ=0.95, respectively. Last, the special case of Japan market, the deviation against LAD beta is -25.93% at θ=0.05.

Consequently, the ICAPM model with quantile-varying beta measures established in this investigation identifies two covariance risk dynamics in international stock markets: (1) "beta smile" and (2) "beta skew". Moreover, for benchmarking purposes, this study considers the LAD beta estimate and uses it to calculate the beta difference percentage across various return quantiles:

Beta difference % of the θ-th beta [against OR versus] LAD beta =-100(the θ-th beta estimate - LAD beta estimate)/ (LAD beta estimate)*

Table 5 lists the difference percentage of the quantile-varying beta versus the LAD beta. Notably, most of the deviation percentage estimates exceed 10% in the tail regions. Specifically, using the LAD beta estimate as a benchmark, the three selected stock markets: Italy, U.S. and U.K. with "beta smile" characteristics experience 20.35%, 19.41% and 18.38% (21.93%, 11.44% and 9.43%) inequality in the right (left tail) region, namely θ=0.95 (θ=0.05). Furthermore, the three stock markets exhibiting "beta skew" phenomena, namely Canada, France and Germany, exhibit 17.60% deviation at θ=0.05, 15.55% deviation at θ=0.95 and 16.94% deviation at θ=0.95, respectively. Finally, for the special case of the Japanese market, the deviation versus LAD beta is -25.93% at θ=0.05[18].

---

[18] Using the OLS beta estimate as the benchmark, most deviation magnitudes exceed 10% in the tail regions.

Table 6. Statistic tests of the equality of quantile-varying beta versus one-single (LAD) beta

	0.05 vs. 0.5 (LAD)	0.1 vs. 0.5 (LAD)	0.25 vs. 0.5 (LAD)	0.75 vs. 0.5 (LAD)	0.9 vs. 0.5 (LAD)	0.95 vs. 0.5 (LAD)
Canada	**2.98**	0.36	1.51	0.03	0.06	0.11
	(0.0856)*	(0.5513)	(0.2199)	(0.8693)	(0.8066)	(0.7356)
France	0.02	0.38	0.04	0.51	0.47	**3.00**
	(0.8898)	(0.5358)	(0.8387)	(0.4751)	(0.4917)	**(0.0837)***
Germany	0.00	0.20	0.10	0.08	**4.83**	**8.68**
	(0.9772)	(0.6539)	(0.7540)	(0.7813)	**(0.0284)****	**(0.0033)*****
Italy	**4.41**	2.64	0.18	0.55	**3.29**	**3.58**
	(0.0361)**	(0.1046)	(0.6731)	(0.4591)	**(0.0703)***	**(0.0741)***
Japan	**13.59**	**5.88**	0.00	0.15	0.00	0.19
	(0.0002)***	**(0.0156)****	(0.9968)	(0.6943)	(0.9793)	(0.6617)
U.K.	0.90	1.61	1.40	0.73	1.28	**4.23**
	(0.3434)	(0.2048)	(0.2377)	(0.3927)	(0.2577)	**(0.0401)****
U.S.	0.70	1.72	1.11	0.15	0.89	**6.25**
	(0.4018)	(0.1900)	(0.2922)	(0.6940)	(0.3472)	**(0.0127)****

Notes:

This study adopts the beta estimate at 0.5 quantile, namely the LAD beta estimate, as a benchmark and the differences between the quantile-varying and the LAD beta estimates is examined.

This table presents the values of the F-statistic for the test of equality of beta parameters across various quantiles. The figure in the parenthesis denotes the p-value of the F-statistic.

The inequality test is based on the benchmark of the beta estimate with 0.5 quantile, namely the LAD beta estimate. The ***, ** and * denote the significance at 1%, 5% and 10%.

Notably, the inequality of beta estimates across various quantiles is more/less pronounced at the tail/central regions. Specifically, at the two central regions, namely θ=0.75 vs. θ=0.5 and θ=0.25 vs. θ=0.5, the inequality of beta estimates is insignificant for all cases. However, at the extreme left-tailed and right-tailed regions, namely θ=0.05 vs. θ=0.5 and θ=0.95 vs. θ=0.5, the difference is more remarkable.

Canada market has significantly higher beta estimate at θ=0.05 against the LAD beta. By contrast, the quantile-varying beta estimate with θ=0.95 is significantly higher than the LAD beta for the case of France and Germany.

For the case of the Italy stock market with "beta smile" phenomena, both of the θ=0.05 and θ=0.95 quantile-varying beta estimates are significantly higher than the LAD (θ=0.5) beta estimate. However, the beta deviation of θ=0.95 vs. θ=0.5 (θ=0.05 vs. θ=0.5) is significant (insignificant) in the U.S. and U.K. stock markets.

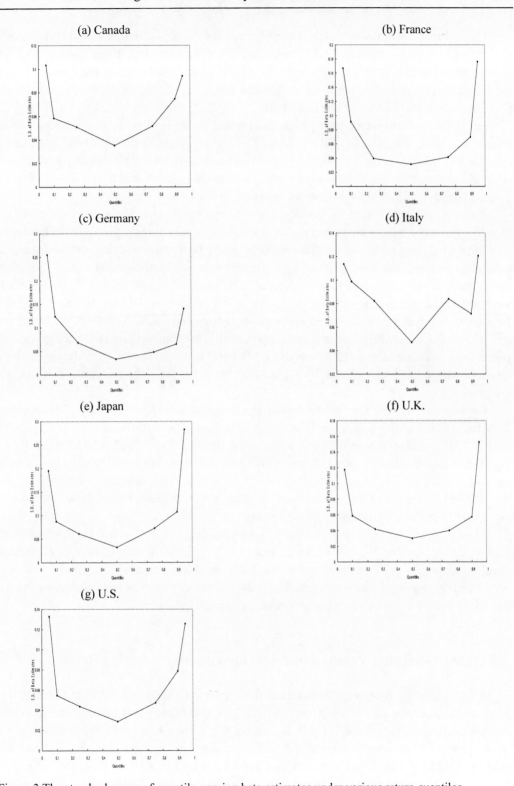

Figure 3 The standard errors of quantile-varying beta estimates under various return quantiles

The following conclusion thus is clear. Except for the Japanese stock market, the model with one-single beta considerably underestimates the covariance risk of the Italian, U.K. and U.S. stock markets in both the right and left-tailed regions. Furthermore, the one-single beta model underestimates the covariance risk in the left-tailed (right-tailed) region only for the Canada (France and Germany) stock markets.

Fig. 3 shows the standard error estimates of quantile-varying beta estimates under various return quantiles. Interestingly, the standard error of quantile-varying beta estimate is considerably higher in the extreme left- and right-tailed regions. This finding is consistent with the notion that the co-movement processes among global stock markets during the volatile (steady) periods are substantially unstable (stable).

Table 6 lists the F test of the equality of beta parameters across various quantiles. Notably, this work adopts the beta estimate at the 0.5 quantile, namely the LAD beta estimate, as a benchmark, and examines the differences between the quantile-varying and the LAD beta estimates. Notably, the inequality of beta parameters across various quantiles is more/less pronounced at the tail/central regions. Specifically, near the central regions, namely $\theta=0.75$ vs. $\theta=0.5$ and $\theta=0.25$ vs. $\theta=0.5$, the inequality of beta estimates is insignificant in all cases. However, in the extreme left-tailed and right-tailed regions, namely $\theta=0.05$ vs. $\theta=0.5$ and $\theta=0.95$ vs. $\theta=0.5$, the difference is greater. Specifically, the Canadian market has significantly higher beta estimate at $\theta=0.05$ versus the LAD beta. In contrast, the quantile-varying beta estimate with $\theta=0.95$ is significantly higher than the LAD beta for the case of France and Germany.

Furthermore, for the case of the Italian stock market with the "beta smile" phenomena, both the $\theta=0.05$ and $\theta=0.95$ quantile-varying beta estimates significantly exceed the LAD ($\theta=0.5$) beta estimate. However, the beta deviation of $\theta=0.95$ vs. $\theta=0.5$ ($\theta=0.05$ vs. $\theta=0.5$) is significant (insignificant) in the U.S. and U.K. stock markets. This finding is consistent with the notion that the "beta smile" pattern in the U.S. and U.K. stock markets is less promising in the left-tailed region. One explanation is that the quantile-varying beta estimate is significantly unstable in the tail regions (See Fig. 3).

Finally, in the case of Japan, the quantile-varying beta estimate at $\theta=0.05$ is significantly lower, not higher, than the LAD beta estimate ($\theta=0.5$). This empirical finding is consistent with the extremely poor performance of the Japanese stock market through the 1990s. In a world with increasingly integrated financial markets, Japanese stocks nevertheless performed extremely poorly compared to all other countries through 1990s.

3.3 Quantile-varying Versus Time-varying and State-varying Betas

Table 7 lists the parameter estimates of the bivariate GARCH model (See Equs. 10-16). First, the sum of the two GARCH parameter estimates, namely $\eta_{i,1}$ and $\lambda_{i,1}$ for individual market returns, and $\eta_{w,1}$ and $\lambda_{w,1}$ for world market returns, are approximately equal to unity in most cases. In the case of Canada-EWW, the sum of the $\eta_{i,1}$ and $\lambda_{i,1}$ estimates is $0.9314(=0.0832+0.8482)$, while that of $\eta_{w,1}$ and $\lambda_{w,1}$ is $0.9139(=0.0901+0.8238)$. This result is consistent with the notion that the variance setting in the GARCH model suffers from a problem of high persistence. Furthermore, this work hypothesizes that the high persistence of GARCH models results from structural changes in the volatility process during estimation.

Table 7. Parameter estimates of the bivariate GARCH model

	Canada-EWW	France-EWW	Germany-EWW	Italy-EWW	Japan-EWW	U.K.-EWW	U.S.-EWW
Individual Market Equ.							
$\varphi_{i,0}$	0.1827 (0.0848)**	0.1551 (0.0999)***	0.1900 (0.1110)	0.1710 (0.1357)	0.1776 (0.1125)	0.1162 (0.0798)	0.1793 (0.0765)***
$\varphi_{i,1}$	-0.0189 (0.0355)	-0.1558 (0.0347)***	-0.0447 (0.0329)	-0.0326 (0.0539)	-0.0593 (0.0334)*	-0.1026 (0.0346)***	-0.1406 (0.0364)***
$\eta_{i,0}$	0.4042 (0.1143)***	2.1099 (0.6090)***	1.4685 (0.3704)***	6.1618 (3.0644)**	0.3383 (0.1316)***	1.3970 (0.4309)***	0.4640 (0.1352)***
$\eta_{i,1}$	0.0832 (0.0203)***	0.1239 (0.0320)***	0.1224 (0.0254)***	0.1178 (0.0452)***	0.0893 (0.0193)***	0.1647 (0.0378)***	0.1082 (0.0249)***
$\lambda_{i,1}$	0.8482 (0.0314)***	0.5941 (0.0930)***	0.7083 (0.0519)***	0.3300 (0.2695)	0.8819 (0.0215)***	0.5274 (0.1078)***	0.7920 (0.0407)***
World Market Equ.							
$\varphi_{w,0}$	0.0634 (0.0731)	0.0589 (0.07380)	0.0671 (0.0828)	0.0724 (0.0790)	0.1884 (0.0736)***	0.0916 (0.0808)	0.0930 (0.0765)
$\varphi_{w,1}$	-0.0868 (0.0355)***	-0.0420 (0.0349)	-0.0398 (0.0318)	-0.0058 (0.0598)	-0.0908 (0.0338)***	-0.0132 (0.0257)	-0.0775 (0.0352)**
$\eta_{w,0}$	0.3797 (0.1666)**	0.7310 (0.2457)***	0.7014 (0.2232)***	0.3738 (0.1611)***	0.0617 (0.0361)	0.5395 (0.1811)***	0.4505 (0.1843)***
$\eta_{w,1}$	0.0901 (0.0271)***	0.0794 (0.0260)***	0.0769 (0.0246)***	0.0971 (0.0323)***	0.0893 (0.0191)***	0.0916 (0.0250)***	0.0682 (0.0219)***
$\lambda_{w,1}$	0.8238 (0.0549)***	0.7510 (0.0701)***	0.7604 (0.0634)***	0.8185 (0.0590)***	0.9042 (0.0203)***	0.7841 (0.0527)***	0.8275 (0.0521)***
Correlation							
ρ	0.6326 (0.0248)***	0.7835 (0.0161)***	0.7746 (0.0169)***	0.6158 0.0257	0.7805 0.0162	0.7021 (0.0210)***	0.6589 (0.0242)***
Log-likelihood function	-2515.21	-2468.91	-2517.68	-2731.11	-2534.62	-2393.87	-2427.55

Notes:
1. The weekly data cover the period January 1993 through the last week of August 2004 for 608 observations. All the stock prices are in terms of dollar.
2. Please refer to Equs. 10-16 for the model specification of the ICAPM with time-varying betas. The ***, ** and * denote the significance at 1%, 2.5% and 5%.
3. The value in the parenthesis denotes the estimated standard error of the estimate.
4. The sum of the two GARCH parameter estimates, namely $\eta_{i,1}$ and $\lambda_{i,1}$ for individual market returns and $\eta_{w,1}$ and $\lambda_{w,1}$ for world market returns, are approximately unity for most cases. Taking the case of Canada-EWW as an example, the sum of the $\eta_{i,1}$ and $\lambda_{i,1}$ estimates is 0.9314 (=0.0832+0.8482), while that of $\eta_{w,1}$ and $\lambda_{w,1}$ is 0.9139 (=0.0901+0.8238). This result is consistent with the notion that the variance setting in the GARCH model suffers from a problem of high persistence. Furthermore, this study hypothesizes that the high persistence of GARCH models results from structural changes in volatility process during estimation.

Table 8. Parameter estimates of the ICAPM with state-varying betas

Canada-EWW	France-EWW	Germany-EWW	Italy-EWW	Japan-EWW	U.K.-EWW	U.S.-EWW
0.9721 (0.0175)***	0.9232 (0.0369)***	0.9933 (0.0071)***	0.9916 (0.0081)***	0.9885 (0.0083)***	0.8691 (0.0697)***	0.9955 (0.0039)***
0.9918 (0.0054)***	0.9421 (0.0230)***	0.9862 (0.0143)***	0.9935 (0.0055)***	0.9901 (0.0081)***	0.8877 (0.0530)***	0.9956 (0.0058)***
0.1172 (0.0680)*	0.0666 (0.0646)	0.1209 (0.071)*	0.0295 (0.0822)	-0.1063 (0.061)*	0.0446 (0.0670)	0.0898 (0.0601)
0.6589 (0.0397)***	0.8869 (0.0446)***	0.5082 (0.0942)***	0.9294 (0.0411)***	1.4188 (0.0442)***	0.5884 (0.0556)***	0.3568 (0.0520)***
1.0335 (0.0977)***	1.2546 (0.0747)***	1.3099 (0.0587)***	0.9782 (0.1276)***	0.9334 (0.0644)***	0.8991 (0.0695)***	0.8533 (0.0379)***
2.1868 (0.1903)***	1.5034 (0.2066)***	1.8862 (0.3447)***	2.9231 (0.3114)***	1.2017 (0.1273)***	1.0914 (0.2505)***	1.2374 (0.1480)***
0.0828 (0.0516)	0.0013 (0.0344)	0.0886 (0.0525)*	0.1131 (0.0613)*	0.0707 (0.0429)*	0.0012 (0.0571)	0.0455 (0.0518)
0.0017 (0.1351)	0.0002 (0.1257)	0.0032 (0.1812)	0.0232 (0.1238)	0.0081 (0.1275)	0.0003 (0.1239)	0.0031 (0.1371)
2.7432 (0.4564)***	3.1759 (0.507)***	1.6510 (0.3548)***	3.6352 (0.5276)***	4.8703 (0.6307)***	3.3422 (0.6514)***	2.3079 (0.3363)***
-1212.76	-1172.39	-1195.17	-1397.10	-1206.59	-1102.69	-1115.54

The weekly data cover the period January 1993 through the last week of August 2004 for 608 observations. All the stock prices are in terms of dollar.

Please refer to Equs. 18-22 for the model specification of the ICAPM with state-varying betas.

The value in the parenthesis denotes the estimated standard error of the estimate. The ***, ** and * denote the significance at 1%, 2.5% and 5%.

The g2 estimates are significantly greater than one for all cases. Taking the case of Canada-EWW as an example, the g2 estimate is 2.7432 with the standard error of 0.4564. The present result means that the volatility of regime II is 2.7432 times to regime I. Furthermore, the corresponding 95% confidence interval of the g2 estimate is [1.8487, 3.6377] and does not overlap the unity, namely the value of g1. Consequently, this study defines regime II (regime I) as the high (low) volatility state.

Except the case of Japanese stock market, the beta estimate with individual stock market at the high volatility state (namely, $\beta_{i,2}$) is significantly higher than that with individual stock market at the low volatility state (namely, $\beta_{i,1}$). Taking the case of Canada-EWW as an example, the $\beta_{i,2}$ ($\beta_{i,1}$) estimate is 1.0335 (0.6589) with the standard error of 0.0977 (0.0397) and its corresponding 95% confidence interval is [1.2250, 0.8420] ([0.7357, 0.5811]). Notably, one special case of Japan market, the $\beta_{i,2}$ estimate (0.9334) at high volatility regime is significantly lower, not higher, than the $\beta_{i,1}$ estimate (1.4188) at low volatility regime.

Table 8 lists the parameter estimates of ICAPM with state-varying betas (See Eqs. 18-22). The empirical findings are consistent with the following notions. First, the g_2 estimates significantly exceed one for all cases. Taking the case of Canada-EWW as an example, the g_2 estimate is 2.7432 and has standard error of 0.4564. The present result means that the volatility of regime II is 2.7432 times that of regime I. Furthermore, the corresponding 95% confidence interval of the g_2 estimate is [1.8487, 3.6377], and does not overlap the unity, namely the value of g_1. This study thus defines regime II (regime I) as the high (low) volatility state.

Second, except for the Japanese stock market, the beta estimate for individual stock markets at the high volatility state (namely, $\beta_{i,2}$) significantly exceeds that of individual stock markets at the low volatility state (namely, $\beta_{i,1}$). Taking the case of Canada-EWW as an example, the $\beta_{i,2}$ ($\beta_{i,1}$) estimate is 1.0335 (0.6589) with the standard error of 0.0977 (0.0397) and its corresponding 95% confidence interval is [1.2250, 0.8420] ([0.7357, 0.5811])[19]. Notably, for the special case of the Japan market, the $\beta_{i,2}$ estimate (0.9334) under the high volatility regime is significantly lower, not higher, than the $\beta_{i,1}$ estimate (1.4188) in the low volatility regime.

Figs. 4 (a) and (b) display the individual market returns and time-varying beta estimates derived from the GARCH model (See Eq. 17) for the case of U.S.-EWW, respectively. Additionally, the smoothing probabilities of the high volatility state are plotted in the third panel and the observations are classified using the system of Hamilton (1989), in which an observation belongs to the high volatility state if the corresponding smoothed probability exceeds 0.5, and otherwise it belongs to a low volatility state[20]. The fourth panel of Fig. 4 plots the state-varying beta estimates implied by the Markov-switching model. Apparently, these state-varying betas in Fig. 4 (d) mirror Fig. 4 (c), which displays the smoothing probabilities of high volatility state. Furthermore, the U.S. high volatility state is characterized by the period from late 1995 to the middle of 2003, and thus the beta estimate increases from 0.3568 to 0.8533.

Theoretically, the quantile-varying betas developed in this study, the state-varying betas derived from Markov-switching models and the time-varying betas implied by GARCH models are not nested and thus are not directly comparable. However, intuitively, the perspective of quantile-varying betas presented in this study resembles the state-varying beta framework of Ramchand and Susmel (1998). However, a key limitation of the two-state Markov switching model of Ramchand and Susmel (1998) is that the dynamics of beta are very simple with only two betas being possible. The switching process between the two possible states appears quite dramatic.

By contrast, this investigation states that a system involving quantile-varying betas can expand the modeling options for stock markets that exhibit smooth beta dynamics.

---

[19] The significance could also be demonstrated by the fact that the 95% confidence levels of the two measures of beta estimate do not overlap.

[20] Although the state variable, s_t is not observable at time t, the specific regime probability can be estimated based on the data itself. More specifically, when the information set used for estimation includes signals dated up to time t, the regime probability is a filtering probability. Meanwhile, it is also possible to use the overall sample period information set to estimate the state probability at time t. The probability is denoted as a smoothing probability. In contrast, a predicting probability denotes the regime probability for an ex ante estimation, with the information set including signals dated up to period t-1.

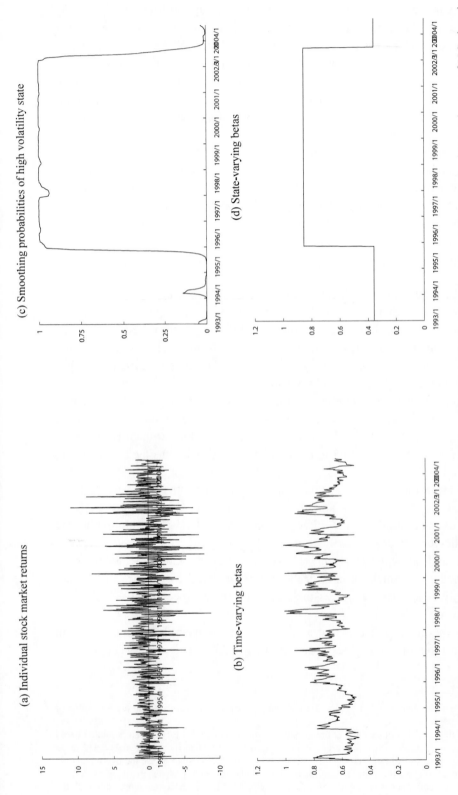

Figure 4 Individual stock market returns, time-varying betas, smoothing probabilities of high volatility state and state-varying betas: The case of U.S. plots the state-varying beta estimates implied by the Markov-switching model. Apparently, these state-varying betas in Fig. 4 (d) mirror Fig. 4 (c), which displays the smoothing probabilities of high volatility state. Furthermore, the U.S. high volatility state is characterized by the period from late 1995 to the middle of 2003, and thus the beta estimate increases from 0.3568 to 0.8533.

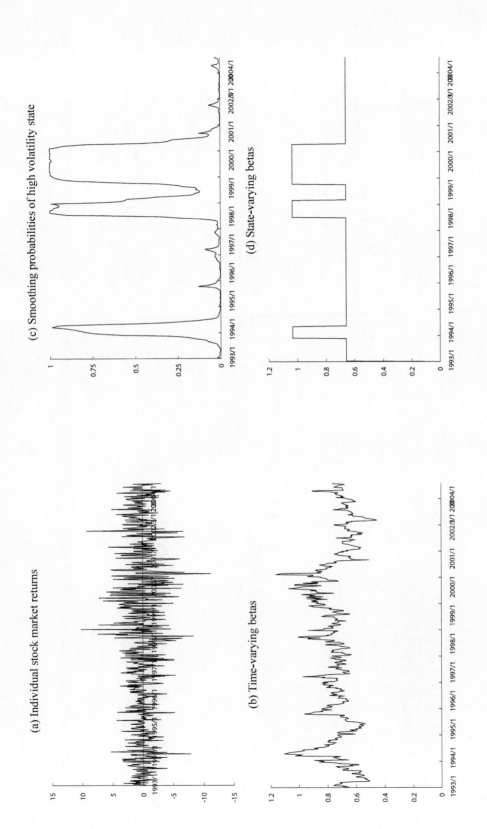

Figure 5. Individual stock market returns, time-varying betas, smoothing probabilities of high volatility state and state-varying betas: The case of Canada

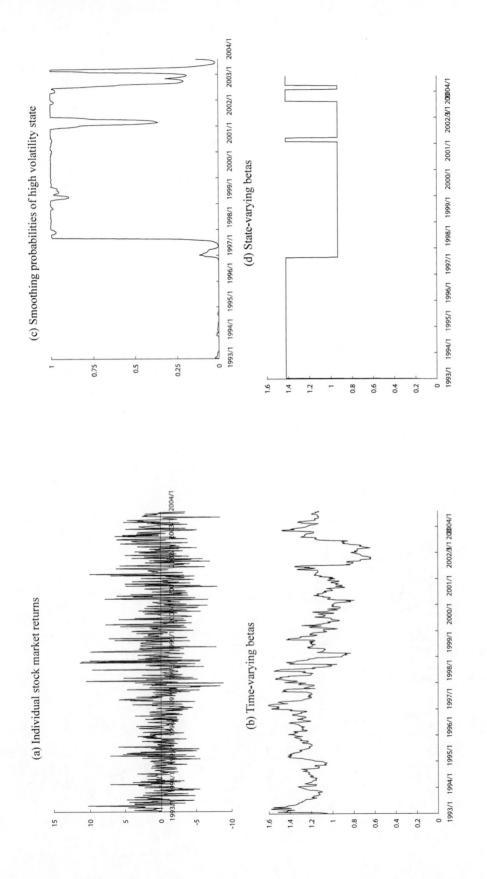

Figure 6 Individual stock market returns, time-varying betas, smoothing probabilities of high volatility state and state-varying bBetas: The case of Japan

Furthermore, Ramchand and Susmel (1998) generated a different beta for each volatility state, but did not consider the possible asymmetry dynamics derived from positive/negative stock returns. In contrast, the framework containing quantile-varying betas could picture the asymmetry dynamics. Specifically, this work denotes the U.S. stock market using the "beta smile" characteristic; however, beta estimates become significantly distorted at the right-tailed region, but the distortion is less promising in the left-tailed region.

As can be seen from Fig. 4(b), the GARCH-betas are unstable over time. One explanation is that GARCH models fail to capture the structural change in variance dynamics, resulting in less stable beta dynamics design. Notably, the higher (lower) state-varying beta estimate for the high (low) volatility regime, namely $\beta_{i,2}$ ($\beta_{i,1}$) for the U.S. market is comparable with the higher (lower) than average time-varying betas estimated using the GARCH model[21].

The key advantage of the quantile-varying beats and the state-varying betas against the time-varying betas lies in providing meaningful implications for stock returns. Specifically, the evidence presented by quantile-varying and state-varying betas is consistent with previous findings in the literature of high correlations among international stock markets during periods of high volatility. Particularly, the results of the proposed quantile-varying betas suggest that the beta estimates differ significantly across various return quantiles, particularly in the extreme tail regions. Furthermore, these results are consistent with the framework of state-varying betas in which betas differ significantly across low and high variance states.

Figs. 5 and 6 do the same as described above with respect to the Canadian and Japanese stock markets, respectively. First, as with the U.S. stock market, the finding of the higher (lower) beta estimate in a high (low) volatility regime, namely $\beta_{i,2} > \beta_{i,1}$, is implied by the volatility-switching model in the Canadian case. However, the evidence from our quantile-varying betas specifies the "beta skew" distortion in Canada; that is; the increasing process of beat estimates is mostly confined to the left-tail region, namely the extreme bust market state. Finally, in the special case of the Japanese market, the state-varying framework identifies a lower (higher) beta estimate at the high (low) volatility state, namely $\beta_{i,2} < \beta_{i,1}$. Nevertheless, the quantile-varying betas presented in this study demonstrate that beta disorder is concentrated in the left-tailed region. Additionally, this finding is consistent with the poor performance of the Japanese stock market during the 1990s.

Consequently, two key advantages of the system with quantile-varying betas established by this study are presented. First, the system with quantile-varying betas comparing that with time-varying betas implied by GARCH models provides meaningful implications regarding correlation-volatility relationship among global stock markets. Secondly, the quantile-varying beta design releases simple dual beta setting implied by Ramchand and Susmel (1998) and can identify asymmetry dynamics in betas. Additionally, our present results also show different types of beta distortions among various markets and insight discussions and explanations are presented as follows.

First, when an individual market singly experiences an extreme bear/bull market state (namely, $\theta = 0.05/0.95$), this study denotes a notable "stock-to-stock" asset reallocation process across various countries; specifically, a capital flight from one stock market (other stock markets) to other stock markets (one stock market) when a specific stock market is

---

[21] This implies that the quantile-varying implied by the univariate quantile regression model and the state-varying beta estimate derived from the univariate Markov-switching model are qualitatively consistent with the time-varying betas estimated using the bivariate GARCH model.

experiencing an extreme bear/bull market state. This study states that this "within-market-hedging" strategy, namely simultaneous short selling (purchase) of one stock market asset and purchase (short selling) of other stock market assets, clearly causes stock prices of a specific market and global markets to tend to move in opposite directions and thus reduces the scale of covariance risk of between them. Taking the Japanese market an example again, during the 1990s, Japanese stock market experienced a recession period alone; while other countries performed well. Apparently, Japanese stock market's covariance risk with global stock markets at the left-tailed region (namely, θ=0.05) should be significantly lower, not higher under this within-market-hedging strategy process.

Inversely, during periods of stock markets globally experiencing an extremely bust/boom state (namely, θ=0.05/0.95), this study hypothesizes the "stock-to-bond" asset reallocation process. Specifically, during periods of universally bust/boom state occurred at stock markets, this investigation states that there is a decrease/increase in capital flows to stock markets and an increase/decrease in fund to bond markets. This study thus posits that this "across-market-hedging strategy", namely simultaneous short selling (purchase) of stock assets and purchase (short selling) of other assets, such as bond assets, apparently causes stock prices tend to move in similar directions and thus enhances the scale of covariance risk of global stock markets [26].

To conclude, this study states that the "stock-to-stock" ("stock-to-bond") asset reallocation process decreases (increases) covariance risk across global stock markets, particularly during dramatic periods. Moreover, for the case of Italy with beta-smile phenomenon, the increasing beta distortions are significant at both tail regions (namely, θ=0.05 and 0.95). This finding is consistent with the notion that the "stock-to-bond" reallocation process fully dominates the "stock-to-stock" process for the case of Italy. By contrast, the beta-smile phenomenon of the U.S. and U.K. markets is insignificant at the left-tailed region, namely θ=0.05. This finding shows that the increasing covariance risk pattern among global stock markets derived from the "stock-to-bond" process might be partially offset by the effects of the "stock-to-stock" process; consequently, the increasing beta distortion at the left-tailed region is insignificant in statistic for the two markets.

Furthermore, the beta estimates of the France and Germany markets skew to the right-tailed region only; by contrast, the beta estimates just skew to the left-tailed region for the case of Canada. This finding denotes that the "stock-to-bond"

Apparently, stock and bond prices are prone to move in opposite directions and their co-movement process decreases at this condition reallocation process fully controls the three markets; however, it mostly occurs at θ=0.95 (θ=0.05) quantile level for the case of France and Germany (Canada). Last, the special case of Japanese market is fully dominated by the "stock-to-stock" process and its beta estimate given θ=0.05 thus is significantly lower than the average.

4. CONCLUSIONS AND EXTENSIONS

This study represents one of the first studies to establish the ICAPM with quantile-varying beta coefficients. Previous studies have demonstrated the instability of covariance risk in international stock markets. This investigation establishes a statistical framework in which the beta coefficient varies with the phase of the return quantile. The model is tested in G7 stock markets. Furthermore, two conventional random-coefficient frameworks including time-varying betas derived from GARCH models and state-varying betas implied by Markov-switching models are adopted for purposes of comparative analysis.

The empirical findings of this work are consistent with the following notions. First, the size of beta estimates changes with return quantile level and two types of beta distortions are demonstrated. Specifically, the "beta smile" ("beta skew") characteristic occurs in the Italian, U.S. and U.K. markets (Canada, France and Germany) markets. Second, the Japanese market provides a special case, and its beta estimate at the left-tailed region is significantly lower, not higher than the LAD beta estimate. Third, two key advantages of the quantile-varying betas are identified. Specifically, the system with quantile-varying betas comparing that with time-varying betas implied by GARCH models provides meaningful implications regarding correlation-volatility relationship among global stock markets. Furthermore, the quantile-varying beta design releases simple dual beta setting implied by Ramchand and Susmel (1998) and can identify asymmetry dynamics in betas.

Three caveats should be noted in interpreting the analytical results of this investigation. First, the present empirical results are limited to G7 stock markets. Future studies could examine a range of stock markets, especially emerging stock markets. As is well known, a key feature of the quantile-varying regression model is capturing the characteristics at tail regions of return distributions. Furthermore, emerging stock markets generally experience more extreme crisis events than mature stock markets. Consequently, comparative analysis of mature versus emerging stock markets would be useful. Second, the quantile-varying beta patterns clearly differ across various G7 contries. Specifically, Italy U.K and U.S. exhibit a "beta smile" curve, while Canada, France and Germany exhibit a "beta skew" curve and Japan serves as one special case. More insight discussions dealing with different types of beta distortions among various markets are encouraged. Third, although three alternatives for beta dynamics, including quantile-varying, time-varying and state-varying betas, are adopted and compared, comparisons should also be made with other dynamic beta models.

REFERENCES

Bekaert, G. and C. Harvey (1995), "Time-varying World Market Integration," Journal of Finance, 50, 2, 403-444

Bhardwaj, R.K., and L.D. Brooks (1993), "Dual Betas from Bull and Bear Markets: Reversal of the Size Effect," Journal of Financial Research, 17, 241-254

Braun, P.A., D. Nelson and A. Sunier (1995), "Good News, Bad News, Volatility and Betas," Journal of Finance, 50, 5, 1575-1603

Bollerslev, T. (1986), "Generalized Autoregressive Conditional Heteroskedasticity," Journal of Econometrics, 31, 307-327

Bollerslev, T. and R.F. Engle (1986), "Modeling the Persistence of Conditional Variance," Econometric Reviews, 5, 1-50

Bollerslev, T., R.Y. Chou and K.F. Kroner (1992), "ARCH Modeling Finance, A Review of the Theory and Empirical Evidence," Journal of Econometrics, 52, 5-59

Buchinsky, M. (1995), "Estimating the Asymptotic Covariance Matrix for Quantile Regression Models: A Monte Carlo Study," Journal of Econometrics, 65, 109-154

Buchinsky, M. (1998), "Recent Advances in Quantile Regression Models: A Practical Guideline for Empirical Research," Journal of Human Research, XXXIII, 88-126

Cai, J. (1994), "A Markov Model of Unconditional Variance in ARCH," Journal of Business and Economic Statistics, 12, 309-316

De Santis G. and B. Gerard (1997), "International Asset Pricing and Portfolio Diversification with Time-varying Risk," Journal of Finance, 5, 1881-1912

Diebold, F.X. (1986), "Modeling the Persistence of Conditional Variance: A Comment," Econometric Reviews, 5, 51-56

Dumas, B. and B. Solnik (1995), "The World Price of Foreign Exchange Risk," Journal of Finance, 50, 445-479

Engel, R.F. (1982), "Autoregressive Conditional Heteroscedasticity with Estimates of Variance of United Kingdom Inflation," Econometrica, 50, 987-1007

Engle, R.F. and C. Mustafa (1992), "Implied ARCH Models from Option Prices," Journal of Econometrics, 52, 289-311

Ferson, W.E. and C.R. Harvey (1993), "The Risk and Predictability of International Equity Returns," Review of Financial Studies, 6, 527-566

Fletcher, J. (2000), "On the Conditional Relationship between Beta and Return in International Stock Returns," International Review of Financial Analysis, 235-245

Gregory, K. and K. Johan (2002), "Time Variation and Asymmetry in Systematic Risk: Evidence from the Finnish Stock Exchange," Journal of Multinational Financial Management, 12, 261-271

Hamilton J.D. (1989), "A New Approach to the Economic Analysis of Nonstationary Time Series and the Business Cycle," Econometrica, 57, 357-384

Hamilton, J.D. and R. Susmel (1994), "Autoregressive Conditional Heteroscedasticity and Changes in Regime," Journal of Econometrics, 64, 307-333

Harvey, C.R. (1991), "The World Price Covariance Risk," Journal of Finance, 44, 111-157

Koenker, R. and G. Bassett (1978), "Regression Quantile," Econometrica, 46, 33–50

Koenker, R. (2000), "Galton, Edgeworth, Frisch, and Prospects for Quantile Regression in Econometrics," Journal of Econometrics, 95, 347–374

Koenker, R. and K.F. Hallock (2001), "Quantile Regression," Journal of Economic Perspectives, 15, 143–156

Lamoureux, C.G. and W.D. Lastrapes (1990), "Persistence in Variance, Structural Change and the GARCH Model," Journal of Business and Economic Statistics, 8, 225-234

Lintner, J. (1965a), "The Valuation of Risk Assets and the Selection of Ricky Investments in Stock Portfolios and Capital Budgets," Review of Economics and Statistics, 47, 13-47

Lintner, J. (1965b), "Security Prices, Risk and Maximal Gains from Diversification," Journal of Finance, 20, 587-616

Longin, F. and M.B. Solnik (1995), "Is the Correlation on International Equity Returns Constant: 1960-1990," Journal of international Money and Finance, 14, 3-23

Markowitz, H.M. (1952), "Portfolio Selection," Journal of Finance, 77-91

Mark, N. (1988), "Time-Varying Betas and Risk Premia in the Pricing of Forward Foreign Exchange Contracts," Journal of Financial Economics, 22, 355-354

Mossin, J. (1966), "Equilibrium in a Capital Asset Market," Econometrica, 68-83

Nelson, D.B. (1991), "Conditional Heteroskedasticity in Asset Returns: A New Approach," Econometrica, 59, 347-370

Ng, L. (1991), "Testing the CAPM with Time-Varying Covariances: a Multivariate GARCH Approach," Journal of Finance, 46, 1507-1521

Pettengill, G., S. Sundaram and I. Mathur (1995), "The Conditional Relation between Beta and Return," Journal of Financial Quantitative Analysis, 30, 101-116

Ramchand, L. and R. Susmel (1997), "Volatility and Cross Correlation across Major Stock Markets," Journal of Empirical Finance, 5, 397-416

Ramchand, L. and R. Susmel (1998), "Variance and Covariances of International Stock Returns: the International Capital Asset Pricing Model Revisited," Journal of international Financial Markets, Institutions and Money, 8, 39-57

Sharp, W.F. (1964), "Capital Asset Prices: A Theory of Market Equilibrium under Conditions of Risk," Journal of Finance, 19, 425-442

In: The Stock Market
Editor: Allison S. Wetherby

Chapter 9

STOCK MARKET VOLATILITY AND THE GREAT MODERATION: NEW EVIDENCE BASED ON THE G-7 ECONOMIES[*]

Juncal Cuñado[1], Javier Gomez Biscarri[2] and Fernando Perez de Gracia[1]

[1]Universidad de Navarra, Spain
[2]IESE Business School, Barcelona, Spain

ABSTRACT

In this chapter we look at the dynamic behavior of stock market volatility in the G-7 countries over a long term period which covers from 1960 to 2006. More generally, we ask whether there have been significant changes in the behavior of market volatility in the G-7 countries. We attempt to place the discussion of possible changes in this dynamic behavior in the context of the "Great Moderation": Has the volatility of the stock market gone down in a parallel manner to the volatility of real activity and inflation or are financial markets 'disconnected' from economic fundamentals? Our data analyses and empirical results do not find evidence of a reduction in stock market volatility in most G-7 economies and, when these changes appear, they seem to have come years before the Great Moderation.

INTRODUCTION

Since the mid 1980s, many OECD economies have experienced an unprecedented period of economic stability. This phenomenon is now known as the Great Moderation (Bernanke, 2004). The volatility of aggregate economic activity has fallen significantly -by more than

---

[*] A verison of this chapter was also published in *Emerging Topics in Banking and Finance,* edited by Emma J. Fuchs and Finn Braun, published by Nova Science Publishers, Inc. It was submitted for appropriate modifications in an effort to encourage wider dissemination of research.

one third- in industrialized economies and so has the volatility of inflation (see, for example, Kim and Nelson, 1999; McConnell and Pérez-Quirós, 2000; Blanchard and Simon, 2001; Stock and Watson, 2002; Smith and Summers, 2002 and Mills and Wang, 2003 among many others). A lower level of macroeconomic volatility has numerous benefits. First, lower volatility of inflation improves the functioning of markets, makes economic planning and forecasting significantly easier and reduces the amount of resources that are devoted to hedging inflation risks. Second, lower output volatility comes with more stable employment, which also implies a reduction in the uncertainty that both households and firms have to confront. Given the long-term growing trend of economic activity and output, a reduction in volatility is closely associated with the fact that recessions have become less frequent and less severe.

However, in recent years we have witnessed episodes of major instability that have shocked both developed and developing economies. A main source of major macroeconomic instability during the recent years has come from the evolution of oil prices: the world seems to have entered into an new era of higher crude oil price volatility (see, for example, Fatthouth, 2005). The price of oil was $22 a barrel in January, 2000 whereas the same barrel sold at a price of $69 in March, 2006, and at almost $100 in November 2007. Developed economies seem to be now less sensitive to more expensive oil, but there is no denying the uncertainty introduced in the macroeconomic arena by the wild swings in oil prices.[1]

Additionally, since the beginning of the 1990s financial crises seem to have been frequent and severe, and hit all major economies: recent examples include the European Monetary System crisis in 1992-1993, the Mexican peso crisis -and the subsequent Tequila effect- in 1994, the East Asian currency crisis in 1997, the Russian bond default in 1998, the crises in Brazil and Argentina (1999 and 2000-2001), the Turkish turmoil in 2001 and, more recently, the subprime crisis in the US financial market, the effects of which we are still witnessing. These crises have probably led to deeper concern: as financial markets increase in importance and activity, instability in those markets may become more relevant for overall macroeconomic instability.

In the light of these developments, the question immediately arises of whether the Great Moderation has also affected -reduced- stock market volatility or, alternatively, whether in fact increased activity in the stock market means higher volatility and, therefore, a more evident "detaching" of the financial side from the real side of the economy. Hence, in this chapter we plan to analyze whether the behavior of stock market volatility has changed significantly over the period 1960-2006 for the G-7 countries. The choices of countries and period make the analysis especially relevant. Our sample period includes the years associated with the Great Moderation, which has been generally detected in all seven countries (Summers, 2005). Even though many empirical papers have analyzed the behavior of the stock market volatility (see, for example, Schwert, 1989, 2002; Campbell et al., 2001; Cunado et al., 2004, 2006; Campbell, 2005, and Lettau et al., 2007, among many others), the overall conclusion seems to be that stock market volatility is increasingly unrelated to macroeconomic activity (Ferguson, 2004). For example, in a recent paper, Campbell (2005) examines the incidence of the Great Moderation on the volatility of the US stock market. His

---

[1] At the time of the writing of this chapter, oil keeps being the source of headaches for governments and businesses alike, and the full impact of the 2006-2007 increase in oil prices remains to be seen.

results seem to suggest that indeed the Great Moderation has had no significant impact on stock market volatility.

In this chapter we attempt to ascertain, then, if significant changes in the level -and structure- of stock market volatility have happened during the years of the Great Moderation. In fact, and more relevantly, we try to locate the dates of possible *structural* changes in volatility behavior, which we then try to relate to the Great Moderation. We are therefore particularly interested in addressing the following questions for the G-7 countries:

- How has stock market volatility evolved in the G-7 during the Great Moderation period (i.e. since the 1960s)?
- How has the structure of stock market volatility (i.e., the level of volatility, the persistence and the news effect) changed through time? Are simple statistical models enough to account for the evolution of volatility in the G-7 economies?
- Is it possible to find a relationship between changes in G-7 stock market volatility and the Great Moderation? In what direction?

In order to analyze the structure and evolution of G-7 stock market volatility we use a simple statistical model -of the GARCH family-. This statistical specification has been successfully applied to financial data and have become a popular tool to study financial market volatility. Other recent papers that have already use a GARCH (1,1) model to analyze the dynamic behavior of stock market volatility are Schwert (2002) and Cunado et al. (2004, 2006) among others.

We allow for changes in all three parameters (e.g., the level of volatility, the news effect and the persistent coefficient), thus explicitly looking at a more complete dynamic behavior of volatility: a change in any of the three parameters would generate a change in the level of unconditional volatility, but the meaning of changes in the three parameters is obviously different.

The structure of the chapter is as follows. Section 2 reviews the relationship between the Great Moderation and stock market volatility. In Section 3 we describe the methodology that has been proposed in order to locate changes in unconditional variance. Section 4 provides some empirical evidence on structural changes in stock market volatility. Finally, in Section 5 we offer some concluding remarks.

THE GREAT MODERATION AND STOCK MARKETS

A large numbers of papers have shown evidence of the Great Moderation, the decline in the volatility of macroeconomic variables (both nominal and real variables) that took place in the second half of the 1980s.[2] As Ferguson (2004) mentions,

> "[…] this decline does not appear to be the result of a long term downward trend but appears to conform more to a structural break around the mid-1980s".

---

[2] See, for example, Summers (2005) and Bernanke (2004) for a recent surveys on the Great Moderation.

Since the initial work of Kim and Nelson (1999), McConnell and Pérez-Quirós (2000) and Blanchard and Simon (2001), who detected the increase in the stability of real GDP growth experienced by the US economy after 1984, authors have extended the analysis to other countries (e.g., Dalsgaard et al., 2002; Doyle and Faust, 2002; Smith and Summers, 2002; Del Negro and Otrok, 2003, Fritsche and Kouzin, 2003; Mills and Wang, 2003 and Stock and Watson, 2003,2004 among others) and to other economic variables such as inflation, interest rates or the various components of GDP (e.g., van Dijk et al., 2002 and Sensier and van Dijk, 2004). Other recent studies such as Anderson and Vahid (2003) and Owyang et al. (2007) have documented the decline in macroeconomic variability at a regional (state) level within the US.

If the evidence for the Great Moderation on macroeconomic variables is undisputable, the causes for this phenomenon are still a matter of dispute. First, good luck has been posited as the main source of the increased stability: the size and frequency of shocks received by the developed economies has gone down in the last two decades (see, for example, Ahmed et al., 2002, Stock and Watson, 2003 and Cogley and Sargent, 2005). Second, improved economic policies, especially monetary policy, aided by a better understanding of stabilization mechanisms could also be behind the stability effect (Bernanke, 2004). Third, improved business practices and, in particular, improved inventory technology, which has allowed firms better to use inventories to smooth production in the face of shifts in sales (see, McConnell and Perez-Quiros, 2000 and Kahn et al., 2002). This hypothesis has two pieces of empirical support. First, the volatility of production has declined proportionately more than the volatility of sales, especially in the durables manufacturing sector, which is more cyclically sensitive. Second, prior to 1984 changes in durable goods inventories had a positive correlation with final sales -so that changes in inventories contributed to fluctuations in production- but after 1984 these inventories became negatively correlated with final sales, thereby contributed to a more stable production. Finally, deeper structural changes and, especially, financial innovation have been advanced as a main cause for stability (Bernanke, 2004). Financial market developments allow consumers to smooth shocks to their income, resulting in smoother streams of consumption at the individual level than would have been possible without these reforms.

A question that becomes of interest in the light of the above discussion on the Great Moderation, and especially in the context of the last cause outlined for its occurrence is the issue of whether -and how- financial markets have been affected. The evidence in this regard opens some interesting questions. It seems to be undisputable that asset prices have gone up significantly during the Great Moderation. Price/Earnings ratios or Price/Dividend ratios have been at record levels during the 1990s and the 2000s. Lettau et al. (2007) point at a reduction in consumption volatility as a possible cause associated with the increases in stock prices and, in that sense, the Great Moderation would be behind these extraordinary increases in the level of stock prices of developed economies. Ferguson (2004), however, mentions that it is hard to find a solid connection between macro fundamentals and changes in the level or volatility of asset prices. In fact, when flexible specifications for investor preferences are adopted in models similar to those of Lettau et al. (2007), macro volatility seems to have little net effect on stock prices (Bekaert et al., 2005).

As said above, Ferguson (2004) explicitly mentions the fact that the link between macroeconomic and stock market volatility is even more tenuous. Researchers have since then focused on the possible incidence of the Great Moderation on stock market volatility (see, for example, Bank for International Settlements, 2003; Campbell, 2005; Rogoff, 2006, and Lettau et al., 2007, among others). Here the agreement is more widespread: theoretical models (Lettau et al., 2007) do not predict a relationship between lower consumption volatility and lower stock return volatility and the empirical evidence agrees much more, and it strongly suggests that indeed the relationship between macroeconomic volatility and financial volatility is weak (see, Schwert, 1989; Bank for International Settlements, 2003; and Rogoff, 2006). Ferguson (2004) forcefully makes the point:

> "[...] evidence of a decline in this volatility is scarce. For S&P 500 returns, the annualized standard deviation was 13.2 percent over 1985-2004, about matching the 12.9 percent figure over 1960-1984. For the ten-year Treasury bond, the annualized standard deviation of interest rate changes was 1.1 percentage points over 1985-2004, down only slightly from 1.4 percentage points over 1960-84. These data indicate clearly that the Great Moderation of volatility in GDP and many of its components has not carried over to the volatility of asset prices."

Also along these lines, Rogoff (2006) uses standard volatility break tests to the Dow Jones Industrial Average and the S&P500 and finds that the Great Moderation has not affected the volatility of stock price returns. Campell (2005) and Ferguson (2004) try to explain this phenomenon by decomposing asset volatility into two pieces, one that depends on the volatility of cash flows and is, therefore, related with news in economic fundamentals (e.g., economic growth, inflation rate, interest rate or exchange rate among others) and one that depends on the volatility of the discount rates applied to those cash flows. The empirical results suggest that the variation in dividends or earnings accounts for no more than one-fourth of stock market volatility, whereas variation in the discount rate -risk-free rate plus the risk premium- accounts for the bulk of the volatility. Since it is the first one that has mainly been reduced by the Great Moderation, the final net effect on stock market volatility ends up being quite small (see, Bekaert et al., 2005, for additional evidence on the same finding).

If the connection between macroeconomic volatility and stock market volatility is, at best, tenuous, then it is not clear what consequences of the Great Moderation one would expect to see in the stock market. Ferguson (2004) suggests that the main cause of volatility is liquidity. Given that the liquidity of financial markets has expanded significantly in recent years, increases rather than decreases in volatility would be expected. In particular, three different areas have contributed to the growth in market liquidity: financial innovations -that enable a wider range of risks to be traded-, the trading behavior of large investors, and the growing role of hedge funds.

The above discussion seems to suggest that not only its likely that we will not observe reductions in stock market volatility, but that in fact the opposite could be the case: we might observe increases in volatility, given that the reduced macroeconomic variability may have set the stage for large shifts in liquidity. We plan now to take an agnostic approach and look at long time series of market indexes for the G-7 countries in an attempt to see whether the behavior of stock market volatility in these countries has indeed experienced structural changes such as those detected in macroeconomic variables and, if so, in what direction these changes have occurred.

STRUCTURAL BREAKS IN THE G-7 STOCK MARKET VOLATILITY

In this section we give a formal structure to the behavior of stock market volatility using simple statistical models of the GARCH family. We then use the parameters in the model, which characterize the dynamic behavior of stock return volatility, to search for possible structural breaks in volatility behavior.

The GARCH family of models has been successfully applied to financial data and it has become a popular tool to study financial market volatility. In a simple GARCH(1,1) process, the stock returns and the variance of innovations to stock returns are given by:

$$r_t = \mu_t + u_t, \quad u_t \rightarrow nid\ (0, \sigma_t^2) \qquad \text{[Mean equation]} \qquad (1)$$
$$\sigma_t^2 = \omega_0 + \alpha_1 \sigma_t^2 + \alpha_2 u_{t-1}^2 \qquad \text{[Variance equation]}$$

Where μ_t is the mean (expected) return, which may be modeled as flexibly as desired, and σ_t^2 is the variance of the return innovation u_t. The three parameters in the variance equation determine the -changing- behavior of conditional variance and they all have quite intuitive interpretations: ω_0 drives the level of the variance whereas the other two parameters determine the dynamic behavior of the series. The parameter α_1 can be interpreted as the persistence and the α_2 as the impact in volatility of new information or the "sensitivity to news" of volatility.[3] In the next section we search for significant changes in all three parameters, thus explicitly looking at a more complete dynamic behavior of volatility: a change in any of the three parameters would generate a change in the level of unconditional -long-run- volatility, but the meaning of changes in the three parameters is obviously different.[4]

In order to take a deeper look at the possible existence of changes in the variance of stock markets, we use methodologies designed to locate changes in the level of unconditional variance and in its dynamic properties. The location of endogenous structural breaks in time series has been a matter of intense research in the last few years: One can look at Banerjee et al. (1992), Ghysels et al. (1997), Bai et al. (1998) or Dufour and Ghysels (1996) to realize that the topic is still in its early development stages. The issue of how to estimate the number and location of multiple endogenous structural breaks is also being currently intensely researched and results on the procedure and properties of the tests involved are now being published. Papers by Andrews et al. (1996), García and Perron (1996), Bai (1997, 1999) or Bai and Perron (1998, 2003) are some of the most noticeable examples.

Most of the techniques in the above papers have been developed for estimation and location of endogenous breaks in the mean parameters of trend models. However, as Bai and Perron (1998) mention, they can also accommodate changes in the variance. Given the richer structure of the GARCH variance process, we have to be cautious about how immediately these tests can be extended to changes in the GARCH parameters.[5]

In this chapter we use the general framework in Bai and Perron (1998, 2003) and use their sequential procedure and estimated critical values. This sequential procedure consists of

---

[3] α_1, α_2 is usually interpreted as the persistence of the variance, although it is more exactly the persistence parameter of the process for squared returns implied by the GARCH structure. We believe that an interpretation of α_1 as persistence of the variance is slightly more intuitive.

[4] The unconditional variance of the series implied by the GARCH structure is $\bar{\sigma}_1\bar{\sigma}, \square\bar{\sigma}$

[5] Formal evidence that this type of tests can be extended to GARCH processes is cited in Andreou and Ghysels (2002).

locating the breaks one at a time, conditional on the breaks that have already been located. Thus, we locate the first break and test for its significance against the null hypothesis of no break. If the null hypothesis is rejected, we then look for the second break conditional on the first break being the one already found, and test for the existence of that second break against the null of one single break, and so on.

Our framework consists of a model for stock market volatility of the form in (2). We believe that at some points in time, $\mathbf{t} = \{t_1, t_2, ... t_m\}$ the process generating the variance may change, that is, the parameters α_1, β_1 and γ_1 change at each of the t_i. The specific number of breaks allowed will be determined by the data through the application of the sequential process outlined above, so here we keep the discussion at a general level.

Given a set $\mathbf{t}$ of l points in time at which q of the parameters of the process change, we want to test if there is an additional break and, if so, when the break takes place and the value of the q parameters before and after the new break. The likelihood of the model that contains the l breaks in $\mathbf{t}$ is specified as $L(t,\theta)$. θ is the set of all parameters and it contains both the parameters that do not change over time and the l values of each of the q parameters allowed to change at the breakpoints. In our specific model, and disregarding some constants,

$$L(t,\theta) = -\frac{1}{2}\sum_{t=1}^{t_1}\left[\log\sigma_{1,t}^2 + \frac{u_{1,t}^2}{\sigma_{1,t}^2}\right] - \frac{1}{2}\sum_{t=1+t_1}^{t_2}\left[\log\sigma_{2,t}^2 + \frac{u_{2,t}^2}{\sigma_{2,t}^2}\right] \cdots - \frac{1}{2}\sum_{t=t_1}^{T}\left[\log\sigma_{n,t}^2 + \frac{u_{n,t}^2}{\sigma_{n,t}^2}\right] \quad (2)$$

The alternative model is specified as one which contains an additional break at time τ. Thus, the set of $l+1$ breakpoints becomes now $\mathbf{t}^* = \{t,\tau\}$, and the log-likelihood associated with the alternative model is $L(\mathbf{t}^*,\theta(\mathbf{t}^*))$. The procedure for the detection and timing of the break consists in finding the series of likelihood-ratio statistics of the alternative (unrestricted model) of $l+1$ breaks against the null (restricted model) of l breaks:

$$LR_\tau(l+1 \mid l) = -2[L(\mathbf{t},\hat{\theta}(\mathbf{t})) - L(\mathbf{t}^*,\hat{\theta}(\mathbf{t}^*))] \quad (3)$$

where $\mathbf{t} = \{t_1, t_2, ... t_l\}$ is the first set of l breaks (under the null of no additional break) and $\mathbf{t}^* = \{t_1, t_2, ... t_l\}$ is the set of $l+1$ breaks that includes τ as a new possible time for a break. $L(t,(t))$ is the value of the log-likelihood of a model that includes the breaks in $\mathbf{t}$, where (t) are the ML estimates of all the parameters of the model. The new breakpoint is located by using the Sup-LR test:

$$\sup \text{LR} : \sup_{\tau \in T^*} \text{LR}_\tau (l+1|l) \quad (4)$$

where $\mathbf{T}^*$ is the set of possible times for the new break. Of course, given the series of LR tests and the Sup-LR test, the date of the new breakpoint $\hat{t}$ is:

$$\hat{t} = \arg\max_{\tau \in T^*} L(t^*, \hat{\theta}(t^*)) = \arg\max_{\tau \in T^*} \left[\sup_\tau \text{LR}_\tau (l+1|l)\right]. \quad (5)$$

If the Sup-LR test is above the critical value, then the null of no additional breakpoint is rejected and the date for the new breakpoint is estimated to be $\hat{t}$. The values of the parameters before and after the break correspond to the estimates in $\hat{\theta}(\mathbf{t}^*)$. The different versions of this statistic (Bai et al., 1998; Bai and Perron, 1998, 2003) have a limiting distribution that depends on a q-dimensional Brownian motion, where q is the number of parameters allowed to change at the time of the break. Thus, the critical values of the $LR(l+1\,|\,l)$ test depend on l and on q and are usually calculated by simulation of the q dimensional Brownian motion.

One final comment is that $\mathbf{T}^*$ the set of possible times for the break, must exclude a number of observations around the initial and final dates and around the dates in $\mathbf{t} = \{t_1,t_2,...t_i\}$ that ensures that each subperiod defined by the breakpoints contains enough observations for the parameters to be accurately estimated. In our analysis we have used a trimming proportion of 0.15.[6] That is, we start by locating the first breakpoint in $\mathbf{T}^* =\{0.15T,\ 0.85T\}$ and then every time we locate a new breakpoint, we exclude from $\mathbf{T}^*$ the 15% observations to both sides of the last breakpoint estimated.

The critical values have been tabulated by the authors, and are available in their papers. It also has to be said that the tests explained above can consistently estimate not the dates of the breaks but the proportion of the total sample at which the breaks occur. That is, we estimate consistently that the break happens at "the 0.2 quantile" of the sample. Of course, one can then back up the specific time of the event, given a fixed number of observations T in the sample.

EMPIRICAL EVIDENCE ON STOCK MARKET VOLATILITY ACROSS THE G-7 ECONOMIES

This section is divided in two sub-sections. In the first one we present some stylized facts about the behavior of the stock market volatility in the G-7 economies. These include some basic descriptive statistics along with a rolling variance, which gives an intuitive visual image of the time evolution of volatility. The second sub-section is devoted to the analysis of the existence of breaks in the volatility processes, and we use the procedures described in Section 3. We focus our comments on the results of the Sup-LR procedure.

The data we use in this chapter are long time series of monthly data on stock returns for Canada, France, Germany, Italy, Japan, the UK and the US. These data have been obtained from the Global Financial Data web site.[7] The series run from 1960:01 to 2006:06, thus yielding a total of 556 observations.[8] Empirical evidence are based on stock returns in local currency and stock returns expressed in US dollars for comparative purposes.

---

[6] This proportion is usually taken to be 0.15. The results are not sensitive to the choice of this trimming proportion, unless the break is located too close to the endpoints of the sample. In small samples or in settings where low frequency data are used a trimming proportion of 0.1 may be more advisable for reasons of data availability.

[7] These stock market indexes are denominated in local currency. In our analysis we also use dollar denominated price indexes of the stock markets. In order to compute the stock returns denominated in US dollars for all G-7 economies, exchange rate data were used. For further information on the stock indexes, consult www.globalfindata.com.

[8] Data availability and comparability dictated the final sample period. Some local indexes were available for longer periods, but we opted for using a uniformly calculated index to make comparison across countries more meaningful and not subject to the different methodologies used by the countries. Still, one would ideally use as long a series as possible.

Some Initial Stylized Facts

We show some descriptive statistics of the G-7 stock market returns and then move to a graphical analysis of volatility. Table 1 reports basic univariate statistics for the annualized regular returns of our seven economies.[9]

Average returns denominated in local currency during the sample period range between -1.6% in Italy to 2.5% in the US while the average returns denominated in US dollars range between −3.5% in Italy to 4.8% in Japan. In terms of standard deviation (volatility), the markets in Italy and Japan have been the most volatile whereas Canada and the US seem to have had the most stable markets.

Table 1. Some basic statistics of the returns, 1960:01-2006:06

	Canada	France	Germany	Italy	Japan	UK	US
Local Currency							
Mean	0.0243	0.0163	0.0146	-0.0160	0.0234	0.0175	0.0257
SD	0.5485	0.6397	0.6083	0.7794	0.6511	0.6536	0.516
SK	-0.9483	-0.440	-0.677	0.1962	-0.4482	-0.1338	-0.614
κ	6.759	4.8354	6.2964	4.137	4.0368	10.614	5.414
ρ_1	0.09**	0.13**	0.11**	0.098**	0.05	0.122**	0.038
Q(4)	8.19*	11.28**	8.92**	8.25*	2.49	12.78**	0.814
JB	411	96.2	294	33.6	43.06	1347	170
US dolar							
Mean	0.0277	0.0154	0.0361	-0.0352	0.0481	0.0085	0.0257
SD	0.5239	0.6999	0.6591	0.8184	0.7511	0.7122	0.516
SK	-0.801	-0.4025	-0.4186	-0.0423	-0.0934	0.1038	-0.614
κ	6.270	4.8968	5.1284	3.8749	3.6424	8.4283	5.414
ρ_1	0.095**	0.10**	0.05	0.09**	0.07*	0.10**	0.038
Q(4)	8.29*	9.71**	2.76	11.17**	8.90*	9.17**	0.814
JB	307	96	121	17.99	10.4	684	170

Returns are calculated as $12(\ln P_t - \ln P_{t-1})$ where P_t is the value of the stock index at month t.
SD: standard deviation.
SK: skewness coefficient.
κ: kurtosis coefficient.
ρ_1: first order autocorrelation coefficient.
Q(4): Ljung-Box(4) statistic for autocorrelation of returns.
JB: Jarque-Bera normality test.
* and ** denote statistical significance at the 10% and 5% levels, respectively.
All data are obtained from Global Financial Data web site. The stock indices are the following: S&P/TSX 300 Composite Index for Canada, SBF 250 Index for France, CDAX Composite Index for Germany, Banca Commerciale Italiana Index for Italy, Nikkei 225 Stock Average for Italy, Nikkei 225 Stock Average for Japan, FTSE All Share Index for the UK and S&P 500 Composite Price Index for the US.

---

[9] We calculate returns as $r_t = 12(\log P_t - \log P_{t-1})$.

A simple look at the dynamic behavior of stock market volatility can be taken in Figure 1. The graphs show the evolution of stock returns during the sample period along with a nonparametric measure of return volatility, a twelve-month rolling variance. This annualized rolling variance is calculated as follows:

$$\sigma^2(\mathbf{r}_t) = \left[\sum_{k=1}^{12} \frac{(r_{t-k} - \mu_{12})^2}{11} \right] \quad (6)$$

where r_t is the return of the stock market index over period t and μ_{12} is the sample mean over the twelve-month window. This rolling variance gives a first idea of the evolution of both the conditional -short-term ups and downs- and the unconditional -longer-run level- variance of the different stock markets. We note that the graphs already suggest the possible existence of changes in the unconditional volatility that is, in the medium-to-long run level of the variance. Specifically, the graphs identify some episodes of high instability: 2003 in Germany, 1988 in France, 1980-1981 in Italy, 1990 in Japan, 1974-1975 in the UK and 1988 in the US.

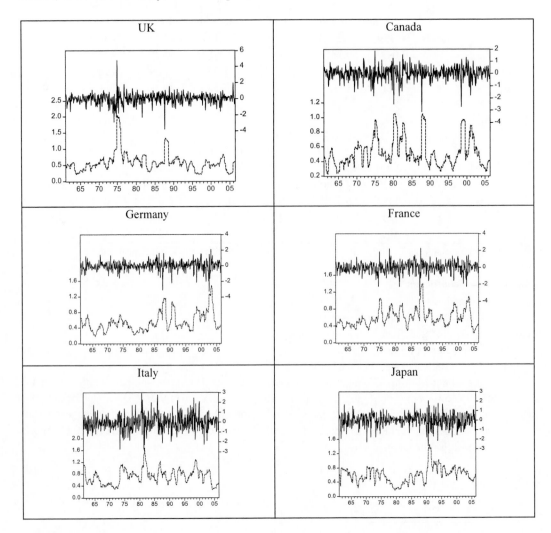

Figure 1a. Stocks returns and rolling variance (local currency).

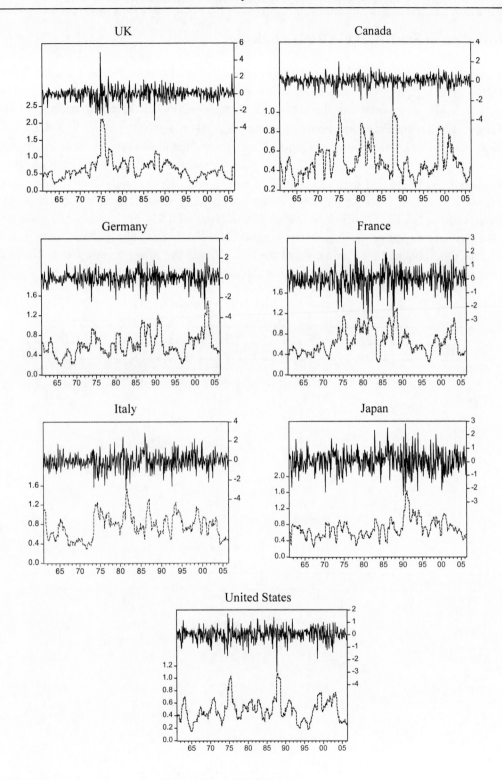

Figure 1b. Stocks returns and rolling variance (US dollars).

Estimation of Statistical GARCH Models

We have initially fitted simple GARCH(1,1) models with no break to the stock market index, with the mean equation in (1) modeled as an autoregressive process of order one, which is usually enough to account for the weak autocorrelation present in mean returns. In the variance equation there are four relevant parameters in our analysis: the *level* of volatility -ω_0-, the *persistence* of volatility -α_1-, the *news* effect -α_2- and the *unconditional variance* implied by the estimates –UV = $\omega_0/(1-\alpha_1-\alpha_2)$–. The parameters of the empirical estimation -done by quasi-maximum likelihood with u_t assumed to be conditionally normally distributed- appear in Table 2. As we can see in the table, when we consider stock returns in local currency, estimates of the level of volatility go from 0.005 in Japan to 0.034 in Canada while estimates of the persistence range from 0.79 in Canada 0.91 in Japan. The highest news effect parameters are obtained for Germany and the UK whereas the lower news effect is obtained for Japan. Finally, the unconditional variance ranges from 0.27 to 0.57.

Table 2. GARCH (1,1) model

	ω_0	α_1	α_2	UV
US dollar				
Canada	0.041	0.799	0.051	0.273
	(0.32)	(4.61)	(0.32)	
France	0.008	0.913	0.066	0.426
	(0.22)	(15.51)	(0.41)	
Germany	0.019	0.856	0.102	0.477
	(0.35)	(11.79)	(0.80)	
Italy	0.015	0.895	0.085	0.81
	(0.24)	(8.66)	(0.34)	
Japan	0.088	0.709	0.133	0.564
	(0.38)	(2.72)	(0.51)	
UK	0.009	0.920	0.057	0.438
	(0.27)	(23.1)	(0.54)	
US	0.013	0.860	0.092	0.278
	(0.33)	(13.48)	(0.85)	
Local currency				
Canada	0.034	0.796	0.089	0.305
	(0.31)	(4.56)	(0.41)	
France	0.032	0.823	0.095	0.401
	(0.22)	(2.91)	(0.23)	
Germany	0.011	0.851	0.125	0.486
	(0.27)	(8.21)	(0.61)	
Italy	0.032	0.823	0.095	0.402
	(0.22)	(2.92)	(0.23)	
Japan	0.005	0.916	0.075	0.571
	(0.22)	(15.29)	(0.42)	
UK	0.029	0.806	0.125	0.438
	(0.35)	(7.41)	(0.79)	

t-statistics use QML standard errors assuming Gaussian distributions for ε_t. The sample size is 556 months.

These results are quite interesting: Canada and Italy present the highest level of stock market volatility, Japan presents the stock market with more persistent volatility -that is, the market takes longer time to return to normal volatility- and the higher UV. Finally, the news effect, which measures how large the reaction of market volatility is to new information, is highest for Germany.[10] Results do not change much for local currency vs. US dollars, suggesting that exchange rates have not induced major distortions in the cross-country comparability of stock return volatility.

We comment now on the results of the likelihood-based estimation that includes the possible existence of one potential structural break in the three parameters of the variance equation. We present critical values of the test (for the null hypotheses of no break) in Table 3 along with the estimated values of the Sup-LR tests for the seven countries in our analysis.

Table 3. Likelihood-based tests (Sup-LR(l+1|l))

Critical values for changes in 3 parameters			Local Currency	US dollars
α	l=0	Canada	12.06	11.91
90%	13.43	France	20.52*	15.48*
95%	15.37	Germany	10.11	6.94
		Italy	16.75*	20.57*
		Japan	13.16	11.12
		UK	11.75	13.38
		US	9.50	9.50

The critical values come from Table II, Bai and Perron (1998). Only results on tests for l=0 (i.e. one structural break) are shown. *: break significant at the 5% level. Evidence for a second break is weak in those cases where it can be estimated. Those results are available from the authors.

Estimates of the parameters are shown in Table 4. The table presents the date of the break, the value of the Sup-LR test, the parameters and standard errors of the two subsamples determined by the break and the unconditional variance implied for each subsample.

The main results can be summarized as follows. When stock returns are denominated either in local currency or in US dollars we detect that there has been one structural change in the stock market volatility of France and Italy whereas for the other five countries (Canada, Germany, Japan, the UK and the US) we find no evidence of a break. The dates of the breaks, however, differ depending on whether we use local currency or US dollars: using stock returns in local currency, the break dates detected are 1971:06 for France and 1972:11 for Italy whereas for returns expressed in US dollars the breaks are 1973:07 for France and 1972:10 for Italy. Given the small difference between the location of the two dates, we omit further comment on the US dollar series and focus on the results obtained for returns expressed in domestic currency.

---

[10] When we consider stock returns in US dollars, Canada also presents the higher level of volatility while France is the more persistent stock market and Japan and Italy have the highest news effect and unconditional variance respectively.

Table 4. GARCH (1,1) model with 1 break

	Break	LR	ω_{01}	α_{11}	α_{21}	UV_1	ω_{02}	α_{12}	α_{22}	UV_2
US dolar										
France	1971:06	15.48	0.005	0.934	0.052	0.38	0.029	0.812	0.132	0.533
			(0.16)	(15.6)	(0.27)	3	(0.91)	(4.77)	(0.57)	
Italy	1972:11	20.57	0.016	0.893	0.089	0.96	7e-14	0.987	4e-14	5e-12
			(0.28)	(11.5)	(0.46)	2	(0.004)	(264)	(6e-7)	
Local currency										
France	1973:07	20.52	0.009	0.927	0.047	0.37	0.018	0.683	0.314	7.37
			(0.20)	(13.1)	(0.25)	9	(0.84)	(0.17)	(0.05)	
Italy	1972:10	16.75	0.059	0.756	0.158	0.69	0.158	0.351	0.350	0.534
			(0.40)	(5.15)	(0.89)	1	(1.19)	(0.99)	(0.93)	

t-statistics use QML standard errors assuming Gaussian distributions for ε_t. The sample size is 556 months. UV denotes the unconditional variance. Coefficients of the mean equation are not shown, but are available upon request. Parameters have been found by estimating separately the two subsamples.

We comment now on the results of the endogenous break analysis. Parameter estimates of the estimations with one break are shown in Table 4 for the only two countries for whom we found structural breaks. The results for both France and Italy suggest a clear change in the behavior of stock market volatility before and after the break and, in both cases, the main parameters of interest change *in the same direction*. In both countries we find that after the break, the parameter that drives the conditional level of volatility, that is, the size of the shocks that are received by the system, goes up. In other words, these two countries are subject to larger shocks. Second, the persistence of volatility decreases: the market returns faster to "normal" levels of volatility. Third, the news effect parameter increased, which suggests that these two financial markets react more intensely to new information. To sum up, we find financial markets that react more intensely to larger shocks, but where the persistence of volatility is reduced. All these three features suggest an enhanced maturity of the financial markets, that are more open to trade (thus the larger size of shocks and the intense reaction to these shocks) but also incorporate faster the relevant information (so that persistence is reduced). The final effect on unconditional volatility, which is a consequence of the changes in all three parameters, is not uniform, and we do not place much emphasis on it.

Both structural breaks are located almost simultaneously in time, in the early 1970's. Events related to the French and Italian economy that may be behind these changes could be the movement toward European union, the begining of the financial liberalization and the significant impact of the first oil price shock in 1973-1974.

In summary, the previous results suggest that stock market volatility has not behaved in a different manner over the period 1960-2006 for most of the G-7 countries: we only find structural breaks in the model parameters that characterize volatility behavior in France and Italy. The empirical evidence for the G7 countries therefore does not support a decline in stock market volatility in line with the decline in macroeconomic volatility (and in line with the findings and discussion in Schwert, 1989; Ferguson, 2004; and Campbell, 2005). We have mentioned above that this could be the case, and, indeed, that the opposite result could be found: the period from 1970 to 1990 was a period of development and deepening of the financial markets in all the G-7 countries and therefore one could expect more trading and more liquidity in those markets, which would induce *higher* rather than *lower* volatility. The results for France and Italy seem to suggest precisely this effect. Finally, the fact that we do not find evidence of significant structural changes in the other five G-7 countries may be explained in two ways. One could be related to the duration of these changes. If the determinants of the change in volatility behavior -financial innovation or structural institutional changes such as financial liberalization- take place gradually rather than at a specific point in time, the effects may not be detectable with an analysis that specifies that the break happens in one specific period. Second, and in line with the comments in Section 2, the combined effect of higher liquidity (and higher volatility in discount rates) and lower macroeconomic volatility (and lower volatility of cash flows) may somehow cancel out the final effect on stock market volatility. The distinction between these two possible causes for the apparent lack of changes in volatility behavior is outside the scope of this paper, but it opens an interesting avenue for research. The analysis for the US has been done already by Campbell (2005), but the application to the other G-7 countries could shed light on the determinants of the evolution of financial volatility.

CONCLUSION

In this chapter we have looked at the evolution of stock market volatility in the G-7 economies, placing the results in the context of the Great Moderation process. In particular, we looked at whether structural breaks are necessary to account for the evolution of stock market volatility and whether these breaks can be associated with the significant decline in macroeconomic volatility. Additionally, we tried to analyze in what direction this decrease in macro volatility could have affected, if at all, stock market volatility.

Using a simple statistical model that, nevertheless, accounts quite well for the time evolution of volatility, we looked for endogenous structural breaks in the dynamic behavior of volatility during a long sample period that included the years of the Great Moderation. Our results show little evidence for structural breaks in volatility behavior for most G-7 countries: Canada, Germany, Japan, the UK and the US. Indeed, only France and Italy show evidence of significant changes in volatility behavior, and these seem to have come prior to the Great Moderation and in the direction of *higher volatility*, rather than lower. We commented how the process of development of the financial market could be behind this result, and that the result tends to confirm that stock market volatility is detached from macroeconomic volatility and responds more to trading or liquidity considerations rather to fundamental volatility within the economy.

The result has important implications for policymakers, who need to watch financial markets carefully for any warning signs that may appear, and not rely on the good news about the economy. It seems that market liquidity, investor behavior, and the asset price volatility that these induce are more important considerations now than they were decades ago, and that traditional stabilization policies may in fact have a different objective now: rather than output and inflation, one may think that stabilization of the financial system could become a top priority. We need look back only a few months in time to see that this could well be the case.

REFERENCES

Ahmed, S., Levin, A., & B.A. Wilson (2002). Recent U.S. Macroeconomic Stability: Good Policies, Good Practices, or Good Luck? *Board of Governors of the Federal Reserve System, International Finance Discussion Paper* 2002-730 (July).

Anderson, H., & Vahid, F. (2003). The decline in income growth volatility in the United States: Evidence from regional data. *Monash Econometrics and Business Statistics Working Paper* 21/2003.

Andreou, E., & Ghysels, E. (2002). Multiple breaks in financial market volatility dynamics. *Journal of Applied Econometrics,* 17, 579-600.

Andrews, D.W., Lee, I., & Ploberger, W. (1996). Optimal changepoint tests for normal linear regression. *Journal of Econometrics,* 70, 9-38.

Bai, J. (1997). Estimating multiple breaks one at a time. *Econometric Theory,* 13, 315-332.

Bai, J., & Perron, P. (1998). Estimating and testing linear models with multiple structural changes. *Econometrica,* 66, 47-78.

Bai, J., & Perron, P. (2003). Computation and analysis of multiple structural change models. *Journal of Applied Econometrics,* 18,1-22.

Bai, J., Lumsdaine, R.L., & Stock, J.H. (1998). Testing for and dating breaks in stationary and nonstationary multivariate time series. *Review of Economic Studies,* 65, 395-432.

Banerjee, A., Lumsdaine, R.L., & Stock, J.S. (1992). Recursive and sequential tests of the unit root and trend-break bypotheses: Theory and international evidence. *Journal of Business and Economic Statistics,* 10, 271-287.

Bank for International Settlements (2003). The recent behaviour of financial market volatility. *BIS Papers* 29.

Bekaert, G., Engstrom, E., & Xing, Y. (2005). Risk, uncertainty, and asset prices. *FEDS Working Paper* 2005-40, Board of Governors of the Federal Reserve System.

Blanchard, O., & Simon, J. (2001). The long and large decline in US output volatility. *Brookings Papers on Economic Activity,* 1, 135-174.

Campbell, J., Lettau, M., Malkiel, B., & Zu, Y. (2001). Have individual stocks become more volatile? An empirical exploration of idiosyncratic risk. *Journal of Finance,* 56, 1-43.

Campbell, S.D. (2005). Stock market volatility and the Great Moderation. *Finance and Economics Discussion Serires, Divisions of Research and Statistics and Monetary Affairs, Federal Reserve Board, Washington*, D.C., 2005-47.

Cogley, T., & Sargent, T. (2005). Drifts and volatilities: Monetary policies and outcomes in the post-WWII U.S.. *Review of Economic Dynamics*, 8, 262-302.

Cunado, J., Gomez Biscarri, J., & Perez de Gracia, F. (2004). Structural changes in volatility and stock market development: Evidence for Spain. *Journal of Banking and Finance,* 28, 1745-1773.

Cunado, J., Gomez Biscarri, J., & Perez de Gracia, F. (2006). Changes in the dynamic behavior of emerging market volatility: Revisiting the effects of financial liberalization. *Emerging Markets Review,* 7, 261-278.

Dalsgaard, T., Elmeskov, J., & Park, C.Y. (2002). Ongoing changes in the business cycle. Evidence and causes. *OECD Economics Department Working Paper no.* 315.

Del Negro, M., & Otrok, C. (2003). Time-varying European business cycles. *Mimeo,* University of Virginia.

Doyle, B.M., & Faust, J. (2002). An investigation of co-movements among the growth rates of the G-7 countries. *Federal Reserve Bulletin*, October, 427 – 437.

Dufour, J.M., & Ghysels, E. (1996). Recent developments in the Econometrics of structural change. *Journal of Econometrics, 70*, 1-316.

Fritsche, U., & Kouzine, V. (2003). Declining output volatility and monetary policy in Germany. *Manuscript -German Institute for Economic Research (DIW Berlin).*

García, R., & Perron, P. (1996). An analysis of the real interest rate under regime shifts. *Review of Economics and Statistics, 78*, 111-125.

Ghysels, E., Guay, A., & Hall, A. (1997). Predictive tests for structural change with unknown breakpoint. *Journal of Econometrics, 82*, 209-233.

Fattouh, B. (2005). The causes of crude oil price volatility. *Middle East Economic Survey, XLVIII*, 13, 28-March-2005.

Ferguson, R.W. (2005). Asset price levels and volatility: Causes and implications. *Remarks to the Banco de Mexico International Conference*, Mexico City, Mexico.

Kim, C.J., & Nelson, C.R. (1999). Has the US economy become more stable? A bayesian approach based on a Markov-Switching model of the business cycle. *Review of Economics and Statistics, 81*, 608-616.

Lettau, M., Ludvigson, S.C., & Wachter, J. A. (2007). The declining equity premium: What role does macroeconomic risk play? *Review of Financial Studies*, Forthcoming.

McConnell, M.M., & Pérez Quirós, G. (2000). Output fluctuations in the US: What has changed since the early 1980´s?. *American Economic Review, 90*, 1464-1476.

Mills, T.C., & Wang, P. (2003). Have output growth rates stabilised? Evidence from the G-7 economies. *Scottish Journal of Political Economy, 50*, 232-246.

Owyang, M., Piger, J., & Wall, H.J. (2007). A state level analysis of the Great Moderation. *Federal Reserve Bank of Sant Louis, Working Paper Series* 2007-003B.

Rogoff, K. (2006). Impact of globalization on monetary policy. *Mimeo.*

Pritsker, M., (2005). Large investors: Implications for equilibrium asset returns, shock absorption, and liquidity. *FEDS Working Paper* 2005-36, Board of Governors of the Federal Reserve System.

Schwert, G. (1989). Why does stock market volatility change over time?. *Journal of Finance, 44*, 1115-1154.

Schwert, G. (2002). Stock volatility in the new millenium: How wacky is Nasdaq?. *Journal of Monetary Economics, 49*, 3-26.

Sensier, M., & van Dijk, D. (2004). Testing for volatility changes in US macroeconomic time series. *Review of Economics and Statistics, 86*, 833-839.

Simon, J. (2001). The decline in Australian output volatility. *Manuscript, Reserve Bank of Australia.*

Smith, P.A., & Summers, P.M. (2002). Regime switches in GDP growth and volatility: Some international evidence and implications for modeling business cycles. *Mimeo.*

Stock, J.H., & Watson, M.W. (2002). Has the business cycle changed and why? In M. Gertler and K. Roggoff, eds., *NBER Macroeconomics Annual 2002.* Cambridge, Mass: MIT Press.

Stock, J.H., & Watson, M.W. (2003). Has the business cycle changed? Evidence and explanations. Prepared for the Federal Reserve Bank of Kansas City symposium, *Monetary Policy and Uncertainty*, Jackson Hole, Wyoming, August 28-30.

Stock, J.H., & Watson, M.W. (2004). Understanding changes in international business cycle dynamics. *Princeton University, Working Paper*.

Summers, P.M. (2005). What caused the Great Moderation? Some cross-country evidence. *Federal Reserve Bank of Kansas City Economic Review, (Third Quarter)*, 5-30.

Van Dijk, D., Osborn, D., & Sensier, M. (2002). Changes in variability of the business cycle in the G7 countries. *CGBCR – Working Paper*, 16.

INDEX

T